THE WORLD
SPLIT OPEN

THE WORLD SPLIT OPEN

FOUR CENTURIES OF WOMEN POETS IN ENGLAND AND AMERICA, 1552–1950

Edited, and with an
introduction, by

LOUISE BERNIKOW

Vintage Books
A Division of Random House, New York

VINTAGE BOOKS EDITION, November 1974
First Edition
Copyright © 1974 by Louise Bernikow

Library of Congress Cataloging in Publication Data
Bernikow, Louise, 1940–   comp.
    The world split open.
        1. American poetry. 2. Women's writings, American.
3. English poetry.   4. Women's writings, English.
I. Title.
PS589.B4   821'.008   74–8582
ISBN 0–394–71072–X

Manufactured in the United States of America

The title is a line from the poem by Muriel Rukeyser entitled "Käthe Kollwitz."

"The Other Side of a Mirror," "Mortal Combat," "Eyes," "The Witch," "Regina," and "Horror" from *Collected Poems of Mary Coleridge*, edited by Theresa Whistler, published by Rupert Hart-Davis, 1954. Reprinted by permission of Theresa Whistler.

"Parentage," "Saint Catherine of Siena," "Maternity," "Easter Night," "A Father of Women: Ad Sororem E. B.," "The Sunderland Children," "In Time of War" and "To Conscripts" from *The Poems of Alice Meynell 1847–1923*, edited by Sir Francis Meynell. Centenary edition. The Newman Press, Westminster, Maryland, 1955.

"Gift to a Jade," "Divorce," "Nervous Prostration," "The Economist" and "Inspiration" from *The Contemplative Quarry and the Man with a Hammar* by Anna Wickham.

What would happen if one woman told the truth about her life?
The world would split open

—Muriel Rukeyser, "Käthe Kollwitz"
from *The Speed of Darkness*

WOMEN OF WORDS
A PREFATORY NOTE

Why should there be a book of poems by women? "If they are any good," a publisher (male) says, "they can stand up in an anthology with men." What will such a book be, a kind of wastebasket?

Why does a woman write a poem? This question has not come up during all the rising questions now being asked; and this moment, the time of publication of this book, may be the last moment for such questions. You will hear queries about equal rights, about dominance, about orgasm —is there a vaginal orgasm? The answer to that is: Since there is orgasm every other inch of the body, why not there?

But deeper, as deep as these, are the questions concerning the poems of women, and they are answered here. Or partly answered. Because this race of women, the women poets, have opened a music in their lives that out of a mixture of strength and weakness, sex and protest, visibility and invisibility, offers us a glimpse of possibility that we may be on the edge of claiming.

Have you ever known the curious happiness and sadness of the young woman poet, who is such a source of confusion to her family and the people around her, if they are culturally tied, hobbled, spancelled, as the Irish say? Have you ever lived in a jail for women, and felt the solidarity and frustration of that suffering, imposed so wildly and lopsidedly? Have you known the double joy and despair of women as daughters and poets? Or the joy and until recently the despair of women homosexuals; or wives or mothers? These may be extremes of what we see here, but they may not be. These cries, these formalities, these bursts of song, this formal music, seen in a brief sampling of four hundred years, will let you make your own decision. We have had Men of Letters; here are the Women of Words.

We have seen many of these writers before. They have

appeared in glorious anthologies—I think of Louis Unter-
meyer's, with his critical building and introducing of the
poets I first met—or in books by women devoted to one
woman poet, like Marya Zaturenska's work on Christina
Rossetti. But here they stand in a procession that says
extraordinary things to us.

That procession begins, for me, with Miriam and
Deborah and Sappho. The last will be found in Louise
Bernikow's sharp and fascinating introduction, but the
other two—who dealt with triumph and justice—are not
mentioned. It is the haunting beauty of that long procession that stays with me, along with certain poems and
songs which you will find here. That beauty has been
selected out for you. You do not feel it when all the poems,
by women and men, are grouped together.

How do poems by women reach students in the schools
today? One undergraduate said to me, "There are no
women until after Easter." In this book, Queen Elizabeth,
Aphra Behn, and a few others, come "before Easter," and
if the book were opened to poetry in translation, of course
there would be many more.

And here we come to poems by black women, mill
workers, blues singers, set with the "literary" forms. Many
music.

Often there are gaps, for the heroes can be the "ten
anonymous women," of my "Ann Burlak" poem in the
thirties. And some of the questions are not here—"Will
the male voice answer?" Marya Zaturenska asks in a poem.
And Sara Bard Field, Elizabeth Bishop, Leonie Adams,
Marie Welch—they come in the same procession. The
poets I have just named were publishing widely before
1950, the cut-off date of this book. It is a good stopping-
place, the end of one stage of what I called in "Ajanta"
(1941) "the journey, and the struggles of the moon." The
journey reached a turning-point; the moon—in all the
senses with which we reach her—took on new meaning.

But, even after those years, I remember reviews of books

by women poets grouped in a "liberal" magazine under the title "Ladies' Day."

There are traces in the poems here of the attempt to get through the burden of sorrow that the speech—speech alone—of women has brought on them; attempts to get through the hostility engendered by that frustration; attempts to find one's own voice, clear of those choking emotions. These are poems, not simply of protest, not simply of the cunt, but of the person entire, the woman.

Yesterday, in a city park, I saw fifty flying children, girls, boys, running along the stone in what looked like free patterns. One girl lifted up a small bright cape, and ran. Maybe those children will be spared the weight of the burden that even their parents—brought up since 1950 —have felt. Maybe their poems. Or does it take forty years in the desert, clear of that "Egypt" of women, those idols, those fleshpots, those pyramids of death and power, before we can make an art that is not branded?

But that is the next book. Here is this one, a good one.

MURIEL RUKEYSER

EDITOR'S NOTE

I have tried in this book to uncover a lost tradition in English and American poetry. My desire is to bring out into the open many poets now lost to our eyes, and also to bring some specific kinds of content, things that have been said and experiences that have been shaped into various poetic forms now lost to our ears. I do not think the loss has been an accident, but rather a result of the patriarchal structure of literary life and work in both countries. I explain this, at least partly, in the Introduction. All I want to say about it here is that this collection has been made by an ardent lover of poetry who, because she is also a feminist, has made choices that are political. I have looked for the poems that are not often printed, the poems on being a woman, the poems on traditionally "unfeminine" subjects, the poems that sometimes don't quite make it on purely esthetic grounds, whatever those grounds are, but make attempts that are interesting and often revolutionary.

I hope that this explanation prevents the reader or critic with the quick sneer who finds some of this collection not to his taste from wasting his time thinking about why. I also hope that the reader who feels engaged understands why.

A word about the time-span of the book. This anthology cuts off around 1950. That is, it includes poets who were writing during the Second World War and just after. My cut-off date does an odd thing to the work of poets who lived and continued writing after that, many of them among the best still at work today. I apologize for the amputation, offering only the decision that space was limited and that the more recent work of those poets can be found elsewhere.

I couldn't have done this alone. I know that everyone says such things, but this particular book has involved a staggering amount of reading and thinking and a fair share of tedium. People have made it happen. Judith

Brandt in London and Leeny Sack in New York have lent me their intelligence—unstintingly, un-repayably. In their own ways, at different times, I have been bolstered, nourished, turned on and enlightened by the help of Honor Moore, Kristen Booth Glen, Quandra Stadler, Susan Kleckner, Edward Tayler and John Simon. I want to thank Janet Kafka for her patience and her confidence that this unwieldy project was worth doing and would happen. The world is full of sisters who inspired me, validated the work and kept it going in a hostile cultural environment; sisters who wrote their own poems and did what they had to. Without all that I might well have spent this time writing about some devious males in Washington or the metrics of John Milton. I do owe, also, a debt to the academy—its members gave me the tools; its attitudes toward women, past and present, gave me the motivation.

CONTENTS

THE POETS OF AMERICA

THE WORLD
SPLIT OPEN

INTRODUCTION

A conversation based on experience, full of imaginative truth. I am talking with a venerable professor of English literature, famous for the scope of his learning and powerful in the liberalism of his concerns. I ask, "What do you know about women poets?"

He: "Women don't make good poets."

I: "Why not?"

He: "Because women are good at accumulation of detail . . ."

He is holding his arms in front of his body, forming a circle with them. He has shaped a pregnant belly.

". . . and not at the sharp, thrusting . . ."

He is making sharp, thrusting motions with one of his arms.

". . . sensibility that is required for good poetry."

This is the sort of person who has written literary history.

WHOSE HISTORY IS LITERARY HISTORY?

What is commonly called literary history is actually a record of choices. Which writers have survived their time and which have not depends upon who noticed them and chose to record the notice. Which works have become part of the "canon" of literature, read, thought about, discussed, and which have disappeared depends, in the same way, on the process of selection and the power to select along the way. Such power, in England and America, has always belonged to white men. That class has written the record called literary history, which is clearly shaped by the attitudes, conscious or unconscious, of white men toward nonwhites and nonmales. As a result of the process whereby male power makes male culture and, therefore, male taste, the literary work of women has either been excluded from literary history or, when included, has been distorted by the values of the class that has transmitted it.

In spite of token talk about Brontës and Dickinsons, most women writers have gotten lost. The professor of the thrusting sensibility claims this is hogwash, that great writers will out whatever the circumstance and that what is lost could not have been very good in the first place. But, asks the antagonist, who lost these women? Who turned out the light and said, "You are obscure"? On what grounds?

Poets have been affected by this class action masquerading as literary history far more than novelists have. Perhaps this is because the novel, living in and being about the social order, includes men more often than not, and women who write about men are more likely to be acknowledged, whatever they are saying, than women who do not. Poems, those sly reports on private experience, voices of the inner self, asocial art forms, may leave men out. Women poets have proven easy to do away with.

Yet one poem by a woman is famous, ingrained in an ordinary grammar-school upbringing with as much insistence as the pledge to the flag. This is Elizabeth Barrett Browning's "How Do I Love Thee?"

Why?

That poem, the emotive voice of a white, heterosexual, married woman, is the "ideal" woman's poem, in men's eyes. It suits male taste. Few know the same poet's tirades against American racism or her feminist verse novel, *Aurora Leigh*. How peculiar it must seem, with that sonnet in mind, that Rilke thought the *Sonnets from the Portuguese* so philosophically compelling and poetically intricate that he translated them into German.

The passing on of those aspects of women's work that are congenial to the male mind both creates and enforces a male value system. The examples in the history of poetry in the English language are endless.

When William Michael Rossetti edited his sister's works, he did not put everything in. Yet something compelled him to set out a list of the poems that were not there:

"Sappho"
"Song: I saw her, she was lovely"
"The pale sad face of her I wronged"
"What Sappho would have said, had her leap
   cured instead of killing her"

Such an act of editorial audacity proceeds from what must have been an honest desire to protect his sister's "reputation." This kind of solicitude has been a consistent pattern in literary history. Thackeray felt obliged to reject one of Elizabeth Barrett Browning's poems for his magazine because he found it "unladylike." Earlier, Aphra Behn was called a whore by her collective public, appalled by the explicit sexuality of her plays and poems. By a curious leap of logic, a woman with a bad reputation, as men defined it, became a woman whose work ought not to be read.

The process by which the work of women poets has been bowdlerized or suppressed, usually on the grounds of "decency," is largely an unconscious one. A man chooses one poem over another for inclusion in his miscellany or anthology or literary review. As far as his consciousness allows, he chooses on the basis of "literary merit," thinking he prefers one poet to another, one poem to another, because he simply likes it better. Such "taste" shapes our sense of the poets of the past.

As long as this process continues, "fame" will continue to be the reward for conformity to class values and a tribute to the skill with which one embodies those values in art. Some poets in this book have achieved fame, but the achievement involves bizarre distortions of their work. I am thinking of Elizabeth Browning and Edna St. Vincent Millay. Each poet seemed to me, when I first collected in my mind what I knew of their lives and work, to conform to what is expected of women. Mrs. Browning was the invalid poetess, the devoted wife, the mistress of sentiment. Yet a reading of her complete literary output and a study of her life shows her to be strange, intellectual, and continuously engaged in struggle against those forces that would have her be simple, wifely, and sentimental.

Edna St. Vincent Millay seemed to conform to another place, another time, and a different male stereotype. She, in the general cultural impress and the selections generally made from her work, comes over as the sexually available, bohemian "New Woman" of the twenties. "My candle burns at both ends" is her most-quoted line, but where is the seriousness of her work and the politics of her thinking in what has become of her reputation? Edna Millay is poetry's Marilyn Monroe.

Conditioned to a partriarchal culture, women have had serious problems with the subject matter of their poetry as well. Woman's place in literary life, if she survives to write at all, has been a place from which men grant her leave to write about either love or religion. Everything else threatens male turf. Love is all right because, like conventional religion, it is an expression of adoration, longing, and dependence in relation to a male figure. In the same way that the culture of romance has siphoned off the energy in female lives, women writers have learned by example that if they want in behind the great oak doors of literary tradition, they had best write love poetry.

It is interesting how the preoccupation with love, in life or literature, has been turned against women. When love poetry was an exclusively male occupation, it was respected and exalted; when women came to accept the terms and follow the Provençal poet's lyre, the genre was deflated. Most poetry written in the nineteenth century by women dealt with love and was treated by the (male) arbiters of taste as maudlin and banal, less for its literary style than for its "sentimental" content. The heightened states of emotion out of which male poets were creating poetry were praised as revolutionary; the heightened states of female emotion were denigrated and dismissed as second-rate.

Religion is a more interesting alternative. It is an acceptable subject because it focuses on the men who are God the Father and the Son, and suits patriarchal taste more subtly. The religious experience, a receiving experience, however intense, is never considered unfeminine. On the contrary. Female passivity, in some cultures, is thought of as a state of nature. Socially and psychologically, then, it has always been acceptable for women to write of the religious experience. Many women have, and much of what they wrote has survived while work dealing with "other" subjects has perished.

Writing about "other" subjects has always meant deep trouble. The gap between what interests women and what interests men has locked women poets into a paralyzing contradiction from which some have emerged and to which others have succumbed. Women's lives bore men. The reality of those lives, especially the embarrassing subject of women's bodies, frightens men. Male approval, the condition of a poet's survival, is withheld when a woman shapes her poetry from the very material that contradicts and threatens male reality. Rage and anger, particularly aimed at men, meet resistance in the male reader. Homosexual love between women may meet indulgence but certainly not understanding. Nor have the guardians of tradition taken kindly to the sound of a woman's voice, alive or on the page, chanting anarchy, chaos, or revolution. When women move into the area of political consciousness, particularly feminism, but in fact any political consciousness, we move out of place.

THE POLITICS OF WOMEN'S POETRY

Every poet in this book lived in a world where survival depended upon men, where what women might think, feel, say, or do was defined by men. Every poet lived in a terrible alienation from the culture from which she was to draw her energy and to which she was to look for her response. It is tempting to read this alienation as no more than the "artist's" situation throughout modern history and to find similarity in the situations, for example, of poets like Donne and Johnson and Will Shakespeare, too, who lived dependent on the ruling class and in their work struggled for a way to survive without too grossly offending the hands that fed them. Yet those poets who lived by patronage had each other for support in ways that women poets rarely have had each other. The School of Donne and the Tribe of Ben could adequately compensate for whatever psychic damage a patron might do. The gulf between poet and coin-delivering aristocrat could not have been so vast as the one between Aphra Behn and King Charles or between Emily Dickinson and her Higginson, who hardly understood her.

Existing dependently in a patriarchal literary situation, women writers have a unique demon to overcome in developing as artists: inhibition. The history of women's poetry might be written in terms of the welling up and discarding and welling up again of inhibition. Periods in individual lives and periods in history have followed such a pattern.

A woman poet constantly pits herself against cultural expectations of "womanhood" and "women's writing." She gives her imagination and courage to that struggle, pours energy into it in ways that do not exist for men. Anger is approached, backed away from, returned to. Woman-ness is sometimes seen as authenticity, the essence to be distilled in the poems. Sometimes it appears as a blemish, the thing to be covered by the poems. A woman poet, in danger of drowning in male-inflicted self-hate, needs to declare her independence in ways that her brother poets do not. Women have written more declarations of independence than men, and for good reason. Women are schooled from childhood in the act of resistance, and the poetry we have written reflects that schooling.

Overcoming the demon inhibition has always meant

rebellion. A woman poet, authentic and in rebellion, is subversive of standard economic, political, social, artistic, and psychic orders. She is barred from the high table of literary tradition and assured invisibility in the eyes of future generations. Historically, the poets who have actively embraced this rebellion as part of their work form a literature all their own. They are feminists, living underground in the world of reputation and fame.

The poems in this book were written in a definite context, rarely spoken of, and changing from period to period in literary history. This context is political and involves some aspect of what, for lack of an appropriate language, has to be called class. The idea of class relationships from writer to writer has been buried by the lingering aroma in literary circles of New Critical attitudes that considered "context" a dirty word and "class" even dirtier. Who might have the materials with which to begin to analyze the context of these poems in terms of class relationships? A graduate of our best educational institutions has studied women writers in a department called "Literature" and, if she has become a specialist, she knows little about history, psychology and economics. The job of acquiring that information and putting it together is only now being started in the field of women's studies. Perhaps, in some years, we will have great experts in the field and we will have studies based on the raw material in this collection.

Without context, and as it presently stands in mainline literary history, women have not existed, or they have existed only in relation to men (the wife of Robert Browning, the sister of Dante Gabriel Rossetti, the sister of Philip Sidney, the consort of Robert Graves), or they have existed as peculiar phenomena of one time and one place. It cannot be a bad thing to experience each woman poet individually, but it is an interesting and truthful enterprise to begin to think of them politically and in relation to one another.

Men have written of "women's art" with their noses wrinkled, as though it had a bad smell, like menstruation.

The term implies second-classness, pettiness, frivolity. We have been taught to think of "greatness" as transcending time, space, and gender. In these terms, women artists are simply "artists" and it is insulting to call them anything else. "Poetess" invites a shiver.

But women are not men and men are not women. There is a connection from woman to woman, present to past, artist to artist, that is never spoken of. That connection is based on identification. The direct communication of inner experience that comes from women poets of the past is a heritage for poets in the present time. These poets know it, write poems about it, receive strength from it, as Adrienne Rich on Emily Dickinson:

> **She chose to have it out at last**
> **On her own premises**

and Amy Lowell on Elizabeth Barrett Browning:

> **. . . Mrs. Browning's heart***
> **Was squeezed in stiff conventions. So she lay**
> **Stretched out upon a sofa, reading Greek**
> **And speculating, as I must suppose,**
> **In just this way on Sapho;**

and Elizabeth Bishop's on Marianne Moore.

A feminist theory of poetry would begin to take into account the context in history of these poems and their political connections and implications. It would deal with the fact that women's poetry conveys with the intensity that is native to it a special kind of consciousness. Whether the word be "class" or "caste" or some word not yet invented, a way of thinking about these poems is

* Excerpt from "The Sisters," by Amy Lowell. From *The Complete Poetical Works of Amy Lowell*. Copyright 1955 by Harvey H. Bundy and G. d'Andelot Belin, Jr., Trustees of the Estate of Amy Lowell. Reprinted by permission of Houghton Mifflin Company.

needed that will clarify the relationship between the words on the page and the circumstances of women's lives. Such a theory would talk of political manifestations of women's oppression and of resistance to it, opening the field to thoughts of class struggle in women's poetry (and what but class struggle can anyone call the many poems of rage against the patriarchy, declarations of independence, fear of domination—the "I am not yours" genre that begins as early as women wrote poetry?), and questions would be raised about the function of art in such a struggle. The poems in this book are, in addition to everything else they are, texts for the study of consciousness in poetry.

Inside the patriarchy, historians and critics resist concepts of "class" and, when it comes to women's writing, are hostile to consideration of historical context. Many prefer the words "major" and "minor" when they try, if they try, to see women poets in relation to the men who were writing at the same time in history. Many insist on this hierarchical vision of literary history, "major" and "minor" alternating with "better" and "worse." This is literature as the Great Chain of Being, with men on top, nearest God, and women farther down, just above the animals, or literature seen as an unending baseball game with major and minor leagues in the full tilt of combat.

Feminist theory would refuse to play this game. Concentrating on consciousness and the politics of women's poetry, such theory would evolve new ways of reading what is here. The role that feminism has played in the evolution of women poets will come clearer, in spite of present obstacles to making that analysis. The materials for such a job are scarce, for not only has feminism been banished from history and whitewashed where it has remained, but the feminism of women writers has been so badly mauled in transmission to our understanding that the search must be begun from scratch.

THE LIVES OF
THE POETS

When, at last, the missing women poets are found, in what peculiar shambles do their lives appear! What is presented as biography amounts to translation. Men who have told women's lives (the "biographers," almost exclusively male) saw what they were capable of seeing, leaving out what was not comprehensible, unknowingly interpreting. What emerges in the telling is the kind of simplification whereby these women were either sinners or saints, whores or madonnas, inspiring muses or devouring *femme fatales*. Rarely have they been pictured as real, whole people. Thus, reduced to single traits, Katherine Philips was gentle and Aphra Behn a whore. Lady Mary Wortley Montagu was a virago and Anna Seward a sweet swan. Emily Brontë was plain Jane. For Elizabeth Browning read pale and frail. In Christina Rossetti see other-worldly. Alice Meynell was an angel in the house, while Edith Sitwell resonates in literary history as a shrew.

In fact, each woman might have possessed her share of the single trait that has come to characterize her, yet each was so much more than has been allowed. Aphra Behn, depending upon who is looking at her life, can certainly be described as brave and rebellious. Emily Brontë, far from plain, was a unique, innovative woman and, in her imagination at least, quite a savage one. Christina Rossetti lived in the "real" world far more than has been allowed. The angelic Alice Meynell turns out to have been quite wild and Sitwell the shrew could be, in her life and in her work, a dear sentimental sop.

As biographers and compilers of encyclopedic guides to poetry and headnotes/footnotes to textbooks reduce the rich and complex lives of these poets to embodiments of the angelic or the demonic, most biographers go on to pronounce a value judgment upon those lives. A pattern emerges in many of the biographical details, a pattern so strongly insisted on and so clearly an example of patriarchal thinking: withdrawal from the world. Emily Dickinson, Emily Brontë, Christina Rossetti, Amy Lowell—women who did not marry—are all described in terms of their "withdrawal." The serious scholarship about them belongs to the *cherchez l'homme* school of inquiry, in which men reveal that they find it hard to understand and downright pathological that women would choose to live without them. It is an odd sort of pronouncement, considering that no one, man or woman, is disturbed by the thought of men who choose to live without women. Such men are usually called holy men and are written about with awe, reverence, and compassion. Yet women without men are described as maimed, incomplete, diseased and, at best, objects of pity.

The question arises as to whether it is possible *not* to live in the world of men and still to live in the world. The answer arises nearly as quickly that this can happen only if men are not thought of as "the world." As a feminist would understand it, here is a capsule history of a woman poet, a composite biographical sketch, in which men are not "the world":

As a girl-child, she had some meager schooling, inferior to what her brothers had if there were brothers in the family. She showed signs of literary talent, which nearly everyone with whom she had contact discouraged. One male figure, however, in whom she had invested considerable authority, told her to continue. Women, sisters or friends, lent support. She lived in constant conflict about being or becoming both poet and woman. A middle-class girl, she was prey to proddings about men and marriage. She resisted, seeing her energy deeply divided, preoccupied with earning an independent living for herself if she did not marry, knowing that women were poor and poets were poor and her chances of survival as woman and poet were, at best, minimal. All this time, she wrote poetry in her journal or under her needlework and tried to learn the poet's craft while allowing her imagination and soul to expand as they would. Then, at some point in her life, knowing it or not knowing it, she began to see herself not as prey but as power. She recognized choice.

If she had been alive in the eleventh or twelfth century, she would have entered a nunnery. Instead, since she lived in the modern world, she found for herself a way to work, a "room of her own," whether literally or as an irresistible metaphor. She learned to stay away from relationships that drained her and took energy from her work, while she managed to retain contact with ideas, events, and the affairs of the human heart, with joy and with pain, friendship and love. Long after she died, she became a well-known poet, although most scholars called her "minor."

Busily, the biographers go to work on such a life story. For courage, they read defeat. The affirmation of life, which the practice of art always is, becomes denial. Richness of mind and heart are mysteriously seen as sterility. Never does it occur to the biographer to consider what the woman experienced in the social order, that *ronde* of discouragement, pressure toward domesticity, and state of constant conflict so blithely called "the world." Never is the possibility raised that the much-touted "world" was for this woman no more than a prison, and the decision to live in it as little as possible a glorious bid for freedom.

Considering such a life, allowing perhaps for the "withdrawal" as an idiosyncratic response, the patriarchal critic, scholar or biographer puzzles over the problem of love. It seems to him that women who loved women had no love in their lives. Such men not only see themselves as "the world," they also see themselves as "love." Women who do not love men, and women who do not have sex with men, in the eyes of men, have loveless and sexless lives. Yet, for all obfuscation about it, the truth seems to be that most of these women poets have loved women, sometimes along with loving men. Women have found in other women exactly that companionship, encouragement, and understanding that they did not find in men. Whether all the woman-to-woman relationships that exist in the lives of these poets were explicitly sexual or not is difficult to know, for taboo was always in the way and evidence that might have told the true nature of those relationships is missing. Yet what matters most is not who did what to whom in what bed, but the direction of emotional attention. Mostly, then, these women turned to women—and understanding that might be the beginning and the end of a nonpatriarchal biography.

Perversely, men ignore the evidence as they wander through thickets in search of the missing lovers they wish to find in these women's lives. This one rejected her, they insist, and so, *ergo*, she withdrew from the world. This one was married to someone else and so, *ergo*, again, she turned to poetry. Male companionship seems the only comprehensible motivation for living or writing. Yet there is contradiction for such ways of thinking in many things that the women wrote. When such a man, bent on refusing to hear what is said, comes upon a passionate poem addressed clearly to "she" or "her," he twists logic to explain what is to him inexplicable and emerges pronouncing that the text has been corrupted. He asserts on no authority that the authentic version is addressed to "he" or "him." If that does not sound convincing, the critic will turn to accepted literary double-think and declare that in the poem under consideration the woman has adopted the "persona" of the male lover addressing his female beloved. It is hard to know what to say to such a critic. She or he would do well to entertain the possibility that poets who are women mean "she" in poems of passion.

THE INSTITUTIONS
OF LITERARY LIFE

"The School of Donne," "the Tribe of Ben," "the Words-worth Circle," "the Rhymers' Club," "the Pre-Raphaelite Brotherhood"—in such clusters have the intellectual move-ments of the past been brought to us. The labels are appropriate. Poets did generally congregate at court, in men's clubs, at Cambridge, in living rooms, in bars, where they shared whatever was to be shared and spread a certain infectious energy among themselves. Male poets, that is. Women had almost nothing to do with such con-gregating, except perhaps to serve tea or sit in a back room copying over manuscripts so the work of the men would make marks for posterity.

In the beginning, stitchers of songs roamed the country-side saying their poems from place to place while women stayed in whatever version there was of "home" and, having little control over the matter, made children, not poems. So the structure was set and when the church be-came a training ground for poets, some women were al-lowed in, but only some. From medieval nunneries we have inherited the earliest poems by women. On the whole, from the beginning until the present, male culture defined the kind of training that was needed to make a poet, set up institutions to provide that training, and excluded women altogether.

Reading and writing was always important. Education always mattered. Renaissance ladies, for a fortuitous col-lision of reasons, had access to extraordinary humanist educations and did, in fact, write poetry, but that was ladies and not women and the situation did not last long. After the Renaissance, the level of ladies' education fell to needlework and music and harmless smatterings of read-ing, all of which enhanced feminine decorativeness but did little to encourage or enable women to become poets. It is miraculous that the women in this book managed to get what learning they had, considering the circumstances.

Yet access to "learning," as it had been defined in the patriarchy, was always a double problem. Women were kept out, which was bad, but when let in, we were exposed to the male way of looking at things, an exposure not always in our best interest.

For example, today a woman might learn of theories that say the roots of poetry lie, historically, in magic and incantation and are connected to the presence of the force that Graves and the scholars who laid his groundwork call "the White Goddess." A woman would learn that poetry is a woman, either historically or metaphorically. What is she to make of this information? If poetry is a woman, why is every woman not a natural poet? Or is she? If a woman becomes more sophisticated in her study of such matters, she will turn to Eric Neumann and learn that the combination of male poet and female muse symbolizes the erotic aspect of the creative act. She will find that interesting, and then she will begin to wish to apply that information to herself. She will find it difficult.

Do women poets see themselves in homosexual relationship to the muse? Can women poets see themselves in any relationship to the muse? Does the figure become maternal and the relationship of poet to muse fit any analysis yet made by anyone? It is not hard to speculate that if a woman sticks with Neumann's analysis and applies it to herself, the psychic conflict caused by that vision might lead her to eliminate the erotic entirely. Alternatively, she might identify with the male poet in this schema and end up perceiving the muse-poet relationship, like everything else, through the grid of male sensibility. The problem here is the problem of what is called "culture" and learning altogether—that women struggle for access and receive as reward a body of knowledge which we have had little part in making, which does not reflect our psychic or material needs and desires, which has, in fact, little utility for us after all.

Another institution of literary life with enormous influence on the poets in this book is the family. It has had as great an effect as literary circles, closed universities, and the perplexing study of iconography. Rarely have women been allowed to live outside families, yet within them, particularly within literary families, this is what happens:

> fathers encourage daughters when there are no male children
>
> brothers overshadow sisters
>
> husbands overshadow wives.

For example: The sister of Sir Philip Sidney is alleged to have had a hand in the *Arcadia*. She, the Countess of Pembroke, was an excellent poet, but the only surviving works from her hand are those having to do with her famous brother—an elegy on his death and translations from the Psalms of David that were done in collaboration with him.

The sister of William Wordsworth always came second in the eyes of the family and, consequently, in her own eyes. Her education was sacrificed for William's. She records in her journal that while William was at Cambridge studying to be a poet, she was at home, rising before the rest of the household to cram in some furtive hours studying the *Iliad*. Her "real" work was housework; the *Iliad* was, culturally considered, a frivolity for her, and Dorothy kept secret the fact that she was reading it.

THE POETS
OF ENGLAND

The earliest poems collected here date from the sixteenth century, which is not the beginning of the story. For all the riches this book contains, there is much missing. The story is amputated all along the way. The women who wrote before the sixteenth century helped build the earliest traditions of English literature, but most of this work was unsigned. The hovering shadows of these lost women ought to be acknowledged at the start, for their presence is felt in the words of all their descendants.

"Anonymous was a woman," says the old joke that is probably not a joke at all. Women have been reluctant to acknowledge authorship of their own work for reasons that have less to do with timidity or masochism than with real historical considerations. Until the nineteenth century, it was considered a violation of morality and a ruination of "virtue" for a woman to write and present her work to a public audience. The history of anonymity for reasons of "virtue" and the sexual politics of such an enterprise does not begin in the English Renaissance, but it was in that period that it was so frequently talked about.

The English Renaissance lady, with whom this history begins, lived quashed in a double bind. If her family was rich and powerful enough, she was encouraged to develop her mind, learn languages, absorb the best of ancient wisdom, be abreast of her times. She was not, as happened to ladies after her, shut away from the world. If her mind made use of what it had been given and created some lines of verse, the lady was thought charming. If by some chance she was taken seriously, she walked thump against a wall that would effectively stop even the most passionately creative soul. The wall was called reputation.

A lady, to be a lady, had to be modest. Her virtue was to be praised and therein lies the problem, for more poets have been lost to "virtue" than to death in childbirth or early starvation or disease in factories and mines. Lady Elizabeth Carew, early in the seventeenth century, set it out in her own words:

'Tis not enough for one that is a wife
   To keep her spotless from an act of ill;
But from suspicion she should free her life,
   And bare herself of power as well as will.
'Tis not so glorious for her to be free,
   As by her proper self restrain'd to be.

When she hath spacious ground to walk upon,
　　Why on the ridge should she desire to go?
It is no glory to forbear alone
　　Those things that may her honour overthrow:
But 'tis thankworthy, if she will not take
All lawful liberties for honour's sake.

That wife her hand against her fame doth rear,
　　That more than to her lord alone will give
A private word to any second ear;
　　And though she may with reputation live,
Yet tho' most chaste, she doth her glory blot,
And wounds her honour, tho' she kills it not.

When to their husbands they themselves do bind,
　　Do they not wholly give themselves away?
Or give they but their body, not their mind,
　　Reserving that, tho' best, for others' prey?
No, sure, their thought no more can be their own,
And therefore should to none but one be known.

Then she usurps upon another's right,
　　That seeks to be by public language grac'd;
And tho' her thoughts reflect with purest light
　　Her mind, if not peculiar, is not chaste.
For in a wife it is no worse to find
A common body, than a common mind.

From the time those words were written, woman's
strength, the root of the word "virtue" in patriarchal
dictionaries, lay in her invisibility, her passivity, the force
with which she kept all doors closed. Women knew quite
well that if one woman signed her work with her own
name, she opened herself to moral and social abuse. To
become anonymous was the only way to survive the social order, if one cared to survive.

　　The pressure against woman's visibility still existed in
the nineteenth century, when great numbers of writers

signed their work with male pseudonyms. This is the same old story dressed in a new pair of trousers. In that period, the most patriarchal of times, to become an ersatz male was the only road to distinction. The outpouring of what was signed as "women's literature" was sneered at, for "women's literature" meant, without further explanation, frivolous, saccharine, decorative, and inconsequential. For a woman with her eye fixed on the company of Shakespeare, Milton, and Wordsworth, the only way to be taken seriously was to become "Acton Bell" or to invent the name "Vernon Lee," which was done by two women who published as though they were one man.

For these reasons, what exists in the literature, signed by women, is but a hint of what was actually written. Al though there were women who wrote poetry before the Renaissance, it is in that period that a body of literature begins to form. Mary Sidney, Countess of Pembroke, is an important germinal figure, representative of women of her class at that time—those ladies in contact with the classics of the ancient world, the art of rhetoric, natural philosophy, ladies able to read, if not to write, Latin and the modern languages of Europe. These ladies, exposed at court or in great country estates to the likes of Shakespeare and Donne, ladies with advantage, had a chance of becoming poets themselves. Many surely did. In 1589, Puttenham wrote in *The Art of English Poesie:*

> **Dark word or doubtful speech are not so narrowly to be looked upon in a large poem, nor especially in the pretty poesies and devices of Ladies and Gentlewomen-makers, whom we would not have too precise poets lest with their shrewd wits, when they were married they might become a little too fantastical wives**

thereby indicating, among other things, the existence of poets who have disappeared. Women who, like Mary Sidney, survived are known to us as patrons of the great male poets. Yet they had voices of their own, now unheard. The reign of Elizabeth was a time of splendid, learned, intellectual, and powerful women. A proverb of the time said that "England is a paradise for women, a prison for servants, and a hell or purgatory for horses."

The poetry written by men and women in the sixteenth and early part of the seventeenth centuries was intellectual, learned, aristocratic, as the audience for poetry was intellectual, learned, and aristocratic. The multiple revolutions of the seventeenth century, political, scientific, economic, artistic—all that unsettlement and rapid change—affected the lives of women of all classes and had a great deal to do with the poetry written by them in the latter part of the century.

The different sound of the poets after the Civil War corresponds generally to what is said in literary history about the transition from ancient to modern ways of thinking and writing poetry at the time. Katherine Philips, Aphra Behn, Ann Collins, and the Countess of Winchilsea are less corseted than their ancestors by the bounds of modesty, chastity, and virtue.

Enter now the middle-class lady, masquerading as aristocrat, longing for the old order. The daughter of a London merchant, educated at one of the best boarding schools, a woman with a husband of small importance in the literary life of the country. The first woman, then, to stand on her own was Katherine Philips. Enter, also, the accepted feminine lifestyle of she-poets: a comfortable country house, a literary circle with herself at the center, a set of pastoral names, old-fashioned and "literary" in that self-conscious sense—a *précieuse*. Orinda, as she called herself, acquired a literary reputation, against which she quite modishly protested. The first volume of poetry by an English woman to appear in print was prefaced by a self-deprecatory note from its author:

. . . **She who never writ any line in my life with an intention to have it printed** . . .

> I am so far from expecting applause for any thing I
> scribble that I can hardly expect pardon; and sometimes
> I think that employment so far above my reach and un-
> fit for my sex that I am going to resolve against it for
> ever . . .

> The truth is, I have an incorrigible inclination to that
> folly of riming and intending the effects of that humour
> only for my own amusement in a retired life, I did not
> so much resist it as a wiser woman would have done.

In the poems that follow her note, Orinda neatly re-
moves herself from public themes ("I think not on the
State, nor am concerned/Which way soever the great
helm is turn'd"), except to attack the murderers of King
Charles I. Instead of the topical poems Aphra Behn was
to write, Orinda stayed close to classical themes, writing
of love and of women, often of both together, for the first
time since Sappho. In an age that made so much of
friendship, in literature as well as in life, little on that
theme by women has endured and Orinda's words are,
therefore, a true historical gold mine. That friendship becomes love in the poems and in her few remaining letters.
The critics who have noticed her work have overlooked
this, one of her persistent themes, knowing less what to
say about it than critics used to know what to say of
Shakespeare's love for the young man.

The first professional woman writer, Aphra Behn,
managed, in a time grown more repressive and restrictive
of women than the golden age of Elizabethan England,
to earn a living for herself by her wits. Being both
astonishingly verbal and very much experienced of the
world, the living came from writing.

Behn was a considerable presence in "the World"—
that is, the world as men defined it, organized it, participated in it. Both Katherine Philips, who lived just before
her, and the Countess of Winchilsea, who lived just after,
as well as most women poets down to the twentieth cen-

tury, lived on the fringe of that world. But Aphra Behn created for herself, seized, in fact, a life in the open, a life among the affairs of men. Her report on that world is the content of her writing.

She says, in the poems, things so far unheard from women's pens. And she often says them slyly, with wit and learning, great good humor and brilliant language. She is an iconoclast, smashing the tidy dreams of state and lawful rule, telling the truth about the sweet confectionary world of love between nymph and swain in idealized landscapes. "Love in fantastic triumph sat" is more than a baroque conceit. It is a poem about the unequal power of men and women in the enterprise of love. "A thousand martyrs I have made" sounds a voice singing what men are most displeased to hear—a woman with a sense of her own pleasure, a woman not always the victim of men, a woman capable of realism and of cynicism about sexual encounters. It is a voice made famous three centuries later in America by Edna St. Vincent Millay.

Aphra Behn wandered her own way through the landscape of love and sex, and told what she saw there: that women spend too much time and energy making themselves attractive to men; that women are constrained by the inability to control the means of reproduction; that women like sex; that men are sometimes impotent; that women respond erotically to other women.

Such a voice had not been heard in English literature before and would not be again for some time to come. It invented itself without precedent out of the life of the woman who owned it, was vilified and occasionally admired in its own time and then fell silent.

The literature of the period after Aphra Behn, to which the work of the Countess of Winchilsea provides a bridge, was urbane. It was made in the city, related to a literary marketplace, a circle of wits, a stylish mode not much preoccupied with being a serious writer. Alongside the urbanity was a strain of pomposity and didacticism unparalleled in literature. It was a period in which women entered more fully into the literary life of the nation, still mostly ladies, but more and more from the class nourished by the city. From the poetry written at the time, women came into literary life with a need to defend their right to existence. Who can surmise what the energy that was poured into peculiar poems like "In Answer to a Lady Who Advised Retirement" or "To One Who Questioned Her Being the Author of some Verses"—who would dare guess what such defensive energy might have produced were it freed from the need to protest so much?

The best work of the period was not in poetry, but in prose: the essay, the novel, uncategorizable forms of what is now journalism. Also, in talk. And therein enter the ladies, militant. They are bored with card parties and they do not drink. Having seen what was accomplished in neighboring France, they organize English reflections of the salon. Social life, the lady's domain, merges uneasily with literary life and produces two generations of extraordinary women, while having some side effect on the general opinion of "the fair sex" in the process.

Still, from the Bluestockings, as they came to be called (the term indicated casual dress. "Come in your blue stockings; don't worry about dress," said one of the first, Mrs. Vesey, to a man who protested he hadn't a thing to wear), with their talk and their theories and the tracts about the need to educate women, with their powerful allies among the men (Richardson, Defoe, Swift, Addison, Steele), with their own accomplishments (book-length studies of Shakespeare, the whole of Epictetus put into English), came no poets worth reading, except for information on how it was with them at the time. Even then, prose tells more.

More people were readers than before, and among them more were women. The demands of the audience produced a suitable commodity; the eighteenth century contains the beginning of that species called "female literature" which has been with us ever since. But what ladies would want to read was decided, in the beginning at least, by men. Mister Steele's *Tatler* and *Spectator* were popular because they took women into account as part of the reading public, with articles on housewifery, dress, manners, and cookery. Quite early on, Mrs. Eliza Haywood started her *Female Spectator*, not very different, in spite of its female editorship, from what Steele put out. Mrs. Haywood, however, for the boldness of her participation in a patriarchal enterprise, was said to have a "doubtful reputation."

Most serious female literary energy went into prose. Women went along with the mainstream in that sense. The poems included in this book indicate that when women did turn to poetry, they did so with that odd mixture of self-assertion and self-deprecation that appears in so many other periods of history. The best poems of the time are the most personal. Although many Bluestockings wrote on political themes, they did so in a way that tries the modern ear.

By the nineteenth century, literary life was locked in patriarchy, with the gentlemanly profession of publishing confined largely to the upper-middle class. A poet was dependent upon the editors of the many literary reviews and magazines published at the time, particularly toward the end of the century. Men ruled the magazines, with a few exceptions. Men defined what was proper for women to read or to publish. Consequently, Thackeray could quite easily reject Elizabeth Browning's poem "Lord Walter's Life" because it was about "unlawful passion" and therefore an unsuitable subject for a woman.

After the drought of the eighteenth century, women's writing in the nineteenth was a deluge. The literary life of those hundred years was a din of women's voices whining, declaiming, inventing, discovering, departing. Some poets of the period were awful, now unreadable, dribbling a treacle of women's verse. Two—Emily Brontë and Christina Rossetti—were among the finest poets of English literature. Many more were very good in endless varieties of ways, and one—Elizabeth Barrett Browning—

however the poetry may have failed, had a vision of women and of the world that is shattering still in its clarity and revolutionary impact.

The actual changes in women's lives had much to do with the sudden explosion of writers and the appearance among the scores of a few great ones. The world into which Mary Wollstonecraft dropped her bombshell book, *The Vindication of the Rights of Woman*—this world in which women were the most exploited class of laborers, the least educated children, the most disenfranchised adults—such a world convulsed again and again through the course of the century. Out of that convulsion came the greatest poems of the period in their multitude and their brilliance.

The context of women's literature is women's politics. The decades of the 1830s and 1840s saw, in England, an accumulation and outburst of feminist energy on a large and visible scale, a coming to consciousness that even though it was muted for thirty years after, sprung out again at the end of the century with such force that no poet was unaware of it and few were untouched by it. In spite of the fact that Darwin was censored in the household of Mary Coleridge and that Christina Rossetti pasted over the "offensive" passages in Swinburne, women at the end of the nineteenth century began throwing off Victorian "protectiveness" and freeing themselves from the social corset of chivalry. By that time a woman might write, although she did not descend from the best families in the realm, although she had desultory schooling instead of a private tutor, and although the act of publishing her own work under her own name remained an oddity and, in some circles, a social sin.

A hundred women marching were and are both cause and equivalent of ten women writing.

Emily Brontë went out into the early-nineteenth-century world a few times, went to school, found it all intolerable and stayed home instead in a parsonage out on the Yorkshire moors. For companionship in the thirty short years of her life, she had Charlotte, the eldest sister,

Anne, the youngest, and Branwell, the only brother. Together, the Brontë children, these isolated people smothered by money worries, spun Gothic lives in their imaginations out on the heath with the wind and the force of the terrain appearing in their novels and poems.

All of them, from the father to the children, wrote from their earliest days. Writing was psychic survival. For years the Brontë children worked on the construction of their elaborate make-believe world, Gondal, writing stories and poems that often came from several hands together. Gondal was full of medieval and romantic pageantry, dungeons, deaths, and love songs. It was a collective passion on the part of the children for the interesting lives that were not to be had.

Emily Brontë's poems, some of them, were part of the Gondal enterprise. A difficulty of Brontë scholarship involves settling on which ones were, for some poems were private snatches written only for herself. Charlotte Brontë had more passion than the others for living in the ways of the world, a passion more commonly called ambition. From Charlotte's impetus, this private poetry found its way into a published book. The *Poems by Currer, Ellis and Acton Bell* was, upon payment of thirty guineas by the authors, published and ignored in 1846.

Emily Brontë's poems are the first large body of work in which that strange and wonderful voice so rarely heard manages to come through. It is the private and inner voice of a woman who, unlike her precedessors, is not speaking for the world, has no audience in mind, has not shaped herself to charm or impress anyone, does not seem to be writing for men's eyes in any way. This authentic woman's voice—what you hear when no one is listening—is probably that elusive quality people later found so hard to nail down as indication of what is so great in the work of Emily Dickinson.

Emily Brontë's voice is full of violence. Her poetry is as brutal as the prose of *Wuthering Heights*, which so perplexed and offended its first readers. The poetry is hurled by a force that is new. Everything in it takes place in the inner landscape and the poet pours out passion, hope, despair, ecstasy, an uncensored range of emotions. She pits her mind and her heart against death. In many ways, Emily Brontë belongs to the period and is historically a Romantic poet. In the deepest ways, however, she belongs only to herself.

Technically, Emily Brontë is far ahead of her time. What in Hopkins would be called innovative some fifty years after, Brontë experimented with early: the sprung rhythm, the colliding words, the invented language. Her subjects are "modern" in the same way: the expressionistic wrestle with one's unwilling soul, the entrapment of the spirit in the body, the recoil from the contemporary world. For premonitions of the spiritual intensity coupled with poetic eccentricity that draws readers to Hopkins, Emily Brontë's "I saw thee, child" might be laid for a moment beside Hopkins' "Spring and Fall: To a Young Child."

Emily Brontë constantly calls up comparison with the other Emily, the one on the other side of the Atlantic. In the work of Emily Dickinson is that register of dreams, sensations, thoughts, hallucinations as they came to a poet who similarly refused to live as a woman of her time was meant to.

A woman encountering the world on her own terms, without the mediation of men, having a face-on confrontation with existence somehow, miraculously, stripped of the conventions of female life—all this Emily Brontë managed by renunciation of what "the empty world," in her words, offered. Charlotte Brontë took that world on and the outcome of her struggle is in the novels. The conflict of women's desires with the social order, so brilliantly articulated in the novels, is inchoate in the poetry of both Brontë sisters.

Enter the legend: sweet, invalid, dear Miss Barrett. Pale, frail "Ba" in the closed room, victim of perpetual illness. Doll's face, those ringlets round her head. Dear

Miss Barrett, lying there the day long, wasting away, waiting for—at last, it comes, the life-force incarnate, virile Robert Browning! Free from the sickness unto death, the pale desert of the years before, Miss Barrett runs away with Mr. Browning into the warm sun, cured. Somewhere along the way she commits to paper these delicate lines, expressing the sum of what is on her mind:

> How do I love thee? Let me count the ways
> I love thee to the depth and breadth and height
> My soul can reach . . .

Such an Elizabeth Browning is fictive. The mythology about her comes from a play called *The Barretts of Wimpole Street* and that play, with the several films it spawned, lodged quite firmly in the mind such a revolting set of associations to the name of Elizabeth Browning that few since have been interested in reading her work.

In truth, she was a strange and progressive woman with a wild imagination and a head full of grotesque images. She struggled from beginning to end to disenchain herself from her role as Lady. She was probably, as a consequence of the medication doled out mercilessly for her vague illnesses, somewhat addicted to opium, and this shows in the poems. By the time Browning came into her life, she was an established poet, considered formidably intellectual and difficult to understand. Browning was drawn to her by her work. She was, also, an intensely political woman, supporting the liberation struggle in Greece in the twenties and in Italy thirty years later. After she and Browning eloped to Italy, she became totally involved in that country's struggle.

Her life in the Italian sunshine extended for fifteen years and in that time she enraptured herself with spiritualism, reached out for realities beyond the material, opened her husband's mind to worlds he had never dreamt, and published a manifesto for intellectual freedom for women, *Aurora Leigh*, a verse novel which Susan

B. Anthony carried in her trunk across the American continent. Four years after *Aurora Leigh,* Elizabeth Barrett Browning hurled at the world a pamphlet called *Poems before Congress,* cursing the American nation for its racism. She and Browning had a child when she was forty-three years old and she brought the child up with a disregard for convention considered bohemian among the bohemians living in Florence.

Such a life shows the poet suffering less (if it is possible to judge another's suffering) from the physical disease that confined her to her darkened room in the house of her father than from the curse of being born a Lady in the nineteenth century. Her youthful education, compared to her brothers', was scanty. What learning she did acquire was largely on her own. It was the prodigious self-education that Browning so much admired in her. As a Lady-in-Training, Elizabeth was blessed with endless leisure and an enormous emptiness of expectation. The tyrannizing father was no more and no less a patriarch than most gentlemen of the time, but he managed somehow to become the first person to acknowledge his daughter's poetry, financing the private publication of an adolescent fantasy of hers called *The Battle of Marathon.* His active Whig politics influenced her first interests in slavery, the Corn Laws and the struggle in Greece. But the patriarch drew back as the poet matured and took on her own voice, drew back further when she left his home for Italy and Browning. Not from Mr. Barrett did the young poet learn what she was later to write about the oppression of women. She had her own experience to rely on and she read Mary Wollstonecraft at fourteen.

Without the legend in the way, Elizabeth Browning and her work are impressive. Her literary production includes translation of the *Prometheus* of Aeschylus, impressionistic lyrics about the sea, verse musings on the nature of poetry, criticism of her contemporaries, political lyrics and polemics, pseudo-medieval ballads of languishing ladies, poems about British class consciousness, child labor, Adam and Eve, studies of the early Greek Christian poets. The list of subjects alone is a tribute to the courage of the poet. She grappled for years with the question of the woman artist, and with few precedents before her, unknown to her, produced *Aurora Leigh*, an exploration of contention between society's attitude toward women and the vision of one female poet, a meditation and polemic on the damage life does to art.

Conspicuously absent from this scan of what the poet wrote about is the subject of love. But, of course, she wrote about love. *Sonnets from the Portuguese* are the private meditations of a forty-year-old woman on the subject of heterosexual married love. As such, embodying all that is expected of women, they currently are both held in contempt and considered typical of what women can do with poetry. They are little read these days. In her own lifetime, Elizabeth Barrett made little fuss over those sonnets and had them published, in fact, in a two-volume edition of *Poems* (1850), most of which had been in print before. There was no critical stir at the time.

In the same period of time, another woman was quietly writing, a woman who was to be completely overshadowed by her poet-brother. Dante Gabriel Rossetti's fame is large —for his poetry, for his aesthetics, for his painting—and his fame is intimately connected with a movement and a group. What space was there for Christina Rossetti in the legendary Pre-Raphaelite brotherhood? None.

She, Christina, sat to her brother as model for his paintings of the Virgin. She, Christina, had little to say in the ponderous talk of form, content, and ideal beauty that went on in her presence. She, Christina, observed the actualization of the Pre-Raphaelite idealization of haunted, ethereal female beauty, saw how it led to the passion of her brother for Elizabeth Siddons, saw how it destroyed, disembodied, laid waste both the woman Elizabeth who was its object and the brother Dante who was its victim.

She had nothing to do with any of it. Here, then, is another recluse, another woman shut off from the world.

Sickly as Elizabeth Browning, sunk deep in a world of her own, with a set of visions of the other side filling her days, a pain, joy, anguish having little to do with court-ships gone sour or ambition thwarted, little to do with the ordinary sense of life. She was one of the greatest religious poets in the English language.

Again, "recluse" is wrong. There were women in her life, a mother, a sister, friends. Toward the end of her life there were more intimate relationships with women; perhaps the fear of the world's contempt for that passion had passed toward the end. There are innumerable love poems to women in her collected work.

Brontë, Browning, and Rossetti are a richness of the past. The poets who lived after them owe them a debt for the sheer audacity of the way each of them lived and for the brilliance of their contribution to our literature. By the twentieth century, it was no longer fashionable to argue whether or not women had souls. It was under-stood that souls and brains come caged in female bodies as equally as they do in male bodies. The streets of Ox-ford and Cambridge had been trod by scholarly female feet for thirty years when the century began. Victoria was in her grave. Albert Hall was used for women's meetings.

So modernism arrived. Out of the patriarchal past, from behind the bars walling women away from the world, came a parade of poets, the mothers of the literature of our time. Alice Meynell. The suffragettes in Holloway. Charlotte Mew. Anna Wickham. Sitwell. Virginia Woolf and Virginia Moore.

Before, during, and after the First World War, shaping the consciousness of England and America, the woman movement carried along with it not only opportunities for lower, middle, and higher education, not only enfranchise-ment of women, not only protective labor laws and divorce laws, not only a wedge in the wall of Victorian men guarding their professions and their possessions, but a shattering sense of feminist consciousness, a bridge from woman to woman, a direct assault upon the institutions of social and economic life, an attack which demolished the myth of the pale frail maiden and created instead a community of strong, brave, and visible women.

This was a revolution that did not pass with time, although it often passed out of the historical record. Not everyone was affected by this revolution. Male poets paid little attention and went on thinking and writing of women the way they always had. The impact on women, however, and on the poetry women wrote, was enormous.

There was a second tide, and a third. The consciousness, if not always the content, of the woman movement in the early part of the century and the writers who reflected it, was felt in the thirties, in the forties, and in the fifties. Many poets wrote directly out of that consciousness, not as solitary figures peering for the first time from behind the illusion that literature was a male enterprise, but as women with a shared language, an historical connection to community, and a reasonable expectation of a receptive readership, however small.

When the war came to Spain and then to all of Europe, the war appeared in women's poetry as women experienced it. No apologies. No remoteness. No need to guess at what it was like "out there." Sinking into the personal past, then deeper into the collective past, into the body, into the unconscious, the poets emerged not with male images, not with the history of male experience, but with the Corn Goddess, the Virgin, Anne Boleyn, and the female spider.

In the second and third waves were the poets Edith Sitwell, Elizabeth Daryush, Ruth Pitter, Kathleen Raine, Laura Riding (an American), and Ann Ridler.

The influence of feminism upon these poets, in fact the history of feminism and its relation to intellectual currents of the century, remains unwritten. It will be told when, first of all, it is acknowledged to be a story worth telling. And the teller will have to overcome phenomenal obstacles, wading past the rather thorough record of what all the brilliant men in the ferment before, during, and after the war said to each other, in order to reconstruct what the women said, who knew whom, what kind of influence women had on each other. Such a history, when written, will point to Bloomsbury and the feminism in that circle as an important force in the history of English literature. The ideas among the people in Bloomsbury were important, for they not only spoke of "new" thinking about women and about the equal participation of women in the moral and artistic adventure they saw themselves embarking upon, but Bloomsbury also provided models of women artists, functional, recognized, long before Virginia became a Woolf and Vanessa a Bell.

Bloomsbury is important, too, as an indication of the many ways women absorbed power in the patriarchal literary world at the beginning of the century and, when those women who achieved power were interested in the work of other women, provided access to the means of production, more or less, that had not existed before. For many who might have lived out their lives in obscurity, the Woolfs' publishing enterprise was salvation.

In the same way, Alida Munro is an important figure in twentieth-century English poetry, for it was she who "discovered" Charlotte Mew and published her work, as Sylvia Beach is important and, in America, Harriet Monroe and *Poetry* magazine.

THE POETS OF AMERICA

In America, the history of women poets has a different shape. The earliest period is sparse, but includes the excellent and important poet Anne Bradstreet. The nineteenth century is somewhat less crammed with "poetesses" than the same period in England. Although there was a fair share of women writing and publishing, only Emily Dickinson produced a body of work as arresting as that of the Brontës, Browning, or Rossetti. The "new world," however, is the source of a powerful body of indigenous poetry by women that is not conventionally defined as part of the national literature. The songs of women in the early mill towns, the organizing and protest songs of Aunt Molly Jackson, Ella Mae Wiggins, and Sarah Ogan Gunning, the lyrics written and sung by "Ma" Rainey, Bessie Smith, and Billie Holiday—these forms of women's poetry and the many others in those genres that remain uncollected, not thought of as poetry, the literature in those traditions have no equal in England's history.

America's first poet was born in England and, by the time she was seventeen and had emigrated to Massachusetts, had well in her mind the examples of women writers of the Renaissance. Although, growing up in a Puritan household, she might have been barred from reading her contemporary sister writers, Anne Bradstreet had clearly been infected by the example of Elizabeth I, by the legacy of female intellect of the period. When she sailed from Southampton and by the time she arrived in Salem harbor in 1630, the young Englishwoman brought with her the seeds of a literary ambition that took root in the hardship of her life in those grim New England years. She became America's first poet, against overwhelming odds.

Lacking the structure of English court life, wherein queens and women of rank might assemble brilliant and learned ladies about themselves and acquire whatever knowledge might be imparted by the Erasmuses and Thomas Mores of the time, colonial American women had no literary or intellectual culture of their own making, at first, from which they could draw inspiration and support. As the Puritan culture in which Anne Bradstreet spent her life took on more and more definition, its attitude toward women of intelligence or literary ambition became more severely repressive. The journal of Governor John Winthrop, a document that became the first history of New England, records the "case" of a woman called Anne Yale Hopkins, wife of the governor of Connecticut who, in the early 1640s, seems to have gone mad because she wanted

to write. Winthrop's opinion may be taken as standard for
the time and place, indicative of what Anne Bradstreet
was up against. The governor's journal describes Mrs.
Hopkins as a woman who

> was fallen into a sad infirmity, the loss of her under-
> standing and reason, which had been growing on her
> divers years, by occasion of her giving herself wholly
> to reading and writing, and had written many books
> . . . if she attended her household affairs, and such
> things as belong to women, and not gone out of her
> way and calling to meddle in such things as are proper
> for men, whose minds are stronger, etc., she had kept
> her wits, and might have improved them usefully and
> honourably in the place God had set her.

Anne Bradstreet's life in such a culture was full of
implicit danger to the development of her selfhood and
her poetry. Additionally, her life was full of immediate
dangers. She had eight children, all of whom survived.
Her own survival is against all the death-in-childbirth
statistics of the time. She was often ill and still survived,
in conditions where medical aid was hard to come by. Her
place in the early colony was severely defined by the men
in her life, father and husband, by their duties in admin-
istration of the colonial government and their social standing and what they required of her as wife and daughter.
What knowledge she had of the world of affairs—in a
time when the world of affairs was in constant riot—came
through the men around her. News of the Civil War in
England, an event that engaged her and became one of the
subjects she wrote poems about, came across the sea in
the form of dispatches that were communicated to her
husband and her father. She never heard the news except
through them. She never, judging from what has been recorded of her life, met another writer face-to-face. She
lived through the Anne Hutchinson controversy and must
have been affected by the spectacle of the mustered patri-

archal forces of Massachusetts bent on crushing the woman who claimed to speak of divine things because of her contact with the source of divinity. Some parallel must have occurred to Anne Bradstreet, uncertain and apologetic as she would have been about it, for she in her own way was committed to speaking out what her mind and sensibility told her.

Uncertain and apologetic—how consistently those moods appear in periods where women who wrote poetry did so in a cultural desert. Anne Bradstreet's attitude toward the definition of women's place, expressed in Winthrop's journal, took the form, as it did for so many women, of self-mockery. Throughout her life, she called herself, in the poems, "thus weak-brained I" or wrote, "My Subject's bare, my Brain is bad."

"The Prologue" is a poem similar to Ann Finch's answer to Pope, taking up the same argument on behalf of female intelligence, playing the same falsely ingratiating game with the imagined males to whom the poem is addressed. In that poem, Bradstreet mutes the self-deprecatory tone somewhat and writes instead of the cultural context that caused it in the first place:

> I am obnoxious to each carping tongue
> Who says my hand a needle better fits,
> A Poets pen all scorn I should thus wrong,
> For such despite they cast on Female wits:
> If what I do prove well, it won't advance,
> They'l say it's stoln, or else it was by chance.

"A Dialogue between Old England and New," which may be the earliest literary record from the colonies of feelings about the English Civil War, is told in terms of symbolical female figures. "Old England" is the mother, a weeping, satin-draped, formerly splendid old woman, and "New England" is her daughter, a sensible young woman in homespun cloth, someone like Anne Bradstreet. Throughout the poet's work, female figures are prominent. One of her first poems is an elegy on Sir Philip Sidney in which the poet quarrels with the Muses, who seize her pen from her and prevent her, for some hundred lines, from completing the poem. Possibly the opposition Anne Bradstreet felt to the usurping act of writing poems came not only from men but from the good wives in the young colony who kept their places as instructed.

There is no evidence of what Anne Bradstreet had in her mind about the possible publication of what she wrote. She did nothing to have the work published, but she did show it to others. She had not the adamant resistance of Emily Dickinson, but then "publication" did not mean in the seventeenth century the same kind of editorial meddling that Emily Dickinson rightly feared. It is appropriate that the Bradstreet poems published in her lifetime were printed and sold in England, from where their original energy had come.

Supposedly it was the poet's brother-in-law who took a manuscript of her poems to England without her knowledge. They were printed in 1650 with the title *The Tenth Muse, Lately Sprung Up in America*. Whether the poet was genuinely ignorant of that daring act of publication, or simply following the convention that a woman not actively seek a public audience, is impossible to tell. Clearly, her aspirations were high. Bradstreet undertook ambitious poetic projects, including an epic about the kingdoms of man, and seems altogether to lack the temperament that would have sought what Katherine Philips, in England, was at that very time describing as "submissive greatness," the modest woman's rightful place in history.

The few other women from whom poetry survives in America's eighteenth century were tied to practical affairs, contemporary events in what they wrote. Lucy Terry, a slave who managed surreptitiously to learn to write, composed a "verse account" of an Indian raid on Old Deerfield. No other work of hers has been found. Mercy Warren, a privileged woman from one of the original Plymouth families, was educated by her parish minister and then by her famous brother James, who had been in Harvard University's class of 1743. Mercy Warren poured her energy and intelligence into the first contemporary account of the American Revolution, a three-volume enterprise published in 1805 under the unwieldy title *The History of the Rise, Progress and Termination of the American Revolution, Interspersed with Biographical, Political and Moral Observations.* There were a few poems from her hand, none particularly arresting.

Phyllis Wheatley is more interesting as a phenomenon than as a poet. This slave girl, brought from Senegal into the service of a fine Boston family, showed an aptitude for learning which was recognized by her owner, who taught her to write. If it had not been politically propitious to do so, she would not likely have received the kind of fame she was accorded in her lifetime. Wheatley was taken up as a *cause célèbre* by antislavery forces. The "Negress Poetess" she was called, and it was talked about as remarkable that a black person and "a girl to boot" could produce acceptable poetry. A reader looking to Phyllis Wheatley for early manifestations of black consciousness and woman consciousness will be disappointed. Her blackness is hardly present in the poems, her womanliness never. Phyllis Wheatley's poems pleased the ruling class from which she won her freedom as payment of a sort for being pleasing. In London, her poetry was issued in a collection and the poet traveled to England, where she was much celebrated for a while. On her return to America, her life trailed off into marriage, poverty and, having outlived her social usefulness, no more poems.

Margaret Fuller once wrote that women in Athens, "shut out from the market place, made up for it at religious festivals. For human beings are not so constituted that they can live without expansion. If they do not get it in one way, they must in another or perish."

In the nineteenth century, American women of literary bent began to create ways of "getting it." Although the lives of women poets are usually told in isolation from other women of their time, the truth is, and it was particularly true in the nineteenth century, both in England and America, that women have always formed circles, quilting bees, coffee klatches, whatever the patriarchy calls them. American women of Margaret Fuller's time who came together in groups to discuss literature had what ought to be called early consciousness-raising sessions in those talks. Abolition became a magnet, drawing to the cause a circle of women who became, in varying degrees, feminists, political activitists, and poets.

Still, in a social context that strangled the development of female selfhood, in a world where the suggestion that ladies' garments be worn more loosely and that the road to mental health lay in allowing ladies to move their bodies around, to swing their arms down country lanes, was regarded as outrageous (and the proponent of such a program was hooted out of the towns in which she spoke), one poet managed to make a miracle. She found a way to breathe.

In 1862 Emily Dickinson wrote to Thomas Higginson asking if her poems "breathed." Living as she did in the stifling gentility of upper-middle-class Amherst, the poet had cause to worry about breathing. Well inside the patriarchy, in a household that revolved, in all the traditional ways, around a domineering father, in a culture whose established heritage was that "ladies"—and Emily Dickinson was an American "lady"—were charming, acquiescent, and voiceless, she did in her poetry what she could never have done out loud. Or could never have done without suffering severely dislocating consequences. She found a voice both original and strange in which to speak with the kind of honesty that exists in no other poet of her time, male or female. That voice *is* the poems and through that voice, she breathes.

In an earlier time, Dickinson would have been burned as a witch, for she spoke in tongues and she spoke against authority. She is not only the poet of consciousness, the register of that mysterious interaction between the inner self and the world of nature, but the poet who has set herself against religious orthodoxy, the social order, and the poetic standards of her time. She assumes control, in the poems, of her own vocabulary, rhymes, meter, line length. She usurps control of the world, too, in those poems, making herself its ruler, its arbiter, at times its god. She was, of course, considered queer, and Higginson thought her mad.

Emily Dickinson shows little sense anywhere in her work of having been moved by other writers, with one important exception. In a body of poetry that is nowhere literary, it is astonishing to come upon three poems of tribute to another poet: Elizabeth Barrett Browning. For a poet of such an allegedly nonpolitical nature, those tributes to Elizabeth Browning are quite extraordinary.

Charlotte Perkins Gilman is not known as a poet, but her single volume is interesting because she set down in poetry, early in her life, what she would later hone, intensify, and deliver to the world from lecterns and in prose. The woman consciousness in her work pervades what women wrote in America during the last years of the nineteenth century and the early part of the twentieth.

Adelaide Crapsey led a life that seems, like so many others, to have been lived in consciousness, in reading, in the study of metrics and the teaching of poetry. She was called "overwrought" like so many others—like Dickinson and Teasdale and many more, the "neurotics" in the eyes of critics, all suffering from "nerves." This Adelaide Crapsey, mysteriously obscure, invented a poetic form of her own, the cinquain. She came early and without apparent commerce with the others to the kind of metric experimentation and linguistic spareness that was to characterize one major poetic movement of the first part of the current century.

A rotting copy of Adelaide Crapsey's *Verse*, published in 1915, one year after her death, has the judgment of some long-dead anonymous reader scrawled on nearly every page. "Morbid!" he says, as though in protest. It is easy to trace that mood called morbid both backward and forward in the history of women's poetry. The anonymous scribbler in Crapsey's volume has made an astute literary judgment. Emily Brontë, Christina Rossetti, Mary Coleridge, Emily Dickinson, the forgotten writers of treacle-verse in ladies' magazines, many of the first poems of any young woman trying out her voice—all these are morbid. They are preoccupied with death, turned inward, melancholy and despairing, strange in a chilling and not altogether "healthy" way.

Why? The sadness, suffering, lamentation in those poems is real enough, but still some analysis is needed to explain the extraordinary degree of morbidity in what women have written. Perhaps such an analysis ought to begin with what has already been so well understood in the psychology of women: anger. The relationship between stifled anger and depression in any of its forms, including morbidity, is the place to begin understanding what amounts to a specific genre of its own in the history of poetry. The unexpressed, unacceptable rage, the lack of a woman's culture revolving around real consciousness and strength—in such a context, psychological and literary, were most of the poems in this book written.

Adelaide Crapsey does not have a greater share of the morbid mood in her work, but some of her poems might be considered as examples. She takes as her theme the witch, a most common theme for women poets who see themselves in one way or another, speaking in tongues, as the odd people out in society. On the fate of the witch, here is Crapsey's closing quatrain:

> And have you heard (and I have heard)
> Of puzzled men with decorous mien,
> Who judged—the wench knows far too much—
> And hanged her on the Salem green?

With such a history of the fate of the gender behind us, with the anger caused by all that, with the lid kept on that anger so that it must come out in archness and irony, as Crapsey manages, is it any wonder that poets in less direct touch with that anger, in cultural contexts more stifling than the early years of the twentieth century when Crapsey was writing, could go no further than to lament what this poet observes ironically, could find no mood but sadness out of which to write poetry, and could elevate that mood no further than the drone of depression and a monody of morbidity?

Other poets of Crapsey's time, making the same kind of observations about women as she had, and using "women" as the subject of their poetry, lived quite different lives and wrote quite different kinds of poetry. Many of them contributed to the "revolution" in poetry at the start of the century. Amy Lowell, for one, made a revolution in terms of her assault on the patriarchy and the male domination of everyday literary life. She stormed the Rhymers' Club, wheedling her way into whatever literary circles (meaning male) that she could, propelled by a fearless energy and a stout conviction about poetry.

Her poems are so passionately feminist that anthologists rarely touch them, preferring instead to reprint the elegant and romantic "Patterns" that most readers must have come across some time in their educations. Of the work by Lowell that is largely unknown, the most interesting pieces are her love poems to women, the preoccupation with Eleonora Duse that Lowell shared with Sara Teasdale and Edna Millay. (For the powerful women are few and far between in recorded history and, once found, are taken up passionately by women writers. If Sappho had not existed, someone would have invented her.) Lowell also wrote a verse parody of her famous ancestor, James Russell Lowell. Her "Fable for Critics" is almost entirely about—and in praise of—women poets.

In America, the class condition of black people and the class condition of women are meshed. The history of poetry written by black people and poetry written by women are also meshed. The two periods that saw an upsurge of race consciousness and pride along with woman consciousness and feminism are the decades of abolitionist agitation in the nineteenth century and the brief years called the Roaring Twenties in the twentieth. The decade of the twenties saw an upsurge of black and white women writing and publishing poetry, and it was poetry of enduring quality. Although the Harlem Renaissance was dominated by black men, there were women in the movement, many of them long before it got labeled a Renaissance. Angelina W. Grimke, a black descendant of the white abolitionist family, Anne Spencer, and Georgia Douglass Johnson, quite early, in periodicals, published poems that came to be associated with the mood and style of the Harlem Renaissance.

Many of the white women who published in the years after the First World War have had some recognition. Sara Teasdale and Elinor Wylie were well known in their lifetimes. So was Edna Millay, although her fame rested largely on the early poems, very libertine, very male-oriented, taken as a symbol of the "new woman"—in male terms, the available bohemian. Somewhere along the way, the Millay canon has come to emphasize the poems of the cynical lover at the expense of the political woman, the supporter of Sacco and Vanzetti, the conscientious objector, the feminist, and the philosophical woman of the later poems.

Two poets not so well known, but who shared in the general euphoria that pervaded the lives of women directly or indirectly part of the woman movement, who caught its energy and translated that into their private art forms, are Lola Ridge and Genevieve Taggard. These poets are part of the buried history within the buried history. Women on the left in America have been banished from contemporary consciousness by the slow erosion of neglect. Ridge's are among the most haunting poems of the period. A working-class woman whose subject is always class struggle, she contributed to Emma Goldman's magazine *Mother Earth*, edited a radical magazine of her own called *Broom*, demonstrated for Sacco and Vanzetti alongside Dorothy Parker and Edna Millay. Genevieve Taggard was a kindred spirit whose early poems, drawn from her childhood in Hawaii, are about white-skinned imperialism. Taggard became a socialist and was published often in *The Liberator*. She was poetry editor of *The Masses*. Radicalism and feminism are the content of most of her poetry and she has been most unfortunately forgotten or unknown to the generations after her.

Between the wars, women in America and England accumulated more power in the literary life of those countries than they had before. Along with the importance of the Woolf press in England and the small magazines there, American poetry of the period owes a great deal of its shape to the work of Harriet Monroe. Her magazine, *Poetry*, afforded many of the poets in this book their first moments of encouragement and their first essential contacts with an audience.

The connection to feminist energy and consciousness of the twenties and thirties has never been really lost to American poets. Margaret Walker and Gwendolyn Brooks, strong, unique voices, have ancestors in the early black poets who formed a black feminist literature. Gertrude Stein may have coined the term "patriarchal poetry," but Babette Deutsch, Marianne Moore, Elizabeth Bishop— each has in her own way understood and found her own voice partly through contact with the heritage of women poets in the struggle against the patriarchal past.

Some poets collected in this book never read Dickinson, Ridge, or Stein, never had access to the newly opened pathways of Cambridge or the Annex of Harvard College. What they wrote arrived at its place in the history of women's poetry by maverick roads. The great blues singers were great poets, speaking woman's experience with intolerable reality in everything they sang. The women who made up songs in the mines and mills of America, Aunt Molly Jackson, Ella Mae Wiggins, and Sarah Ogan Gunning, are only a few among many. The native poetic traditions of America are not necessarily those that emerge from the pages of the *Atlantic Monthly* or *Poetry* magazine, nor from the presses of book-publishing houses. Where women have distilled experience into the verbal art form that in so short a space can create for the reader so total a sensation, where women have found language to shape what is in our imaginations, we have made poetry. We have, from the first, been singers, always.

Louise Bernikow

Cummington, Mass.
1973

THE POETS OF
ENGLAND

QUEEN ELIZABETH I
(1533–1603)

Elizabeth I was one of the last of a long line of aristocratic English women whose humanist education equipped them to read and write in several languages, including Greek and Latin, and to write poetry. At fifteen, Elizabeth "did into English," as it was said, Margaret of Navarre's "Godly Meditation of the Soul." She also did a complete and excellent translation of Boethius' "Consolation of Philosophy." Many original poems have been attributed to her, but the two printed here are indisputably hers. Many women poets lamented the Queen's death as the end of an era that admired intellect and artistic talent in women.

THE DOUBT OF FUTURE FOES

The doubt of future foes exiles my present joy,
And wit me warns to shun such snares as threaten mine
   annoy;
For falsehood now doth flow, and subject's faith doth
   ebb,
Which should not be if reason ruled or wisdom weaved
   the web.
But clouds of joys untried do cloak aspiring minds,
Which turn to rain of late repent by changed course of
   winds.
The top of hope supposed the root upreared shall be,
And fruitless all their grafted guile, as shortly ye shall
   see.
The dazzled eyes with pride, which great ambition
   blinds,
Shall be unsealed by worthy wights whose foresight
   falsehood finds.
The daughter of debate that discord aye doth sow

Shall reap no gain where former rule still peace hath
    taught to know.
No foreign banished wight shall anchor in this port;
Our realm brooks not seditious sects, let them elsewhere
    resort.
My rusty sword through rest shall first his edge employ
To poll their tops that seek such change or gape for
    future joy.

ON MONSIEUR'S DEPARTURE

I grieve and dare not show my discontent,
I love and yet am forced to seem to hate,
I do, yet dare not say I ever meant,
I seem stark mute but inwardly do prate.
    I am and not, I freeze and yet am burned,
    Since from myself another self I turned.

My care is like my shadow in the sun,
Follows me flying, flies when I pursue it,
Stands and lies by me, doth what I have done.
His too familiar care doth make me rue it.
    No means I find to rid him from my breast,
    Till by the end of things it be supprest.

Some gentler passion slide into my mind,
For I am soft and made of melting snow;
Or be more cruel, love, and so be kind.
Let me or float or sink, be high or low.
    Or let me live with some more sweet content.
    Or die and so forget what love ere meant.

MARY SIDNEY HERBERT, COUNTESS OF PEMBROKE (1561-1621)

Mary Sidney's father was one of King Edward's principal gentlemen of the privy chamber and his daughter was exposed to the world of Elizabethan "affairs" and "letters." Her brother, Sir Philip Sidney, went to Christ Church, Oxford, while Mary Sidney was educated by tutors. At sixteen, she became the Countess of Pembroke. Twenty-four years of her life were spent at the Pembroke estate in Wiltshire entertaining a literary circle that included Samuel Daniel, Thomas Kyd, and, possibly, Shakespeare. She was very much respected as a patroness and author, although the only works that survive and can be definitely attributed to her are several translations from the French, the English versions of the Psalms that she began with her brother and completed after his death, and the elegy on Philip Sidney's death. There is considerable speculation about her part in Sidney's *Arcadia*, which she "edited" and published in 1593. Her grave bears this eloquent epitaph:

Underneath this sable hearse
Lies the subject of all verse:
Sidney's sister, Pembroke's mother:
Death, ere thou hast slain another
Fair and learn'd and good as she,
Time shall throw a dart at thee.

Marble piles let no man raise,
To her name: for after days
Some kind of woman born as she,

Reading this, like Niobe
Shall turn marble and become
Both her mourner and her tomb.

Psalm lii
    Tyrant, why swelst thou thus,
        Of mischief vaunting?
    Since helpe from God to us
        Is never wanting.

Psalm lvii
    Thy mercie Lord, Lord now thy mercie show,
        On thee I ly,
        To thee I fly.
    Hide me, hive me as thine owne,
    Till these blasts be overblown,
    Which now do fiercely blow.

Psalm lix
    Save me from such as me assaile,
      Let not my foes,
    O God, against my life prevaile:
      Save me from those
    Who make a trade of cursed wrong,
    And bred in bloud, for bloud doe long.

Psalm lx
    Thy anger erst in field
      Our scatt'red squadrons broke;
    Oh, God, bee reconciled,
      Our leading now retake.
      This land at thee did quake,
    It chinckt and gaping lay:
      Oh sound her ruptures make,
    Her quaking bring to stay.

Psalm lxvii
  God, on us thy mercy show,
  Make on us thy blessings flow,
    Thy faces beames
  From Heav'n upon us show'r
    In shining streames
    That all may see
    The way of thee,
  And know thy saving pow'r.

Psalm lxxi
  Lord, on thee my trust is grounded:
  Leave me not with shame confounded;
    But in justice bring me aide.
  Lett thine eare to me be bended;
  Lett my life, from death defended,
    Be by thee in safety staid.

Psalm lxxii
  Teach the kings sonne, who king hym selfe shall be,
    Thy judgments, Lord, thy justice make hym learn:
  To rule realme as justice shall decree,
    And poore mens right in judgement to discern,
        Then fearless peace,
        With rich encrease
      The mountaynes proud shall fill:
        And justice shall
        With plenty fall
      On ev'ry humble hill.

THE DOLEFULL LAY OF CLORINDA

  Ay me, to whom shall I my case complaine,
  That may compassion my impatient griefe?
  Or where shall I unfold my inward paine,
  That my enriven heart may find reliefe?
    Shall I unto the heavenly powres it show?
    Or unto earthly men that dwell below?

To heavens? ah! they, alas! the authors were,
And workers of my unremèdied wo:
For they foresee what to us happens here,
And they foresaw, yet suffred this be so.
    From them comes good, from them comes also ill,
    That which they made, who can them warne to spill?

To men? ah! they alas like wretched bee,
And subject to the heavens ordinance:
Bound to abide whatever they decree,
Their best redresse is their best sufferance.
    How then can they, like wretched, comfort mee,
    The which no lesse need comforted to bee?

Then to my selfe will I my sorrow mourne,
Sith none alive like sorrowfull remaines:
And to my selfe my plaints shall back retourne,
To pay their usury with doubled paines.
    The woods, the hills, the rivers, shall resound
    The mournfull accents of my sorrowes ground.

Woods, hills and rivers now are desolate,
Sith he is gone the which them all did grace:
And all the fields do waile their widow state,
Sith death their fairest flowre did late deface.
    The fairest flowre in field that ever grew,
    Was Astrophell; that was, we all may rew.

What cruell hand of cursed foe unknowne,
Hath cropt the stalke which bore so faire a flowre?
Untimely cropt, before it well were growne,
And cleane defaced in untimely howre.
    Great losse to all that ever did him see,
    Great losse to all, but greatest losse to me.

Break now your gyrlonds, O ye shepheards lasses,
Sith the faire flowre, which them adornd is gon:
The flowre, which them adornd, is gone to ashes,
Never againe let lasse put gyrlond on.

In stead of gyrlond, weare sad Cypres nowe,
And bitter Elder, broken from the bowe.

Ne ever sing the love-layes which he made,
Who ever made such layes of love as hee?
Ne ever read the riddles, which he sayd
Unto your selves, to make you mery glee.
　Your mery glee is now laid all abed,
　Your mery maker now alasse! is dead.

Death, the devourer of all world's delight,
Hath robbed you, and reft fro me my joy:
Both you, and me, and all the world he quight
Hath robd of joyance, and left sad annoy.
　Joy of the world, and shepheards pride was hee
　Shepheards, hope never like againe to see!

Oh Death, that hast us of such riches reft,
Tell us at least, what hast thou with it done?
What is become of him whose flowre here left
Is but the shadow of his likenesse gone?
　Scarce like the shadow of that which he was,
　Nought like, but that he like a shade did pas.

But that immortal spirit, which was deckt
With all the dowries of celestiall grace,
By soveraine choyce from th' hevenly quires select
And lineally derived from Angels race,
　O! what is now of it become, aread.
　Ay me, can so divine a thing be dead?

Ah! no: it is not dead, ne can it die,
But lives for aie, in blissfull Paradise:
Where like a new-borne babe it soft doth lie,
In bed of lilies wrapt in tender wise;
　And compact all about with roses sweet,
　And dainty violets from head to feet.

Three thousand birds all of celestial brood,
To him do sweetly caroll day and night;

And with straunge notes, of him well understood,
Lull him a sleep in angelick delight;
   Whilest in sweet dreame to him presented bee
   Immortall beauties, which no eye may see.

But he them sees and takes exceeding pleasure
Of their divine aspects, appearing plaine,
And kindling love in him above all measure,
Sweet love still joyous, never feel paine.
   For what so goodly forme he there doth see,
   He may enjoy from jealous rancor free.

There liveth he in everlasting blis,
Sweet Spirit never fearing more to die:
Ne dreading harme from any foes of his,
Ne fearing salvage beasts more crueltie.
   Whilest we here, wretches, waile his private lack,
   And with vaine vowes do often call him back.

But live thou there, still happie, happie Spirit,
And give us leave thee here thus to lament
Not thee that doest thy heavens joy inherit,
But our owne selves that here in dole are drent.
   Thus do we weep and waile, and wear our eies,
   Mourning, in others, our owne miseries.

KATHERINE PHILIPS (1631–1664)

"The Matchless Orinda," "The English Sappho," as
she was known in her time, was born Katherine
Fowler, daughter of a London merchant. She was educated, which was not rare for a daughter of the
middle class, in a boarding school. At seventeen, she

married a Welshman, whose business interests she often managed and who appears in her poetry under the name "Antenor." She established a literary salon called the "Society of Friendship" that included the poets Cowley, Cartwright, Jeremy Taylor and Henry Vaughan. Some "verses" on Vaughan's poems, published in 1650, brought her considerable fame and she lived the life of a successful literary lady until she died of smallpox during an epidemic of that disease in London. Orinda was chiefly known to the public as a translator—her version of Corneille's play *Pompée* was an astounding success in Dublin in 1663—until the publication of a volume of poems. Just before she died, what was called a "pirated" volume of the poetry appeared. Oddly enough, when the "authorized" version was published, three years later, the text differed little from what had already appeared in print. Orinda had a son and a daughter and it is thought that her daughter became a poet.

ORINDA UPON LITTLE
HECTOR PHILIPS

Twice forty months of wedlock I did stay,
Then had my vows crown'd with a lovely boy,
And yet in forty days he dropt away,
O swift vicissitude of human joy.

I did but see him and he disappear'd,
I did but pluck the rose-bud and it fell,
A sorrow unforeseen and scarcely fear'd,
For ill can mortals their afflictions spell.

And now (sweet babe) what can my trembling heart
Suggest to right my doleful fate or thee,
Tears are my Muse and sorrow all my art,
So piercing groans must be thy elegy.

Thus whilst no eye is witness of my moan,
I grieve thy loss (Ah boy too dear to live)
And let the unconcernèd world alone,
Who neither will, nor can refreshment give.

An off'ring too for thy sad tomb I have,
Too just a tribute to thy early hearse,
Receive these gasping numbers to thy grave,
The last of thy unhappy mother's verse.

ORINDA TO LUCASIA

Observe the weary birds ere night be done,
How they would fain call up the tardy sun,
   With feathers hung with dew,
   And trembling voices too.
They court their glorious planet to appear,
That they may find recruits of spirits there.
   The drooping flowers hang their heads,
   And languish down into their beds:
While brooks more bold and fierce than they
   Wanting those beams, from whence
   All things drink influence,
Openly murmur and demand the day.

Thou my Lucasia are far more to me,
Than he to all the under-world can be;
   From thee I've heat and light,
   Thy absence makes my night.
But ah! my friend, it now grows very long,
The sadness weighty, and the darkness strong:
   My tears (its dew) dwell on my cheeks,
   And still my heart thy dawning seeks,
And to thee mournfully it cries,
   That if too long I wait,
   Ev'n thou may'st come too late,
And not restore my life, but close my eyes.

TO MY EXCELLENT LUCASIA, ON OUR FRIENDSHIP

I did not live until this time
    Crown'd my felicity,
When I could say without a crime,
    I am not thine, but thee.

This carcass breath'd, and walkt, and slept,
    So that the world believ'd
There was a soul the motions kept;
    But they were all deceiv'd.

For as a watch by art is wound
    To motion, such was mine:
But never had Orinda found
    A soul till she found thine;

Which now inspires, cures and supplies,
    And guides my darkned breast:
For thou art all that I can prize,
    My joy, my life, my rest.

No bridegroom's nor crown-conqueror's mirth
    To mine compar'd can be:
They have but pieces of the earth,
    I've all the world in thee.

Then let our flames still light and shine,
    And no false fear controul,
As innocent as our design,
    Immortal as our soul.

PARTING WITH LUCASIA: A SONG

I

Well, we will do that rigid thing
    Which makes spectators think we part;
Though Absence hath for none a sting
    But those who keep each other's heart.

II

And when our sense is dispossest,
  Our labouring souls will heave and pant,
And gasp for one another's breast,
  Since their conveyances they want.

III

Nay, we have felt the tedious smart
  Of absent Friendship, and do know
That when we die we can but part;
  And who knows what we shall do now?

IV

Yet I must go: we will submit,
  And so our own disposers be;
For while we nobly suffer it,
  We triumph o'er Necessity.

V

By this we shall be truly great,
  If having other things o'ercome,
To make our victory complete
  We can be conquerors at home.

VI

Nay then to meet we may conclude,
  And all obstructions overthrow,
Since we our passion have subdu'd,
  Which is the strongest thing I know.

AGAINST LOVE

Hence, Cupid! with your cheating toys,
Your real Griefs, and painted Joys,
Your Pleasure which itself destroys.

    Lovers like men in fevers burn and rave,
      And only what will injure them do crave.
Men's weakness makes Love so severe,
They give him power by their fear,
And make the shackles which they wear.
    Who to another does his heart submit,
    Makes his own Idol, and then worships it.
Him whose heart is all his own,
Peace and liberty does crown,
He apprehends no killing frown.
    He feels no raptures which are joys diseas'd,
    And is not much transported, but still pleas'd.

AN ANSWER TO ANOTHER PERSUADING A LADY TO MARRIAGE

Forbear, bold youth, all's Heaven here,
    And what you do aver,
To others, courtship may appear,
    'Tis sacriledge to her.

She is a publick deity,
    And were't not very odd
She should depose her self to be
    A petty houschold god?

First make the sun in private shine,
    And bid the world adieu,
That so he may his beams confine
    In complement to you.

But if of that you do despair,
    Think how you did amiss,
To strive to fix her beams which are
    More bright and large than this.

UPON THE DOUBLE MURTHER OF KING CHARLES I, IN ANSWER TO A LIBELLOUS COPY OF RIMES BY VAVASOR POWELL

I think not on the State, nor am concern'd
Which way soever the great helm is turn'd:
But as that son whose Father's danger nigh
Did force his native dumbness, and untie
The fetter'd organs; so this is a cause
That will excuse the breach of Nature's laws,
Silence were now a sin, nay passion now
Wise men themselves for merit would allow.
What noble eye could see (and careless pass)
The dying Lion kick'd by every ass?
Has Charles so broke God's Laws, he must not have
A quiet crown, nor yet a quiet grave?
Tombs have been sanctuaries; Thieves lie there
Secure from all their penalty and fear.
Great Charles his double misery was this,
Unfaithful friends, ignoble enemies.
Had any heathen been this Prince's foe,
He would have wept to see him injur'd so,
His title was his crime, they'd reason good
To quarrel at the right they had withstood.
He broke God's Laws, and therefore he must die;
And what shall then become of thee and I?
Slander must follow Treason; but yet stay,
Take not our reason with our King away.
Though you have seiz'd upon all our defence,
Yet do not sequester our common sense.
Christ will be King, but I ne'er understood
His subjects built His Kingdom up with blood,
Except their own; or that He would dispense
With his commands, though for His own defence.
Oh! to what height of horror are they come
Who dare pull down a crown, tear up a tomb?

ANNE COLLINS
(c. 1653)

"An. Collins" is merely the name on the title page of a rare and often-overlooked book called *Divine Songs and Meditations* which appeared in 1653. In the prologue, the author says that she has been ill a lot and many of the poems are written in bouts of sickness, but that is the extent of the information we have about her.

SONG (I)

The Winter being over,
   In order comes the Spring,
Which doth green herbs discover,
   And cause the birds to sing.
The night also expirèd,
   Then comes the morning bright,
Which is so much desirèd
   By all that love the light.
     This may learn
     Them that mourn,
To put their grief to flight:
The Spring succeedeth Winter,
   And day must follow night.

He therefore that sustaineth
   Affliction or distress,
Which every member paineth,
   And findeth no release:
Let such therefore despair not,
   But on firm hope depend,
Whose griefs immortal are not,
   And therefore must have end.
     They that faint
     With complaint

Therefore are to blame:
They add to their afflictions,
  And amplify the same.

THE SOUL'S HOME

Such is the force of each created thing
That it no solid happiness can bring,
Which to our minds can give contentment sound;
For, like as Noah's dove no succour found,
Till she return'd to him that sent her out,
Just so, the soul in vain may seek about
For rest or satisfaction any where,
Save in his presence who hath sent her here;
Yea though all earthly glories should unite
Their pomp and splendour to give such delight,
Yet could they no more sound contentment bring
Than star-light can make grass or flowers spring.

SONG (II)

My straying thoughts, reduced stay,
And so a while retired,
Such observations to survey
Which memory hath regist'red,
That were not in oblivion dead.

In which review of mental store,
One note affordeth comforts best,
Chiefly to be preferred therefore,
As in a cabinet or chest
One jewel may exceed the rest.

God is the Rock of his elect
In whom his grace is inchoate,
This note, my soul did most affect,
It doth such power intimate   —
To comfort and corroborate.

God is a Rock first in respect
He shadows his from hurtful heat,
Then in regard he doth protect
His servants still from dangers great
And so their enemies defeat.

In some dry desert lands (they say)
Are mighty rocks, which shadow make,
Where passengers that go that way,
May rest, and so refreshing take,
Their sweltish weariness to slake.

So in this world such violent
Occasions find we still to mourn,
That scorching heat of discontent
Would all into combustion turn
And soon our souls with anguish burn,

Did not our Rock preserve us still,
Whose spirit, ours animates,
That wind that bloweth where it will
Sweetly our souls refrigerates,
And so destructive heat abates.

From this our Rock proceeds likewise,
The saving streams, which graciously
Revives the soul which scorched lies,
Through sense of God's displeasure high,
Due to her for iniquity.

So this our Rock refreshing yields,
To those that unto him adhere,
Whom likewise mightily he shields,
So that they need not faint nor fear
Though all the world against them were.

APHRA BEHN
(1640–1689)

Aphra Behn was the first English woman to make her living by writing. Her biography is full of mystery, contradiction and holes. Many have written about her, but few have agreed. Her parentage is unknown. Some time before 1665, Aphra Behn probably spent time in Surinam (Dutch Guiana), although the circumstances are vague and the veracity of that part of her biography has been questioned. The "new world" did, however, furnish the background for her *Oroonoko,* one of the earliest English novels. She married a Dutch merchant named Behn who died or disappeared after one year. The facts become clearer after 1666, when she traveled from London to Antwerp to act as a secret agent for King Charles, who, it seems, refused to pay for her services. The code named under which the poet sent her intelligence communications, "Astrea," later became one of her literary pseudonyms. Behn spent time in debtors' prison in London and, upon release, began a long writing career. She wrote seventeen plays, several histories and novels, and poems. "Among the rakes of her time" and "not a lady" are some of the kinder remarks made about her in her lifetime. She was a bohemian, feminist, anti-Whig and probably the most famous woman writer in England before the nineteenth century.

THE CABAL AT NICKEY NACKEYS

I.

A Pox of the Statesman that's witty,
Who watches and Plots all the Sleepless Night:
For Seditious Harangues, to the Whiggs of the City;
And Maliciously turns a Traytor in Spight.
Let him Wear and Torment his lean Carrion:
   To bring his Sham-Plots about,
    Till at last King Biship and Barron,
For the Publick Good he have quite rooted out.

II.

—But we that are no Polliticians,
But Rogues that are Impudent, Barefac'd and Great,
Boldly head the Rude Rable in times of Sedition;
And bear all down before us, in Church and in State.
   Your Impudence is the best State-Trick;
    And he that by Law meanes to rule,
   Let his History with ours be related;
And tho' we are the Knaves, we know who's the Fool.

SONG
LOVE ARM'D

Love in fantastic triumph sat
   Whilst bleeding hearts around him flow'd,
For whom fresh paines he did create,
   And strange tyrannic power he show'd;

From thy bright eyes he took his fire,
   Which round about in sport he hurl'd;
But 'twas from mine he took desire,
   Enough to undo the amorous world.

From me he took his sighs and tears,
　　From thee his pride and cruelty;
From me his languishments and fears,
　　And every killing dart from thee.

Thus thou and I the god have arm'd,
　　And set him up a deity;
But my poor heart alone is harm'd,
　　Whilst thine the victor is, and free.

SONG
A THOUSAND MARTYRS
I HAVE MADE

A thousand martyrs I have made,
　　All sacrific'd to my desire;
A thousand beauties have betray'd,
　　That languish in resistless fire.
The untam'd heart to hand I brought,
And fixed the wild and wandering thought.

I never vow'd nor sigh'd in vain
　　But both, tho' false, were well receiv'd.
The fair are pleas'd to give us pain,
　　And what they wish is soon believ'd.
And tho' I talk'd of wounds and smart,
Love's pleasures only touched my heart.

Alone the glory and the spoil
　　I always laughing bore away;
The triumphs, without pain or toil,
　　Without the hell, the heav'n of joy.
And while I thus at random rove
Despis'd the fools that whine for love.

TO ALEXIS IN ANSWER TO HIS POEM AGAINST FRUITION

Ah hapless sex! who bear no charms,
But what like lightning flash and are no more,
   False fires sent down for baneful harms,
Fires which the fleeting Lover feebly warms
    And given like past Beboches o're,
    Like Songs that please (tho bad,) when new,
But learn'd by heart neglected grew.

In vain did Heav'n adorn the shape and face
With Beautyes which by Angels forms it drew:
In vain the mind with brighter Glories Grace,
While all our joys are stinted to the space
    Of one betraying enterview,
With one surrender to the eager will
We're short-liv'd nothing, or a real ill.

Since Man with that inconstancy was born,
To love the absent, and the present scorn,
    Why do we deck, why do we dress
    For such a short-liv'd happiness?
    Why do we put Attraction on,
Since either way tis we must be undon?

    They fly if Honour take our part,
    Our Virtue drives 'em o're the field.
    We lose 'em by too much desert,
    And Oh! they fly us if we yield.
Ye Gods! is there no charm in all the fair
To fix this wild, this faithless, wanderer?

    Man! our great business and our aim,
    For whom we spread our fruitless snares,
No sooner kindles the designing flame,
    But to the next bright object bears
The Trophies of his conquest and our shame:
    Inconstancy's the good supream
The rest is airy Notion, empty Dream!

Then, heedless Nymph, be rul'd by me
If e're your Swain the bliss desire;
Think like Alexis he may be
Whose wisht Possession damps his fire;
The roving youth in every shade
Has left some sighing and abandon'd Maid,
For tis a fatal lesson he has learn'd,
After fruition ne're to be concern'd.

THE DISAPPOINTMENT

I.

One day the Amorous *Lysander*,
By an impatient Passion sway'd,
Surpriz'd fair *Cloris*, that lov'd Maid,
Who could defend her self no longer.
All things did with his Love conspire;
The gilded Planet of the Day,
In his gay Chariot drawn by Fire,
Was now descending to the Sea,
And left no Light to guide the World,
But what from *Cloris* Brighter Eyes was hurld.

II.

In a lone Thicket made for Love,
Silent as yielding Maids Consent,
She with a Charming Languishment,
Permits his Force, yet gently strove;
Her Hands his Bosom softly meet,
But not to put him back design'd,
Rather to draw 'em on inclin'd:
Whilst he lay trembling at her Feet,
Resistance 'tis in vain to show;
She wants the pow'r to say—*Ah! What d'ye do?*

III.

Her Bright Eyes sweet, and yet severe,
Where Love and Shame confus'dly strive,
Fresh Vigor to *Lysander* give;
And breathing faintly in his Ear,
She cry'd—*Cease, Cease—your vain Desire,*
Or I'll call out—What would you do?
My Dearer Honour ev'n to You
I cannot, must not give—Retire,
Or take this Life, whose chiefest part
I gave you with the Conquest of my Heart.

IV.

But he as much unus'd to Fear,
As he was capable of Love,
The blessed minutes to improve,
Kisses her Mouth, her Neck, her Hair;
Each Touch her new Desire Alarms,
His burning trembling Hand he prest
Upon her swelling Snowy Brest,
While she lay panting in his Arms.
All her Unguarded Beauties lie
The Spoils and Trophies of the Enemy.

V.

And now without Respect or Fear,
He seeks the Object of his Vows,
(His Love no Modesty allows)
By swift degrees advancing—where
His daring Hand that Altar seiz'd,
Where Gods of Love do sacrifice:
That Awful Throne, that Paradice
Where Rage is calm'd, and Anger pleas'd;
That Fountain where Delight still flows,
And gives the Universal World Repose.

VI.

Her Balmy Lips incountring his,
Their Bodies, as their Souls, are joyn'd;
Where both in Transports Unconfin'd
Extend themselves upon the Moss.
Cloris half dead and breathless lay;
Her soft Eyes cast a Humid Light,
Such as divides the Day and Night;
Or falling Stars, whose Fires decay:
And now no signs of Life she shows,
But what in short-breath'd Sighs returns and goes.

VII.

He saw how at her Length she lay;
He saw her rising Bosom bare;
Her loose thin *Robes,* through which appear
A Shape design'd for Love and Play;
Abandon'd by her Pride and Shame.
She does her softest Joys dispence,
Off'ring her Virgin-Innocence
A Victim to Loves Sacred Flame;
While the o'er-Ravish'd Shepherd lies
Unable to perform the Sacrifice.

VIII.

Ready to taste a thousand Joys,
The too transported hapless Swain
Found the vast Pleasure turn'd to Pain;
Pleasure which too much Love destroys:
The willing Garments by he laid,
And Heaven all open'd to his view,
Mad to possess, himself he threw
On the Defenceless Lovely Maid.
But Oh what envying God conspires
To snatch his Power, yet leave him the Desire!

IX.

Nature's Support, (without whose Aid
She can no Humane Being give)
It self now wants the Art to live;
Faintness its slack'ned Nerves invade:
In vain th' inraged Youth essay'd
To call its fleeting Vigor back,
No motion 'twill from Motion take;
Excess of Love is Love betray'd:
In vain he Toils, in vain Commands,
Then I sensible fell weeping in his Hand.

X.

In this so Amorous Cruel Strife,
Where Love and Fate were too severe,
The poor *Lysander* in despair
Renounc'd his Reason with his Life:
Now all the brisk and active Fire
That should the Nobler Part inflame,
Serv'd to increase his Rage and Shame,
And left no Spark for New Desire:
Not all her Naked Charms cou'd move
Or calm that Rage that had debauch'd his Love.

XI.

Cloris returning from the Trance
Which Love and soft Desire had bred,
Her timerous Hand she gently laid
(Or guided by Design or Chance)
Upon that Fabulous *Priapus,*
That Potent God, as Poets feign;
But never did young *Shepherdess,*
Gath'ring of Fern upon the Plain,
More nimbly draw her Fingers back,
Finding beneath the verdant Leaves a Snake:

XII.

Than *Cloris* her fair Hand withdrew,
Finding that God of her Desires
Disarm'd of all his Awful Fires,
And Cold as Flow'rs bath'd in the Morning Dew.
Who can the *Nymph's* Confusion guess?
The Blood forsook the hinder Place,
And strew'd with Blushes all her Face,
Which both Disdain and Shame exprest:
And from *Lysander's* Arms she fled,
Leaving him fainting on the Gloomy Bed.

XIII.

Like Lightning through the Grove she hies,
Or *Daphne* from the *Delphick God*,
No Print upon the grassey Road
She leaves, t' instruct Pursuing Eyes.
The Wind that wanton'd in her Hair,
And with her Ruffled Garments plaid,
Discover'd in the Flying Maid
All that the Gods e'er made, if Fair.
So *Venus*, when her *Love* was slain,
With Fear and Haste flew o'er the Fatal Plain.

XIV.

The *Nymph's* Resentments none but I
Can well Imagine or Condole:
But none can guess *Lysander's* Soul,
But those who sway'd his Destiny.
His silent Griefs swell up to Storms,
And not one God his Fury spares;
He curs'd his Birth, his Fate, his Stars;
But more the *Shepherdess's* Charms,
Whose soft bewitching Influence
Had Damn'd him to the *Hell* of Impotence.

TO THE FAIR CLARINDA, WHO MADE LOVE TO ME, IMAGIN'D MORE THAN WOMAN

Fair lovely Maid, or if that Title be
Too weak, too Feminine for Nobler thee,
Permit and Name that more Approaches Truth:
And let me call thee, Lovely Charming Youth.
This last will justifie my soft complaint,
While that may serve to lessen my constraint;
And without Blushes I the youth persue,
When so much beauteous Woman is in view.
Against thy Charms we struggle but in vain
With thy deluding Form thou giv'st us pain,
While the bright Nymph betrays us to the Swain.
In pity to our Sex sure thou wer't sent,
That we might Love, and yet be Innocent:
For sure no Crime with thee we can commit;
Or if we shou'd—thy Form excuses it.
For who, that gathers the fairest Flowers believes
A Snake lies hid beneath the Fragrant Leaves.

Thou beauteous Wonder of a different kind,
Soft Cloris with the dear Alexis join'd;
When e'r the Manly part of thee, wou'd plead
Thou tempts us with the Image of the Maid,
While we the noblest Passions do extend
The love to Hermes, Aphrodite the friend.

SONG
THE WILLING MISTRISS

Amyntas led me to a Grove,
    Where all the Trees did shade us;
The Sun it self, though it had Strove,
    It could not have betray'd us:

The place secur'd from humane Eyes,
   No other fear allows,
   But when the Winds that gently rise,
Doe Kiss the yeilding Boughs.

Down there we satt upon the Moss,
   And did begin to play
A Thousand Amorous Tricks, to pass
   The heat of all the day.
A many Kisses he did give:
   And I return'd the same
Which made me willing to receive
   That which I dare not name.

His Charming Eyes no Aid requir'd
   To tell their softning Tale;
On her that was already fir'd,
   'Twas Easy to prevaile.
He did but Kiss and Clasp me round,
   Whilst those his thoughts Exprest:
And lay'd me gently on the Ground;
   Ah who can guess the rest?

ANNE KILLIGREW
(1660–1685)

As Maid of Honor to Mary of Modena, Anne Killigrew lived for a short while in an atmosphere where female intellect and talent were admired. At court, she would surely have known the accomplished poet Anne Finch, Countess of Winchilsea. Killigrew's name, but not her work, is known because of the Ode to her written by John Dryden after her death. In that poem, Dryden praises her talent at "the two sister-arts" of poesy and painting, describing her work as the heritage of her father, Dr. Henry Killigrew, a Royalist theologian and sometime dramatist. ("Our wonder is the less to find/ A soul so charming from a stock so good;/ Thy father was transfus'd into thy blood:"). At twenty-five, she died of smallpox.

UPON THE SAYING THAT MY VERSES WERE MADE BY ANOTHER

Next Heaven, my vows to thee, O sacred Muse!
I offered up, nor didst thou them refuse.

O Queen of Verse, said I, if thou'lt inspire,
And warm my soul with thy poetic fire,
No love of gold shall share with thee my heart,
Or yet ambition in my breast have part,
More rich, more noble I will ever hold
The Muse's laurel, than a crown of gold.
An undivided sacrifice I'll lay
Upon thine altar, soul and body pay;
Thou shalt my pleasure, my employment be,
My all I'll make a holocaust to thee.

The deity that ever does attend
Prayers so sincere, to mine did condescend.
I writ, and the judicious praised my pen:
Could any doubt ensuing glory then?
What pleasing raptures filled my ravished sense,
How strong, how sweet, Fame, was thy influence!
And thine, false Hope, that to my flattered sight
Did'st glories represent so near and bright!
By thee deceived, methought each verdant tree
Apollo's transformed Daphne seemed to be;
And ev'ry fresher branch, and ev'ry bough,
Appeared as garlands to empale my brow.
The learn'd in love say, thus the winged boy
Does first approach, dressed up in welcome joy;

At first he to the cheated lover's sight
Nought represents but rapture and delight,
Alluring hopes, soft fears, which stronger bind
Their hearts, than when they more assurance find.

Emboldened thus, to fame I did commit
(By some few hands) my most unlucky wit.
But ah, the sad effects that from it came!
What ought t'have brought me honour, brought me
    shame!
Like Aesop's painted jay, I seemed to all,
Adorned in plumes, I not my own could call:
Rifled like her, each one my feathers tore,
And, as they thought, unto the owner bore.
My laurels thus another's brow adorned,
My numbers they admired, but me they scorned:
Another's brow, that had so rich a store
Of sacred wreaths that circled it before;
While mine quite lost (like a small stream that ran
Into a vast and boundless ocean,)
Was swallowed up with what it joined, and drowned.
And that abyss yet no accession found.

Orinda (Albion's and her sex's grace)
Owed not her glory to a beauteous face;
It was her radiant soul that shone within,
Which struck a lustre through her outward skin;
That did her lips and cheeks with roses dye,
Advanced her height, and sparkled in her eye.
Nor did her sex at all obstruct her fame,
But higher 'mong the stars it fixed her name;
What she did write, not only all allowed,
But every laurel to her laurel bowed!

The envious age, only to me alone,
Will not allow what I do write, my own;
But let them rage, and 'gainst a maid conspire,
So deathless numbers from my tuneful lyre
Do ever flow; so, Phoebus, I by thee

Divinely inspired and possessed may be,
I willingly accept Cassandra's fate,
To speak the truth, although believed too late.

ANNE FINCH, COUNTESS OF WINCHILSEA (1661-1720)

Anne Kingsmill Finch was Maid of Honor to Mary of Modena, the wife of King James II. In this position she probably met Anne Killigrew. The Revolution of 1688 changed her life, for by then she had married Heneage Finch, who was devoted to the King and refused to take the Oath of allegiance to William and Mary. The couple moved from court to country and for the rest of her life Anne Finch traveled to and from London, lived in "somewhat reduced" circumstances, had literary friendships, and acquired a reputation as a poet. Her husband collected antiquarian books and was supportive of his "literary" wife, whose work is full of complaints about the general cultural denigration of women writers. She has been variously described as a nature poet out of tune with her time, and as a forerunner of Romanticism. William Wordsworth is responsible for the first opinion, having "discovered" her work and written about it.

A NOCTURNAL REVERIE

In such a night, when every louder wind
Is to its distant cavern safe confin'd;
And only gentle Zephyr fans his wings,

And lonely Philomel, still waking, sings;
Or from some tree, fam'd for the owl's delight,
She, hollowing clear, directs the wand'rers right:
In such a night, when passing clouds give place,
Or thinly vail the Heav'ns mysterious face;
When in some river, overhung with green,
The waving moon and trembling leaves are seen;
When freshen'd grass now bears itself upright,
And makes cool banks to pleasing rest invite,
Whence springs the woodbind, and the bramble-rose,
And where the sleepy cowslip shelter'd grows;
Whilst now a paler hue the foxglove takes,
Yet checquers still with red the dusky brakes:
When scatter'd glow-worms, but in twilight fine,
Shew trivial beauties watch their hour to shine;
Whilst Salisb'ry stands the test of every light,
In perfect charms and perfect virtue bright:
When odours, which declin'd repelling day,
Thro' temperate air uninterrupted stray;
When darken'd groves their softest shadows wear
And falling waters we distinctly hear;
When thro' the gloom more venerable shows
Some ancient fabrick, awful in repose,
While sunburnt hills their swarthy looks conceal,
And swelling haycocks thicken up the vale:
When the loos'd horse now, as his pasture leads,
Comes slowly grazing thro' th' adjoining meads,
Whose stealing pace, and lengthen'd shade we fear,
Till torn-up forage in his teeth we hear:
When nibbling sheep at large pursue their food,
And unmolested kine rechew the cud;
When curlews cry beneath the village walls,
And to her straggling brood the partridge calls;
Their short-liv'd jubilee the creatures keep,
Which but endures, whilst tyrant-man do's sleep:
When a sedate consent the spirit feels,
And no fierce light disturbs, whilst it reveals;
But silent musings urge the mind to seek

Something, too high for syllables to speak;
Till the free soul to a compos'dness charm'd,
Finding the elements of rage disarm'd,
O'er all below a solemn quiet grown,
Joys in th' inferior world, and thinks it like her own:
In such a night let me abroad remain,
Till morning breaks, and all's confus'd again;
Our cares, our toils, our clamours are renew'd,
Or pleasures, seldom reach'd, again pursu'd.

ADAM POS'D

Cou'd our first father, at his toilsome plough,
Thorns in his path, and labour on his brow,
Cloath'd only in a rude, unpolish'd skin,
Cou'd he a vain fantastick nymph have seen,
In all her airs, in all her antick graces,
Her various fashions, and more various faces;
How had it pos'd that skill, which late assign'd
Just appellations to each several kind!
A right idea of the sight to frame;
T' have guest from what new element she came;
T' have hit the wav'ring form, and giv'n this Thing a
    name.

MELINDA ON AN INSIPPID BEAUTY

In imitation of a fragment of Sappho's

You, when your body, life shall leave
Must drop entire, into the grave;
Unheeded, unregarded lie,
And all of you together die;
Must hide that fleeting charm, that face in dust,
Or to some painted cloth, the slighted Image trust,
Whilst my fam'd works, shall through all times surprise
My polish'd thoughts, my bright Ideas rise,
And to new men be known, still talking to their eyes.

THE ANSWER

[To Pope's *Impromptu*]

Disarm'd with so genteel an air,
    The contest I give o'er;
Yet, Alexander, have a care,
    And shock the sex no more.
We rule the world our life's whole race,
    Men but assume that right;
First slaves to ev'ry tempting face,
    Then martyrs to our spite.
You of one Orpheus sure have read,
    Who would like you have writ
Had he in London town been bred,
    And polish'd to[o] his wit;
But he poor soul thought all was well,
    And great should be his fame,
When he had left his wife in hell,
    And birds and beasts could tame.
Yet venturing then with scoffing rhimes
    The women to incense,
Resenting Heroines of those times
    Soon punished his offence.
And as the Hebrus roll'd his scull,
    And harp besmear'd with blood,
They clashing as the waves grew full,
    Still harmoniz'd the flood.
But you our follies gently treat,
    And spin so fine the thread,
You need not fear his aukward fate,
    The lock wo'n't cost the head.
Our admiration you command
    For all that's gone before;
What next we look for at your hand
    Can only raise it more.
Yet sooth the Ladies I advise
    (As me too pride has wrought,)

We're born to wit, but to be wise
    By admonitions taught.

ARDELIA'S ANSWER TO EPHELIA

*who had invited her to come to her in town—reflecting on
the Coquetterie and detracting humour of the Age*

Me, dear Ephelia, me, in vain you court
With all your pow'rfull influence, to resort
To that great Town, where Friendship can but have
The few spare hours, which meaner pleasures leave.
No! Let some shade, or your large Pallace be
Our place of meeting, love, and liberty;
To thoughts, and words, and all endearments free.
But, to those walls, excuse my slow repair;
Who have no businesse, or diversion there;
No daz'ling beauty, to attract the gaze
Of won'd'ring crouds to my applauded face;
Nor to my little witt, th' ill nature joyn'd,
To passe a gen'rall censure on mankind:
To call the yong, and unaffected, fools;
Dull all the grave, that live by moral rules;
To say the souldier brags, who ask'd declares
The nice escapes and dangers of his wars,
The Poet's vain, that knows his unmatch'd worth,
And dares maintain what the best Muse brings forth:
Yett, this the humour of the age is grown,
And only conversation of the Town.
In Satir vers'd, and sharpe detraction, bee,
And you're accomplish'd, for all company.

    When my last visit, I to London made,
Me, to Almeria, wretched chance, betray'd;
The fair Almeria, in this art so known,
That she discerns all failings, but her own.
With a lowd welcome, and a strict embrace,
Kisses on kisses, in a publick place,

Sh' extorts a promise, that next day I dine
With her, who for my sight, did hourly pine;
And wonders, how so far I can remove,
From the beaux monde, and the dull country love;
Yet vows, if but an afternoon 'twoud cost
To see me there, she cou'd resolve allmost
To quitt the Town, and for that time, be lost.
   My word I keep, we dine, then rising late,
Take coach, which long had waited at the gate.
About the streets, a tedious ramble goe,
To see this Monster, or that wax work show,
Or any thing, that may the time bestow.
When by a Church we passe, I ask to stay,
Go in, and my devotions, humbly pay
To that great Pow'r, whom all the wise obey.
Whilst the gay thing, light as her feather'd dresse,
Flys round the Coach, and does each cusheon presse,
Through ev'ry glasse, her sev'ral graces shows,
This, does her face, and that, her shape expose,
To envying beautys, and admiring beaux.
One stops, and as expected, all extolls,
Clings to the door, and on his elbow lolls,
Thrusts in his head, at once to view the fair,
And keep his curls from discomposing air,
Then thus proceeds—
                    My wonder itt is grown
To find Almeria here, and here alone.
Where are the Nymphs, that round you us'd to croud,
Of your long courted approbation proud,
Learning from you, how to erect their hair,
And in perfection, all their habitt wear,
To place a patch, in some peculiar way,
That may an unmark'd smile, to sight betray,
And the vast genius of the Sex, display?
   Pitty me then (she crys) and learn the fate
That makes me Porter to a Temple gate;
Ardelia came to Town, some weeks agoe,
Who does on books her rural hours bestow,

And is so rustick in her cloaths and meen,
'Tis with her ungenteel but to be seen,
Did not a long acquaintance plead excuse;
Besides, she likes no witt, thats now in use,
Dispises Courtly Vice, and plainly sais,
That sence and Nature shou'd be found in Plays,
And therefore, none will 'ere be brought to see
But those of Dryden, Etheridge, or Lee,
And some few Authors, old, and dull to me.
To her I did engage my coach and day,
And here must wait, while she within does pray.
Ere twelve was struck, she calls me from my bed,
Nor once observes how well my toilett's spread;
Then, drinks the fragrant tea contented up,
Without a complement upon the cup,
Tho' to the ships, for the first choice I stear'd,
Through such a storm, as the stout bargemen fear'd;
Least that a praise, which I have long engross'd
Of the best china Equipage, be lost.
Of fashions now, and colours I discours'd,
Detected shops that wou'd expose the worst,
What silks, what lace, what rubans she must have,
And by my own, an ample pattern gave;
To which, she cold, and unconcern'd reply'd,
I deal with one that does all these provide,
Hauing of other cares, enough beside;
And in a cheap, or an ill chosen gown,
Can vallue blood that's nobler then my own,
And therefore hope, my self not to be weigh'd
By gold, or silver, on my garments laid;
Or that my witt, or judgment shou'd be read
In an uncomon colour on my head.
  Stupid! and dull, the shrugging Zany crys;
When, service ended, me he moving spy's,
Hastes to conduct me out, and in my ear
Drops some vile praise, too low for her to hear;
Which to avoid, more then the begging throng,
I reach the coach, that swiftly rowls along,

Least to Hide park, we shou'd too late be brought,
And loose e're night, an hour of finding fault.
Arriv'd, she crys,—
                          that awk'ard creature see,
A fortune born, and wou'd a beauty bee
Cou'd others but believe, as fast as she.
Round me, I look, some Monster to discry,
Whose wealthy acres, must a Title buye,
Support my Lord, and be, since his have fail'd,
With the high shoulder, on his race entayl'd;
When to my sight, a lovely face appears,
Perfect in e'vry thing, but growing years;
This I defend, to do my judgment right,
Can you dispraise a skin so smooth, so white,
That blush, which o're such well turn'd cheeks does rise,
That look of youth, and those enliven'd eyes?
She soon replies,—
                          that skin, which you admire,
Is shrunk, and sickly, cou'd you view itt nigher.
The crimson lining and uncertain light,
Reflects that blush, and paints her to the sight.
Trust me, the look, which you comend, betrays
A want of sence, more then the want of days,
And those wild eyes, that round the cercle stray,
Seem, as her witts, had but mistook their way.
As I did mine, I to my self repeat,
When by this envious side. I took my seat:
Oh! for my groves, my Country walks, and bow'rs,
Trees blast not trees, nor flow'rs envenom flow'rs,
As beauty here, all beautys praise devours.
But Noble Piso passes,—
                          he's a witt.
As some (she sais) wou'd have itt, tho' as yett
No line he in a Lady's fan has writt,
N'ere on their dresse, in verse, soft things wou'd say,
Or with loud clamour ouer powr'd a Play,
And right or wrong, preuented the third day;
To read in publick places, is not known,

Or in his Chariot, here appears alone;
Bestows no hasty praise, on all that's new.
When first this Coach came out to publick view,
Mett in a visit, he presents his hand
And takes me out, I make a willfull stand,
Expecting, sure, this wou'd applause invite,
And often turn'd, that way, to guide his sight;
Till finding him wrapp'd in a silent thought,
I ask'd, if that the Painter well had wrought,
Who then reply'd, he has in the Fable err'd,
Cov'ring Adonis with a monstrous beard;
Made Hercules (who by his club is shewn)
A gentler fop then any of the Town,
Whilst Venus, from a bogg is rising seen,
And eyes a squint, are given to beautys queen
I had no patience, longer to attend,
And know 'tis want of witt, to discomend.
    Must Piso then! be judg'd by such as these,
Piso, who from the Latin, Virgil frees,
Who loos'd the bands, which old Sylenus bound,
And made our Albion rocks repeat the mistick sound,
"Whilst all he sung was present to our eyes
"And as he rais'd his verse, the Poplars seem'd to rise?"
Scarce cou'd I in my brest my thoughts contain,
Or for this folly, hide my just disdain.
When see, she says, observe my best of friends,
And through the window, half her length extends
Exalts her voyce, that all the ring may hear;
How fullsomly she oft repeats my dear.
Letts fall some doubtfull words, that we may know
There still a secret is, betwixt them two,
And makes a sign, the small white hand to shew.
When, Fate be prais'd, the coachman slacks the reins,
And o're my lap, no longer now she leans,
But how her choyce I like, does soon enquire?
    Can I dislike I cry, what all admire,
Discreet, and witty, civil and refin'd,
Nor, in her person fairer then her mind,

Is young Alinda, if report be just;
For half the Caracter, my eyes I trust.
What chang'd Almeria, on a suddain cold,
As if I of your friend, some tale had told?
No, she replyes, but when I hear her praise,
A secret failing does my pitty raise,
Damon she loves, and 'tis my dayly care,
To keep the passion from the publick ear,
I ask, amaz'd, if this she has reveal'd,
No, but 'tis true, she crys, though much conceal'd;
I have observ'd itt long, nor wou'd betray
But to your self, what now with grief I say,
Who this, to none, but Confidents must break,
Nor they to others, but in whispers, speak;
I am her friend and must consult her fame.
More was she saying, when fresh objects came,
Now what's that thing, she crys, Ardelia, guesse?
A woman sure.—
                            Ay and a Poetesse,
They say she writes, and 'tis a comon jest.
Then sure sh' has publickly the skill professt,
I soon reply, or makes that gift her pride,
And all the world, but scribblers, does deride;
Setts out Lampoons, where only spite is seen,
Not fill'd with female witt, but female spleen.
Her florish'd name, does o're a song expose,
Which through all ranks, down to the Carman, goes.
Or poetry is on her Picture found,
In which she sits, with painted lawrel crown'd.
If no such flyes, no vanity defile
The Helyconian balm, the sacred oyl,
Why shou'd we from that pleasing art be ty'd,
Or like State Pris'ners, Pen and Ink deny'd?
But see, the Sun his chariot home has driv'n
From the vast shining ring of spacious Heav'n,
Nor after him Celestial beautys stay,
But crou'd with sparkling wheels the milky way.
Shall we not then, the great example take

And ours below, with equal speed forsake?
When to your favours, adding this one more,
You'll stop, and leave me thank-full, att my door.
How! e're you've in the Drawing-room appear'd,
And all the follys there beheld and heard.
Since you've been absent, such intrigues are grown;
Such new Coquetts and Fops are to be shown,
Without their sight you must not leave the Town
Excuse me, I reply, my eyes ne're feast
Upon a fool, tho' ne're so nicely dresst.
Nor is itt musick to my burthen'd ear
The unripe prating's of our sex to hear,
A noysy girl, who has at fifteen talk'd more
Then Grandmother, or Mother here to fore,
In all the cautious, prudent years they bore.
Statesmen there are, (she crys) whom I can show
That bear the kingdoms cares, on a bent brow;
Who take the weight of politicks by grains,
And to the least, know what each scull contains,
Who's to be coach'd, who talk'd to when abroad,
Who but the smile must have, and who the nod;
And when this is the utmost of their skill,
'Tis not much wonder, if affairs go ill.
Then for the Church-men—
                    hold my lodging's here;
Nor can I longer a re-proof forbear
When sacred things nor Persons she wou'd spare.
  We parted thus, the night in peace I spent,
And the next day, with haste and pleasure went
To the best seat of fam'd and fertile Kent.
Where lett me live from all detraction free
Till thus the World is criticis'd by mee;
Till friend, and Foe, I treat with such dispite
May I no scorn, the worst of ills, excite.

LADY MARY WORTLEY MONTAGU (1690-1762)

Lady Montagu is primarily known as a witty, satirical letter-writer. Her childhood was spent at the home of her father, the Duke of Kingston, where she was educated by her brother's tutor. Pressured, as a young gentlewoman, to marry a titled man of her father's choice, she eloped with Edward Wortley Montagu instead. The letters that she wrote after her marriage show her restless, isolated in a country house. In 1716 she accompanied her husband to the East, leaving in the letters a vivid account of the city of Constantinople. On her return, she introduced into England the Turkish practice of inoculation against smallpox. Her poetry was well-known, and some of it was attributed to Pope or John Gay. Pope became her admirer and friend at first, and then, for reasons that remain unclear, her virulent enemy. In his *Imitation of the First Satire of the Second Book of Horace*, he wrote what she considered libelous things about her. In 1739 she left England, her husband, Pope and the scandal behind, to live on the Continent for the next twenty-two years.

VERSES ADDRESSED TO THE IMITATOR OF THE FIRST SATIRE OF THE SECOND BOOK OF HORACE

In two large columns on thy motley page,
Where Roman wit is strip'd with English rage;
Where ribaldry to satire makes pretence;

And modern scandal rolls with ancient sense:
Whilst on one side we see how Horace thought;
And on the other how he never wrote:
Who can believe, who view the bad and good,
That the dull copyist better understood
That Spirit, he pretends to imitate,
Than heretofore that Greek he did translate?

Thine is just as an image of *his* pen,
As thou thyself art of the sons of men:
Where our own species in burlesque we trace,
A sign-post likeness of the human race,
That is at once resemblance and disgrace.
If *he* has thorns, they all on roses grow;
Thine like rude thistles, and mean brambles show,
With this exception, that tho' rank the soil,
Weeds as they are they seem produc'd by toil.
Satire should, like a polish'd razor keen,
Wound with a touch, that's scarcely felt or seen.
Thine is an oyster-knife that hacks and hews;
The rage but not the talent to abuse;
And is in *hate*, what *love* is in the stews.
'Tis the gross *lust* of hate, that still annoys,
Without distinction, as gross love enjoys:
Neither to folly, or to vice confin'd;
The object of thy spleen is human kind:
It preys on all, who yield or who resist;
To thee 'tis provocation to exist. . . .

If none do yet return th' intended blow,
You all your safety to your dullness owe:
But whilst that armour thy poor corps defends,
'Twill make thy readers few, as are thy friends;
Those, who thy nature loath'd, yet lov'd thy art,
Who lik'd thy head, and yet abhorr'd thy heart;
Chose thee, to read, but never to converse,
And scorn'd in prose, him whom they priz'd in verse;
Even thy shall now their partial error see,
Shall shun thy writings, like thy company,

And to thy books shall ope their eyes no more,
Than to thy person they wou'd do their door.

AN ANSWER TO A LOVE-LETTER

Is it to me, this sad lamenting strain?
Are heaven's choicest gifts bestowed in vain?
A plenteous fortune, and a beauteous bride,
Your love rewarded, gratify'd your pride:
Yet leaving her—'tis me that you pursue
Without one single charm, but being new.
How vile is man! how I detest their ways
Of artful falsehood, and designing praise!
Tasteless, an easy happiness you slight,
Ruin your joy, and mischief your delight,
Why should poor pug (the mimic of your kind)
Wear a rough chain, and be to box confin'd?
Some cup, perhaps, he breaks, or tears a fan
While roves unpunish'd the destroyer, man.
Not bound by vows, and unrestrain'd by shame,
In sport you break the heart, and rend the fame.
Not that your art can be successful here,
Th' already plunder'd need no robber fear:
Nor sighs, nor charms, nor flatteries can move,
Too well secur'd against a second love.
Once, and but once, that devil charm'd my mind;
To reason deaf, to observation blind;
I idly hop'd (what cannot love persuade?)
My fondness equal'd, and my love repaid:
Slow to distrust, and willing to believe,
Long hush'd my doubts, and did myself deceive;
But oh! too soon—this tale would ever last;
Sleep, sleep my wrongs, and let me think them past.
For you, who mourn with counterfeited grief,
And ask so boldly like a begging thief,
May soon some other nymph inflict the pain,
You know so well with cruel art to feign.
Though long you sported with Dan Cupid's dart,

You may see eyes, and you may feel a heart.
So the brisk wits, who stop the evening coach,
Laugh at the fear which follows their approach;
With idle mirth, and haughty scorn despise
The pasesenger's pale cheek and staring eyes:
But seiz'd by Justice, find a fright no jest,
And all the terror doubled in their breast.

IN ANSWER TO A LADY
WHO ADVISED RETIREMENT

You little know the heart that you advise;
I view this various scene with equal eyes:
In crowded courts I find myself alone,
And pay my worship to a nobler throne.
Long since the value of this world I know,
Pity the madness, and despise the show:
Well as I can my tedious part I bear,
And wait for my dismission without fear.
Seldom I mark mankind's detested ways,
Not hearing censure, nor affecting praise;
And, unconcern'd, my future fate I trust
To that sole Being, merciful and just.

EMILY BRONTË
(1818–1848)

Emily Brontë stayed at home most of her life, in
Haworth parsonage in the West Riding of Yorkshire.
She was the fifth of six children—five girls (Maria,
Elizabeth, Charlotte, and Anne) and one boy (Branwell). Her mother died when Emily was three and the
"upbringing" of the children was done by their father
and their mother's sister. The father published a book

Cottage Poems, which he described as "chiefly designed for the lower classes of society." Emily went
to school briefly, but received most of her education
from Charlotte. In 1842, she went with her sister to
the Pensionnat Heger in Brussels, where she stayed
for eight months, and then returned to Haworth to
stay. The *Poems by Currer, Ellis, and Acton Bell* were
published in 1846, subsidized by the Brontës themselves. Two copies were sold. *Wuthering Heights* is
said to have been begun in 1845 or 1846 on Charlotte's suggestion that more money could be made
writing novels. Emily caught a cold at her brother's
funeral and died of consumption, refusing to see a
doctor, refusing medication, in what has been sug-
gested was an "eager death."

I SAW THEE, CHILD,
ONE SUMMER'S DAY

I saw thee, child, one summer's day
Suddenly leave thy cheerful play,
And in the green grass, lowly lying,
I listened to thy mournful sighing.

I knew the wish that waked that wail;
I knew the source whence sprung those tears;
You longed for fate to raise the veil
That darkened over coming years.

An anxious prayer was heard, and power
Was given me, in that silent hour,
To open to an infant's eye
The portals of futurity.

But, child of dust, the fragrant flowers,
The bright blue sky and velvet sod
Were strange conductors to the bowers
Thy darking footsteps must have trod.

I watched my time, and summer passed,
And Autumn waning fleeted by,
And doleful winter nights at last
In cloudy mourning clothed the sky.

And now I'm come: this evening fell
Not stormily, but stilly drear;
A sound sweeps o'er thee like a knell
To banish joy and welcome care;

A fluttering blast that shakes the leaves,
And whistles round the gloomy wall,
And lingering long lamenting grieves,
For 'tis the spectre's call.

He hears me: what a sudden start
Sent the blood icy to that heart;
He wakens, and how ghastly white
That face looks in the dim lamplight.

Those tiny hands in vain essay
To thrust the shadowy fiend away;
There is a horror on his brow,
An anguish in his bosom now;

A fearful anguish in his eyes
Fixed strainedly on the vacant air;
Heavily burst in long-drawn sighs
His panting breath, enchained by fear.

Poor child, if spirits such as I
Could weep o'er human misery,
A tear might flow, aye, many a tear,
To see the road that lies before,
To see the sunshine disappear,
And hear the stormy waters roar,
Breaking upon a desolate shore,
Cut off from hope in early day,
From power and glory cut away.

But it is doomed, and morning's light
Must image forth the scowl of night,
And childhood's flower must waste its bloom
Beneath the shadow of the tomb.

LIGHT UP THY HALLS!
'TIS CLOSING DAY

Light up thy halls! 'Tis closing day;
I'm drear and lone and far away—
Cold blows on my breast the northwind's bitter sigh,
And oh, my couch is bleak beneath the rainy sky!

Light up thy halls—and think not of me;
That face is absent now, thou hast hated so to see—
Bright be thine eyes, undimmed their dazzling shine,
For never, never more shall they encounter mine!

The desert moor is dark; there is tempest in the air;
I have breathed my only wish in one last, one burning
    prayer—
A prayer that would come forth, although it lingered
    long;
That set on fire my heart, but froze upon my tongue.

And now, it shall be done before the morning rise:
I will not watch the sun ascent in yonder skies.
One task alone remains—thy pictured face to view;
And then I go to prove if God, at least, be true!

Do I not see thee now? Thy black resplendent hair;
Thy glory-beaming brow, and smile, how heavenly fair!
Thine eyes are turned away—those eyes I would not
    see;
Their dark, their deadly ray, would more than madden
    me.

There, go, deceiver, go! My hand is streaming wet;
My heart's blood flows to buy the blessing—To forget!
Oh could that lost heart give back, back again to thine,
One tenth part of the pain that clouds my dark decline!

Oh could I see thy lids weighed down in cheerless woe;
Too full to hide their tears, too stern to overflow;
Oh could I know thy soul with equal grief was torn,
This fate might be endured—this anguish might be
  borne!

How gloomy grows the night! 'Tis Gondal's wind that
  blows;
I shall not tread again the deep glens where it rose—
I feel it on my face—"Where, wild blast, dost thou
  roam?
What do we, wanderer, here, so far away from home?

"I do not need thy breath to cool my death-cold brow;
But go to that far land, where she is shining now;
Tell Her my latest wish, tell Her my dreary doom;
Say that *my* pangs are past, but *Hers* are yet to come."

Vain words—vain, frenzied thoughts! No ear can hear
  me call—
Lost in the vacant air my frantic curses fall—
And could she see me now, perchance her lip would
  smile,
Would smile in careless pride and utter scorn the while!

And yet for all her hate, each parting glance would tell
A stronger passion breathed, burned, in this last
  farewell.
Unconquered in my soul the Tyrant rules me still;
Life bows to my control, but *Love* I cannot kill!

UPON HER SOOTHING BREAST

Upon her soothing breast
She lulled her little child;
A winter sunset in the west,
A dreary glory smiled.

THERE LET THY BLEEDING BRANCH ATONE

There let thy bleeding branch atone
For every torturing tear:
Shall my young sins, my sins alone,
Be everlasting here?

Who bade thee keep that cursed name
A pledge for memory?
As if Oblivion ever came
To breathe its bliss on me;

As if, through all the 'wildering maze
Of mad hours left behind,
I once forgot the early days
That thou wouldst call to mind.

TO IMAGINATION

When weary with the long day's care,
And earthly change from pain to pain,
And lost, and ready to despair,
Thy kind voice calls me back again—
O my true friend, I am not lone
While thou canst speak with such a tone!

So hopeless is the world without,
The world within I doubly prize;
Thy world where guile and hate and doubt
And cold suspicion never rise;
Where thou and I and Liberty
Have undisputed sovereignty.

What matters it that all around
Danger and grief and darkness lie,
If but within our bosom's bound
We hold a bright unsullied sky,

Warm with ten thousand mingled rays
Of suns that know no winter days?

Reason indeed may oft complain
For Nature's sad reality,
And tell the suffering heart how vain
Its cherished dreams must always be;
And truth may rudely trample down
The flowers of Fancy newly blown.

But thou art ever there to bring
The hovering visions back and breathe
New glories o'er the blighted spring
And call a lovelier life from death,
And whisper with a voice divine
Of real worlds as bright as thine.

I trust not to thy phantom bliss,
Yet still in evening's quiet hour
With never-failing thankfulness
I welcome thee, benignant power,
Sure solacer of human cares
And brighter hope when hope despairs.

REMEMBRANCE

Cold in the earth, and the deep snow piled above thee!
Far, far removed, cold in the dreary grave!
Have I forgot, my Only Love, to love thee,
Severed at last by Time's all-wearing wave?

Now, when alone, do my thoughts no longer hover
Over the mountains on Angora's shore;
Resting their wings where heath and fern-leaves cover
That noble heart for ever, ever more?

Cold in the earth, and fifteen wild Decembers
From those brown hills have melted into spring—
Faithful indeed is the spirit that remembers
After such years of change and suffering!

Sweet Love of youth, forgive if I forget thee
While the World's tide is bearing me along:
Sterner desires and darker hopes beset me,
Hopes which obscure but cannot do thee wrong.

No other Sun has lightened up my heaven;
No other Star has ever shone for me;
All my life's bliss from thy dear life was given—
All my life's bliss is in the grave with thee.

But when the days of golden dreams had perished
And even Despair was powerless to destroy,
Then did I learn how existence could be cherished,
Strengthened and fed without the aid of joy;

Then did I check the tears of useless passion,
Weaned my young soul from yearning after thine;
Sternly denied its burning wish to hasten
Down to that tomb already more than mine!

And even yet, I dare not let it languish,
Dare not indulge in Memory's rapturous pain;
Once drinking deep of that divinest anguish,
How could I seek the empty world again?

DEATH, THAT STRUCK WHEN I WAS MOST CONFIDING

Death, that struck when I was most confiding
In my certain Faith of Joy to be,
Strike again, Time's withered branch dividing
From the fresh root of Eternity!

Leaves, upon Time's branch, were growing brightly,
Full of sap and full of silver dew;
Birds, beneath its shelter, gathered nightly;
Daily, round its flowers, the wild bees flew.

Sorrow passed and plucked the golden blossom,
Guilt stripped off the foliage in its pride;
But, within its parent's kindly bosom,
Flowed forever Life's restoring tide.

Little mourned I for the parted Gladness,
For the vacant next and silent song;
Hope was there and laughed me out of sadness,
Whispering, "Winter will not linger long."

And behold, with tenfold increase blessing
Spring adorned the beauty-burdened spray;
Wind and rain and fervent heat caressing
Lavished glory on its second May.

High it rose; no wingèd grief could sweep it;
Sin was scared to distance with its shine:
Love and its own life had power to keep it
From all wrong, from every blight but thine!

Cruel death, the young leaves droop and languish!
Evening's gentle air may still restore—
No: the morning sunshine mocks my anguish—
Time for me must never blossom more!

Strike it down, that other boughs may flourish
Where that perished sapling used to be;
Thus, at least, its mouldering corpse will nourish
That from which it sprung—Eternity.

NO COWARD SOUL IS MINE

No coward soul is mine
No trembler in the world's storm-troubled sphere
I see Heaven's glories shine
And Faith shines equal arming me from Fear

O God within my breast
Almighty ever-present Deity
Life, that in me hast rest
As I Undying Life, have power in Thee

Vain are the thousand creeds
That move men's hearts, unutterably vain,
Worthless as withered weeds
Or idlest froth amid the boundless main

To waken doubt in one
Holding so fast by thy infinity
So surely anchored on
The steadfast rock of Immortality

With wide-embracing love
Thy spirit animates eternal years
Pervades and broods above,
Changes, sustains, dissolves, creates and rears

Though Earth and moon were gone
And suns and universes ceased to be
And thou wert left alone
Every Existence would exist in thee

There is not room for Death
Nor atom that his might could render void
Since thou art Being and Breath
And what thou art may never be destroyed.

STANZAS*

Often rebuked, yet always back returning
    To those first feelings that were born with me,
And leaving busy chase of wealth and learning
    For idle dreams of things which cannot be:

To-day, I will seek not the shadowy region;
    Its unsustaining vastness waxes drear;
And visions rising, legion after legion,
    Bring the unreal world too strangely near.

I'll walk, but not in old heroic traces,
    And not in paths of high morality,
And not among the half-distinguished faces,
    The clouded forms of long-past history.

* The authorship of this poem is questioned. It may have
been written by Charlotte.

I'll walk where my own nature would be leading:
    It vexes me to choose another guide:
Where the gray flocks in ferny glens are feeding;
    Where the wild wind blows on the mountain side.

What have those lonely mountains worth revealing?
    More glory and more grief than I can tell:
The earth that wakes one human heart to feeling
    Can centre both the worlds of Heaven and Hell.

CHARLOTTE BRONTË (1816–1854)

Charlotte Brontë's life was a series of lurchings away from the family home at Haworth parsonage. She spent several years alternating between jobs as a teacher or governess and staying on the moors with her sisters and brother. It was Charlotte's idea to start a school with her sisters and to spend a year in Brussels learning French and German in preparation for that. Under the pseudonymn "Currer Bell," she published *Jane Eyre* in 1847, a year after the *Poems*. *Shirley* was published two years later and brought her considerable fame. At the age of thirty-eight, she married, became pregnant and died of an illness resulting from childbirth.

EVENING SOLACE

The human heart has hidden treasures,
    In secret kept, in silence sealed;
The thoughts, the hopes, the dreams, the pleasures,
    Whose charms were broken if revealed.

And days may pass in gay confusion,
  And nights in rosy riot fly,
While, lost in Fame's or Wealth's illusion,
  The memory of the Past may die.

But there are hours of lonely musing,
  Such as in evening silence come,
When, soft as birds their pinions closing,
  The heart's best feelings gather home.
Then in our souls there seems to languish
  A tender grief that is not woe,
And thoughts that once wrung groans of anguish,
  Now cause but some mild tears to flow.

And feelings, once as strong as passions,
  Float softly back—a faded dream;
Our own sharp griefs and wild sensations,
  The tale of others' sufferings seem,
Oh! when the heart is freshly bleeding,
  How longs it for that time to be,
When, through the mist of years receding,
  Its woes but live in reverie!

And it can dwell on moonlight glimmer,
  On evening shade and loneliness;
And, while the sky grows dim and dimmer,
  Feel no untold and strange distress—
Only a deeper impulse given,
  By lonely hour and darkened room,
To solemn thoughts that soar to heaven
  Seeking a life and world to come.

ELIZABETH BARRETT BROWNING (1806–1861)

Elizabeth Browning's childhood was filled with reading, leisure and culture acquired from her brothers' tutors. A narrative poem, *The Battle of Marathon*, was published in fifty copies by her "proud" father when she was fourteen. Her illnesses are vague. The first, at fifteen, was somehow connected to riding a horse. The second occurred much later and is so beclouded that it is impossible to know what it was. From 1841 until her marriage to Robert Browning in 1846, Elizabeth Barrett remained in her room in the house on Wimpole Street in London. After the marriage, she left with Browning for Italy, where she spent the remaining fifteen years of her life. A son, Robert, was born in 1849 and Mrs. Browning was much criticized for treating him as an equal and "forcing him into precocious emotionalism over her own interests in politics and spiritualism." She had been quite accepted as a poet long before she met Browning and, in her early correspondence with him, wrote constantly about her preoccupation with a blank-verse novel that was not to appear for ten years. In the dedication to *Aurora Leigh*, the poet describes it as "the most mature of my works and the one into which my highest convictions upon life and art have entered." Her friendships included the major "progressive" women of her time—Julia Ward Howe, Harriet Martineau, and Margaret Fuller—all of whom shared her sense of the women's struggle and commitment to the abolition of slavery.

A TRUE DREAM

(Dreamed at Sidmouth, 1833)

I had not an evil end in view,
    Tho' I trod the evil way;
And why I practised the magic art,
    My dream it did not say.

I unsealed the vial mystical,
    I outpoured the liquid thing,
And while the smoke came wreathing out,
    I stood unshuddering.

The smoke came wreathing, wreathing out,
    All mute, and dark, and slow,
Till its cloud was stained with a fleshly hue,
    And a fleshly form 'gan show.

Then paused the smoke—the fleshly form
    Looked steadfast in mine ee,
His beard was black as a thundercloud,
    But I trembled not to see.

I unsealed the vial mystical,
    I outpoured the liquid thing,
And while the smoke came wreathing out,
    I stood unshuddering.

The smoke came wreathing, wreathing out,
    All mute, and dark, and slow,
Till its cloud was stained with a fleshly hue,
    And a fleshly form 'gan show.

Then paused the smoke—but the mortal form
    A garment swart did veil,
I looked on it with fixed heart,
    Yea—not a pulse did fail!

I unsealed the vial mystical,
    I outpoured the liquid thing,
And while the smoke came wreathing out,
    I stood unshuddering.

The smoke came wreathing, wreathing out,
  And now it was faster and lighter,
And it bore on its folds the rainbow's hues,
  Heaven could not show them brighter.

Then paused the smoke, the rainbow's hues
  Did a childish face express—
The rose in the cheek, the blue in the eyne,
  The yellow in the tress.

The fair young child shook back her hair,
  And round me her arms did wreathe,
Her lips were hard and cold as stone,
  They sucked away my breath.

I cast her off as she clung to me,
  With hate and shuddering;
I brake the vials, and foresware
  The curse, cursed thing.

Anon outspake a brother of mine—
  'Upon the pavement, see,
Besprent with noisome poison slime,
  Those twining serpents three.'

Anon outspake my wildered heart
  As I saw the serpent train—
'I have called up three existences
  I cannot quench again.

'Alas! with unholy company,
  My lifetime they will scathe;
They will hiss in the storm, and on sunny days
  will gleam and thwart my path.'

Outspake that pitying brother of mine—
  'Now nay, my sister, nay,
I will pour on them oil of vitriol,
  And burn their lives away.'

'Now nay, my brother, torture not,
  Now hold thine hand, and spare.'
He poured on them oil of vitriol,
  And did not heed my prayer.

I saw the drops of torture fall;
  I heard the shriekings rise,
While the serpents writhed in agony
  Beneath my dreaming eyes.

And while they shrieked, and while they writhed,
  And inward and outward wound,
They waxed larger, and their wail
  Assumed a human sound.

And glared their eyes, and their slimy scales
  Were roundly and redly bright,
Most like the lidless sun, what time
  Thro' the mist he meets your sight.

And larger and larger they waxed still,
  And longer still and longer;
And they shrieked in their pain, 'Come, come to us,
  We are stronger, we are stronger.'

Upon the ground I laid mine head,
  And heard the wailing sound;
I did not wail, I did not writhe—
  I laid me on the ground.

And larger and larger they waxed still
  And longer still and longer;
And they shrieked in their pangs, 'Come, come to us,
  We are stronger, we are stronger.'

Then up I raised my burning brow,
  My quiv'ring arms on high;
I spake in prayer, and I named aloud
  The name of sanctity.

And as in my anguish I prayed and named
   Aloud the holy name,
The impious mocking serpent voice
   Did echo back the same.

And larger and larger they waxed still,
   And stronger still and longer!
And they shrieked in their pangs, 'Come, come to us,
   We are stronger, we are stronger.'

Then out from among them arose a form
   In shroud of death indued—
I fled from him with wings of wind,
   With whirlwinds he pursued.

      *   *   *   *

I stood by a chamber door, and thought
   Within its gloom to hide;
I locked the door, and the while forgot
   That I stood on the outer side.

And the knell of mine heart was wildly tolled
   While I grasped still the key,
For I felt beside me the icy breath,
   And knew that *that* was *he*.

I heard these words, 'Who'er doth *taste*,
   Will *drink* the magic bowl;
So her body may do my mission here
   Companioned by her soul.'

Mine hand was cold as the key it held,
   Mine heart had an iron weight;
I saw a gleam, I heard a sound—
   The clock was striking eight.

SONNETS FROM THE PORTUGUESE

I

I thought once how Theocritus had sung
Of the sweet years, the dear and wished-for years,
Who each one in a gracious hand appears
To bear a gift for mortals, old or young:
And, as I mused it in his antique tongue,
I saw, in gradual vision through my tears,
The sweet, sad years, the melancholy years,
Those of my own life, who by turn had flung
A shadow across me. Straightway I was 'ware,
So weeping, how a mystic Shape did move
Behind me, and drew me backward by the hair;
And a voice said in mastery, while I strove,—
"Guess now who holds thee?"—"Death," I said.
　But, there,
The silver answer rang—"Not Death, but Love."

V

I lift my heavy heart up solemnly,
As once Electra her sepulchral urn,
And, looking in thine eyes, I overturn
The ashes at thy feet. Behold and see
What a great heap of grief lay hid in me,
And how the red wild sparkles dimly burn
Through the ashen greyness. If thy foot in scorn
Could tread them out to darkness utterly,
It might be well perhaps. But if instead
Thou wait beside me for the wind to blow
The grey dust up, . . . those laurels on thine head,
O my Belovèd, will not shield thee so,
That none of all the fires shall scorch and shred
The hair beneath. Stand further off then! go.

XXII

When our two souls stand up erect and strong,
Face to face, silent, drawing nigh and nigher,

Until the lengthening wings break into fire
At either curvèd point,—what bitter wrong
Can the earth do to us, that we should not long
Be here contented? Think. In mounting higher,
The angels would press on us and aspire
To drop some golden orb of perfect song
Into our deep, dear silence. Let us stay
Rather on earth, Belovèd—where the unfit
Contrarious moods of men recoil away
And isolate pure spirits, and permit
A place to stand and love in for a day,
With darkness and the death-hour rounding it.

TO GEORGE SAND

I. A Desire

Thou large-brained woman and large-hearted man,
Self-called George Sand! whose soul, amid the lions
Of thy tumultuous senses, moans defiance,
And answers roar for roar, as spirits can!
I would some mild miraculous thunder ran
Above the applauded circus, in appliance
Of thine own nobler nature's strength and science,
Drawing two pinions, white as wings of swan,
From thy strong shoulders, to amaze the place
With holier light! that thou to woman's claim,
And man's, mightst join beside the angel's grace
Of a pure genius sanctified from blame,—
Till child and maiden pressed to thine embrace,
To kiss upon thy lips a stainless fame.

II. A Recognition

True genius, but true woman! dost deny
Thy woman's nature with a manly scorn,
And break away the gauds and armlets worn
By weaker women in captivity?
Ah, vain denial! that revolted cry

Is sobbed in by a woman's voice forlorn!—
Thy woman's hair, my sister, all unshorn,
Floats back dishevelled strength in agony,
Disproving thy man's name! and while before
The world thou burnest in a poet-fire,
We see thy woman-heart beat evermore
Through the large flame. Beat purer, heart, and higher,
Till God unsex thee on the heavenly shore,
Where unincarnate spirits purely aspire.

THE CURSE

I

Because ye have broken your own chain
    With the strain
Of brave men climbing a Nation's height,
Yet thence bear down with brand and thong
On souls of others,—for this wrong
    This is the curse.   Write.

Because yourselves are standing straight
    In the state
Of Freedom's foremost acolyte,
Yet keep calm footing all the time
On writhing bond-slaves,—for this crime
    This is the curse.   Write.

Because ye prosper in God's name,
    With a claim
To honor in the old world's sight,
Yet do the fiend's work perfectly
In strangling martyrs,—for this lie
    This is the curse.   Write.

II

Ye shall watch while kings conspire
Round the people's smouldering fire,
   And, warm for your part,

Shall never dare—O shame!
To utter the thought into flame
   Which burns at your heart.
       This is the curse.   Write.

Ye shall watch while nations strive
With the bloodhounds, die or survive,
   Drop faint from their jaws,
Or throttle them backward to death;
And only under your breath
   Shall favor the cause.
       This is the curse.   Write.

Ye shall watch while strong men draw
The nets of feudal law
   To strangle the weak;
And, counting the sin for a sin,
Your soul shall be sadder within
   Than the word ye shall speak.
       This is the curse.   Write.

When good men are praying erect
That Christ may avenge his elect
   And deliver the earth,
The prayer in your ears, said low,
Shall sound like the tramp of a foe
   That's driving you forth.
       This is the curse.   Write.

When wise men give you their praise,
They shall pause in the heat of the phrase,
   As if carried too far.
When ye boast your own charters kept true,
Ye shall blush; for the thing which ye do
   Derides what ye are.
       This is the curse.   Write.

When fools cast taunts at your gate,
Your scorn ye shall somewhat abate
   As ye look o'er the wall;

For your conscience, tradition, and name
Explode with a deadlier blame
   Than the worst of them all.
      This is the curse.   Write.

Go, wherever ill deeds shall be done,
Go, plant your flag in the sun
   Beside the ill-doers!
And recoil from clenching the curse
Of God's witnessing Universe
   With a curse of yours.
      THIS is the curse.   Write.

A MAN'S REQUIREMENTS

I

Love me, Sweet, with all thou art,
   Feeling, thinking, seeing;
Love me in the lightest part,
   Love me in full being.

II

Love me with thine open youth
   In its frank surrender;
With the vowing of thy mouth,
   With its silence tender.

III

Love me with thine azure eyes,
   Made for earnest granting;
Taking color from the skies,
   Can Heaven's truth be wanting?

IV

Love me with their lids, that fall
   Snow-like at first meeting;

Love me with thine heart, that all
   Neighbors then see beating.

V

Love me with thine hand stretched out
   Freely—open-minded:
Love me with thy loitering foot,—
   Hearing one behind it.

VI

Love me with thy voice, that turns
   Sudden faint above me;
Love me with thy blush that burns
   When I murmur *Love me!*

VII

Love me with thy thinking soul,
   Break it to love-sighing;
Love me with thy thoughts that roll
   On through living—dying.

VIII

Love me in thy gorgeous airs,
   When the world has crowned thee;
Love me, kneeling at thy prayers,
   With the angels round thee.

IX

Love me pure, as musers do,
   Up the woodlands shady:
Love me gaily, fast and true,
   As a winsome lady.

X

Through all hopes that keep us brave,
    Farther off or nigher,
Love me for the house and grave,
    And for something higher.

XI

Thus, if thou wilt prove me, Dear,
    Woman's love no fable,
I will love *thee*—half a year—
    As a man is able.

THE CRY OF THE CHILDREN

"φεῦ, φεῦ, τι προσδερκεσθε μ' ομμασιν, τεκνα."
                                    Medea

Do ye hear the children weeping, O my brothers,
        Ere the sorrow comes with years?
They are leaning their young heads against their
    mothers,—
        And *that* cannot stop their tears.
The young lambs are bleating in the meadows;
        The young birds are chirping in the nest;
The young fawns are playing with the shadows;
        The young flowers are blowing toward the west—
But the young, young children, O my brothers,
        They are weeping bitterly!—
They are weeping in the playtime of the others,
        In the country of the free.

Do you question the young children in their sorrow,
        Why their tears are falling so?—
The old man may weep for his to-morrow
        Which is lost in Long Ago—
The old tree is leafless in the forest—
        The old year is ending in the frost—

The old wound, if stricken, is the sorest—
    The old hope is hardest to be lost:
But the young, young children, O my brothers,
      Do you ask them why they stand
Weeping sore before the bosoms of their mothers,
      In our happy Fatherland?

They look up with their pale and sunken faces,
      And their looks are sad to see,
For the man's grief abhorrent, draws and presses
      Down the cheeks of infancy—
"Your old earth," they say, "is very dreary;"
    "Our young feet," they say, "are very weak!
Few paces have we taken, yet are weary—
    Our grave-rest is very far to seek!
Ask the old why they weep, and not the children,
      For the outside earth is cold,—
And we young ones stand without, in our bewildering,
      And the graves are for the old!

"True," say the young children, "it may happen
      That we die before our time!
Little Alice died last year—the grave is shapen
    Like a snowball, in the rime.
We looked into the pit prepared to take her—
    Was no room for any work in the close clay:
From the sleep wherein she lieth none will wake her,
    Crying, 'Get up, little Alice! it is day.'

If you listen by that grave, in sun and shower,
    With your ear down, little Alice never cries!—
Could we see her face, be sure we should not know her,
    For the smile has time for growing in her eyes,—
And merry go her moments, lulled and stilled in
      The shroud, by the kirk-chime!
It is good when it happens," say the children,
      "That we die before our time!"

Alas, the wretched children! they are seeking
      Death in life, as best to have!

They are binding up their hearts away from breaking,
    With a cerement from the grave.
Go out, children, from the mine and from the city—
    Sing out, children, as the little thrushes do—
Pluck you handfuls of the meadow-cowslips pretty—
    Laugh aloud, to feel your fingers let them through!
But they answer, "Are your cowslips of the meadows
    Like our weeds anear the mine?
Leave us quiet in the dark of the coal-shadows,
    From your pleasures fair and fine!

"For oh," say the children, "we are weary,
    And we cannot run or leap—
If we cared for any meadows, it were merely
    To drop down in them and sleep.
Our knees tremble sorely in the stooping—
    We fall upon our faces, trying to go;
And, underneath our heavy eyelids drooping,
    The reddest flower would look as pale as snow.
For, all day, we drag our burden tiring,
    Through the coal-dark, underground—
Or, all day, we drive the wheels of iron
    In the factories, round and round.

"For, all day, the wheels are droning, turning,—
    Their wind comes in our faces,—
Till our hearts turn,—our heads, with pulses burning,
    And the walls turn in their places—
Turns the sky in the high window blank and reeling—
    Turns the long light that droppeth down the wall—
Turn the black flies that crawl along the ceiling—
    All are turning, all the day, and we with all!—
And all day, the iron wheels are droning;
    And sometimes we could pray,
'O ye wheels' (breaking out in a mad moaning),
    'Stop! be silent for to-day!' "

Ay! be silent! Let them hear each other breathing
    For a moment, mouth to mouth—

Let them touch each other's hands, in a fresh wreathing
     Of their tender human youth!
Let them feel that this cold metallic motion
    Is not all the life God fashions or reveals—
Let them prove their inward souls against the notion
    That they live in you, or under you, O wheels!—
Still, all day, the iron wheels go onward,
     As if Fate in each were stark;
And the children's souls, which God is calling sunward,
     Spin on blindly in the dark.

Now tell the poor young children, O my brothers,
     That they look to Him and pray—
So the blessed One, who blesseth all the others,
     Will bless them another day.
They answer, "Who is God that He should hear us,
    While the rushing of the iron wheels is stirred?
When we sob aloud, the human creatures near us
    Pass by, hearing not, or answer not a word!
And *we* hear not (for the wheels in their resounding)
     Strangers speaking at the door;
Is it likely God, with angels singing round Him,
     Hears our weeping any more?

"Two words, indeed, of praying we remember;
     And at midnight's hour of harm,—
'Our Father,' looking upward in the chamber,
     We say softly for a charm.
We know no other words, except 'Our Father,'
    And we think that, in some pause of angels' song,
God may pluck them with the silence sweet to gather,
    And hold both within His right hand which is strong.
'Our father!' If he heard us, He would surely
     (For they call Him good and mild)
Answer, smiling down the steep world very purely
     'Come and rest with me, my child.'

"But, no!" say the children, weeping faster,
     "He is speechless as a stone;

And they tell us, of his image is the master
    Who commands us to work on.
"Go to!" say the children,— "up in heaven,
  Dark, wheel-like, turning clouds are all we find.
Do not mock us: grief has made us unbelieving:
We look up for God; but tears have made us blind."
Do you hear the children weeping and disproving,
    O my brothers, what ye preach?
For God's possible is taught by his world's loving—
    And the children doubt of each.

And well may the children weep before you!
    They are weary ere they run;
They have never seen the sunshine, nor the glory
    Which is brighter than the sun.
They know the grief of man, without its wisdom;
    They sink in man's despair, without its calm;
Are slaves, without the liberty in Christdom;
    Are martyrs, by the pang without the palm:
Are worn as if with age, yet unretrievingly
    The harvest of its memories cannot reap;
Are orphans of the earthly love and heavenly—
    Let them weep! let them weep!

They look up with their pale and sunken faces,
    And their look is dread to see.
For they mind you of their angels in high places,
    With eyes turned on Deity.
"How long," they say, "how long, O cruel nation,
  Will you stand, to move the world on a child's heart,—
Stifle down with a mailed heel its palpitation,
    And tread onward to your throne amid the mart!
Our blood splashes upward, O gold-heaper,
    And your purple shows your path!
But the child's sob in the silence curses deeper
    Than the strong man in his wrath."

HIRAM POWERS' "GREEK SLAVE"

They say Ideal beauty cannot enter
The house of anguish. On the threshold stands
An alien Image with enshackled hands,
Called the Greek Slave! as if the artist meant her
(That passionless perfection which he lent her,
Shadowed not darkened where the sill expands)
To so confront man's crimes in different lands
With man's ideal sense. Pierce to the centre,
Art's fiery finger, and break up ere long
The serfdom of this world. Appeal, fair stone,
From God's pure heights of beauty against man's
    wrong!
Catch up in thy divine face, not alone
East griefs but west, and strike and shame the strong,
By thunders of white silence, overthrown.

CHRISTINA ROSSETTI (1830–1894)

The model for Rossetti family life was Italian; like her mother, Christina Rossetti did not "go out" in society, was extremely devout and had a life with few external events in it. She was educated by her mother and considerably influenced by her father, an Italian exile poet and Dante scholar. Whereas the men in the family were flamboyant, adventurous and political, the women—Christina, her sister and her mother—were dutiful and submissive. Christina was both a painter and a poet. She contributed to the Pre-Raphaelite magazine *The Germ* under a pseudonym, and it was her poem "Goblin Market" that brought the first critical recognition to the Pre-Raphaelite Movement.

Much of her lifetime was spent struggling with illness and death—in the people close to her and in herself. She had a series of illnesses, the worst of which was Graves' disease, which plagued her during the last twenty years of her life. Nevertheless, she did not live as a recluse, but entertained many friends at home. One of the least often mentioned of her close friends was the man known as Lewis Carroll. Although she was a contemporary of Elizabeth Browning's, the two poets never met and Christina Rossetti never had the kind of fame that Mrs. Browning lived to enjoy. She never had much money, either, her poems often being turned down by magazine editors or, in book form, not very "popular." In addition to the lyric poetry reprinted here, Christina Rossetti wrote serious works of prose, much of it devotional, and several books for children.

SONG

When I am dead, my dearest,
    Sing no sad songs for me;
Plant thou no roses at my head,
    Nor shady cypress tree:
Be the green grass above me
    With showers and dewdrops wet:
And if thou wilt, remember,
    And if thou wilt, forget.

I shall not see the shadows.
    I shall not feel the rain;
I shall not hear the nightingale
    Sing on as if in pain:
And dreaming through the twilight
    That doth not rise nor set,
Haply I may remember,
    And haply may forget.

ECHO

Come to me in the silence of the night;
 Come in the speaking silence of a dream;
Come with soft rounded cheeks and eyes as bright
 As sunlight on a stream;
  Come back in tears,
O memory, hope, love of finished years.

O dream how sweet, too sweet, too bitter sweet,
 Whose wakening should have been in Paradise,
Where souls brimfull of love abide and meet;
 Where thirsting longing eyes
  Watch the slow door
That opening, letting in, lets out no more.

Yet come to me in dreams, that I may live
 My very life again though cold in death:
Come back to me in dreams, that I may give
 Pulse for pulse, breath for breath:
  Speak low, lean low,
As long ago my love, how long ago.

IN AN ARTIST'S STUDIO

One face looks out from all his canvases,
 One selfsame figure sits or walks or leans:
 We found her hidden just behind those screens,
That mirror gave back all her loveliness.
A queen in opal or in ruby dress,
 A nameless girl in freshest summer-greens,
 A saint, an angel—every canvas means
That same one meaning, neither more nor less.
He feeds upon her face by day and night,
 And she with true kind eyes looks back on him,
Fair as the moon and joyful as the light:
 Not wan with waiting, not with sorrow dim;
Not as she is, but was when hope shone bright;
 Not as she is, but as she fills his dream.

THE WORLD

By day she woos me, soft, exceeding fair:
  But all night as the moon so changeth she;
  Loathsome and foul with hideous leprosy,
And subtle serpents gliding in her hair.
By day she woos me to the outer air,
  Ripe fruits, sweet flowers, and full satiety:
  But thro' the night a beast she grins at me,
A very monster void of love and prayer.
By day she stands a lie: by night she stands
  In all the naked horror of the truth,
With pushing horns and clawed and clutching hands.
Is this a friend indeed, that I should sell
  My soul to her, give her my life and youth,
Till my feet, cloven too, take hold on hell?

MONNA INNOMINATA:
A SONNET OF SONNETS

*Beatrice, immortalized by 'altissimo poeta . . . cotanto
amante'; Laura, celebrated by a great though an inferior
bard,—have alike paid the exceptional penalty of exceptional honour, and have come down to us resplendent
with charms, but (at least, to my apprehension) scant of
attractiveness.*

*These heroines of world-wide fame were preceded by a
bevy of unnamed ladies, 'donne innominate,' sung by a
school of less conspicuous poets; and in that land and that
period which gave simultaneous birth to Catholics, to
Albigenses, and to Troubadours, one can imagine many
a lady as sharing her lover's poetic aptitude, while the
barrier between them might be one held sacred by both,
yet not such as to render mutual love incompatible with
mutual honour.*

*Had such a lady spoken for herself, the portrait left us
might have appeared more tender, if less dignified, than
any drawn even by a devoted friend. Or had the Great*

*Poetess of our own day and nation only been unhappy
instead of happy, her circumstances would have invited
her to bequeath to us, in lieu of the 'Portuguese Sonnets,'
an inimitable 'donna innominata' drawn not from fancy
but from feeling, and worthy to occupy a niche beside
Beatrice and Laura.*

1

'Lo di che han detto a' dolci amici addio.'—DANTE
'Amor, con quanto sforzo oggi mi vinci!'—PETRARCA

Come back to me, who wait and watch for you:—
    Or come not yet, for it is over then,
    And long it is before you come again,
So far between my pleasures are and few.
While, when you come not, what I do I do
    Thinking 'Now when he comes,' my sweetest 'when':
    For one man is my world of all the men
This wide world holds; O love, my world is you.
Howbeit, to meet you grows almost a pang
    Because the pang of parting comes so soon;
    My hope hangs waning, waxing, like a moon
    Between the heavenly days on which we meet:
Ah me, but where are now the songs I sang
    When life was sweet because you called them sweet?

2

'Era già l'ora che volge il desio.'—DANTE
'Ricorro al tempo ch' io vi vidi prima.'—PETRARCA

I wish I could remember that first day,
    First hour, first moment of your meeting me,
    If bright or dim the season, it might be
Summer or Winter for aught I can say;
So unrecorded did it slip away,
    So blind was I to see and to foresee,
    So dull to mark the budding of my tree
That would not blossom yet for many a May.
If only I could recollect it, such

A day of days! I let it come and go
  As traceless as a thaw of bygone snow;
It seemed to mean so little, meant so much;
If only now I could recall that touch,
  First touch of hand in hand—Did one but know!

3

'O ombre vane, fuor che ne l'aspetto!'—DANTE
'Immaginata guida la conduce.'—PETRARCA

I dream of you, to wake: would that I might
  Dream of you and not wake but slumber on;
  Nor find with dreams the dear companion gone,
As, Summer ended, Summer birds take flight.
In happy dreams I hold you full in sight,
  I blush again who waking look so wan;
  Brighter than sunniest day that ever shone,
In happy dreams your smile makes day of night.
Thus only in a dream we are as one,
  Thus only in a dream we give and take
    The faith that maketh rich who take or give;
If thus to sleep is sweeter than to wake,
    To die were surely sweeter than to live,
Though there be nothing new beneath the sun.

4

'Poca favilla gran fiamma seconda.'—DANTE
'Ogni altra cosa, ogni pensier va fore,
E sol ivi con voi rimansi amore.'—PETRARCA

I loved you first: but afterwards your love,
  Outsoaring mine, sang such a loftier song
As drowned the friendly cooings of my dove.
  Which owes the other most? My love was long,
  And yours one moment seemed to wax more strong;
I loved and guessed at you, you construed me
And loved me for what might or might not be—
  Nay, weights and measures do us both a wrong.
For verily love knows not 'mine' or 'thine';

With separate 'I' and 'thou' free love has done,
   For one is both and both are one in love:
Rich love knows nought of 'thine that is not mine';
     Both have the strength and both the length thereof,
Both of us, of the love which makes us one.

5

'Amor che a nullo amato amar perdona.'—DANTE
'Amor m'addusse in sì gioiosa spene.'—PETRARCA

O my heart's heart, and you who are to me
   More than myself myself, God be with you,
   Keep you in strong obedience leal and true
To Him whose noble service setteth free;
Give you all good we see or can foresee,
   Make your joys many and your sorrows few,
   Bless you in what you bear and what you do,
Yea, perfect you as He would have you be.
So much for you; but what for me, dear friend?
   To love you without stint and all I can,
To-day, to-morrow, world without an end;
To love you much and yet to love you more,
   As Jordan at his flood sweeps either shore;
   Since woman is the helpmeet made for man.

6

'Or puoi la quantitate
Comprender de l'amor che a te mi scalda.'—DANTE
'Non vo' che da tal nodo amor mi scioglia.'—PETRARCA

Trust me, I have not earned your dear rebuke,—
   I love, as you would have me, God the most;
   Would lose not Him, but you, must one be lost,
Nor with Lot's wife cast back a faithless look,
Unready to forego what I forsook;
   This say I, having counted up the cost,
   This, though I be the feeblest of God's host,
The sorriest sheep Christ shepherds with His crook.

Yet while I love my God the most, I deem
   That I can never love you overmuch;
     I love Him more, so let me love you too;
   Yea, as I apprehend it, love is such
I cannot love you if you love not Him,
    I cannot love Him if I love not you.

7

'Qui primavera sempre ed ogni frutto.'—DANTE
'Ragionando con meco ed io con lui.'—PETRARCA

'Love me, for I love you'—and answer me,
   'Love me, for I love you': so shall we stand
   As happy equals in the flowering land
Of love, that knows not a dividing sea.
Love builds the house on rock and not on sand,
   Love laughs what while the winds rave desperately;
   And who hath found love's citadel unmanned?
   And who hath held in bonds love's liberty?—
My heart's a coward though my words are brave—
   We meet so seldom, yet we surely part
   So often; there's a problem for your art!
   Still I find comfort in his Book who saith,
Though jealousy be cruel as the grave,
    And death be strong, yet love is strong as death.

8

'Come dicesse a Dio, D'altro non calme.'—DANTE
'Spero trovar pietù non che perdono.'—PETRARCA

'I, if I perish, perish'—Esther spake:
   And bride of life or death she made her fair
   In all the lustre of her perfumed hair
And smiles that kindle longing but to slake.
She put on pomp of loveliness, to take
   Her husband through his eyes at unaware;
   She spread abroad her beauty for a snare,
Harmless as doves and subtle as a snake.

She trapped him with one mesh of silken hair,
　　She vanquished him by wisdom of her wit,
　　　　And built her people's house that it should stand:—
　　If I might take my life so in my hand,
And for my love to Love put up my prayer,
　　And for love's sake by Love be granted it!

9

'O dignitosa coscienza e netta!'—DANTE
'Spirto più acceso di virtuti ardenti.—PETRARCA

Thinking of you, and all that was, and all
　　That might have been and now can never be,
　　I feel your honoured excellence, and see
Myself unworthy of the happier call:
For woe is me who walk so apt to fall,
　　So apt to shrink afraid, so apt to flee,
　　Apt to lie down and die (ah woe is me!)
Faithless and hopeless turning to the wall.
And yet not hopeless quite nor faithless quite,
Because not loveless; love may toil all night,
But take at morning; wrestle till the break
　　Of day, but then wield power with God and man:—
　　So take I heart of grace as best I can,
Ready to spend and be spent for your sake.

10

'Con miglior corso e con migliore stella.'—DANTE
'La vita fugge e non s'arresta un' ora.'—PETRARCA

Time flies, hope flags, life plies a wearied wing;
　　Death following hard on life gains ground apace;
　　Faith runs with each and rears an eager face,
Outruns the rest, makes light of everything,
Spurns earth, and still finds breath to pray and sing;
　　While love ahead of all uplifts his praise,
　　Still asks for grace and still gives thanks for grace,
Content with all day brings and night will bring.

Life wanes; and when love folds his wings above
  Tired hope, and less we feel his conscious pulse,
  Let us go fall asleep, dear friend, in peace:
  A little while, and age and sorrow cease;
  A little while, life reborn annuls
Loss and decay and death, and all is love.

11

'Vien dietro a me e lascia dir le genti.'—DANTE
'Contando i casi della vita nostra.'—PETRARCA

Many in aftertimes will say of you
  'He loved her'—while of me what will they say?
  Not that I loved you more than just in play,
For fashion's sake as idle women do.
Even let them prate; who know not what we knew
  Of love and parting in exceeding pain,
  Of parting hopeless here to meet again,
Hopeless on earth, and heaven is out of view.
But by my heart of love laid bare to you,
  My love that you can make not void nor vain,
Love that foregoes you but to claim anew
Beyond this passage of the gate of death,
  I charge you at the Judgment make it plain
My love of you was life and not a breath.

12

'Amor che ne la mente mi ragiona.'—DANTE
'Amor vien nel bel viso di costei.'—PETRARCA

If there be any one can take my place
  And make you happy whom I grieve to grieve,
  Think not that I can grudge it, but believe
I do commend you to that nobler grace,
That readier wit than mine, that sweeter face;
  Yea, since your riches make me rich, conceive
  I too am crowned, while bridal crowns I weave,
And thread the bridal dance with jocund pace.

For if I did not love you, it might be
That I should grudge you some one dear delight;
But since the heart is yours that was mine own,
Your pleasure is my pleasure, right my right,
Your honourable freedom makes me free,
And you companioned I am not alone.

13

'E drizzeremo gli occhi al Primo Amore.'—DANTE
'Ma trovo peso non da le mie braccia.'—PETRARCA

If I could trust mine own self with your fate,
Shall I not rather trust it in God's hand?
Without Whose Will one lily doth not stand,
Nor sparrow fall at his appointed date;
Who numbereth the innumerable sand,
Who weighs the wind and water with a weight,
To Whom the world is neither small nor great,
Whose knowledge foreknew every plan we planned.
Searching my heart for all that touches you,
I find there only love and love's goodwill
Helpless to help and impotent to do,
Of understanding dull, of sight most dim;
And therefore I commend you back to Him
Whose love your love's capacity can fill.

14

'E la Sua Volontade è nostra pace.'—DANTE
'Sol con questi pensier, con altre chiome.'—PETRARCA

Youth gone, and beauty gone if ever there
Dwelt beauty in so poor a face as this;
Youth gone and beauty, what remains of bliss?
I will not bind fresh roses in my hair,
To shame a cheek at best but little fair,—
Leave youth his roses, who can bear a thorn,—
I will not seek for blossoms anywhere,
Except such common flowers as blow with corn.

Youth gone and beauty gone, what doth remain?
  The longing of a heart pent up forlorn,
    A silent heart whose silence loves and longs;
  The silence of a heart which sang its songs
    While youth and beauty made a summer morn,
Silence of love that cannot sing again.

A BETTER RESURRECTION

I have no wit, no words, no tears;
  My hearth within me like a stone
Is numbed too much for hopes or fears.
  Look right, look left, I dwell alone;
I lift mine eyes, but dimmed with grief
  No everlasting hills I see;
My life is in the falling leaf:
  O Jesus, quicken me.

My life is like a faded leaf,
  My harvest dwindled to a husk:
Truly my life is void and brief
  And tedious in the barren dusk;
My life is like a frozen thing,
  No bud nor greenness can I see;
Yet rise it shall—the sap of Spring;
  O Jesus, rise in me.

My life is like a broken bowl,
  A broken bowl that cannot hold
One drop of water for my soul
  Or cordial in the searching cold;
Cast in the fire the perished thing;
  Melt and remould it, till it be
A royal cup for Him, my King:
  O Jesus, drink of me.

INTROSPECTIVE

I wish it were over the terrible pain,
Pang after pang again and again:
First the shattering ruining blow,
Then the probing steady and slow.

Did I wince? I did not faint:
My soul broke but was not bent:
Up I stand like a blasted tree
By the shore of the shivering sea.

On my boughs neither leaf nor fruit,
No sap in my uttermost root,
Brooding in an anguish dumb
On the short past and the long to come.

Dumb I was when the ruin fell,
Dumb I remain and will never tell;
O my soul, I talk with thee,
But not another the sight must see.

I did not start when the torture stung,
I did not faint when the torture wrung:
Let it come tenfold if come it must,
But I will not groan when I bite the dust.

IS THIS THE END?

Is this the end? Is there no end but this?
    Yea, none beside:
    No other end for pride
And foulness and besottedness.

Hath she no friend? hath she no clinging friend?
    Nay, none at all;
    Who stare upon her fall
Quake for themselves with hair on end.

Will she be done away? vanish away?
  Yea, like a dream;
  Yea, like the shades that seem
Somewhat, and lo are nought by day.

Alas for her amid man's helpless moan,
  Alas for her!
  She hath no comforter:
In solitude of fire she sits alone.

MARY ELIZABETH COLERIDGE (1861–1907)

Mary Coleridge came of a traditional Victorian family, growing up in a household that revolved around an imposing *paterfamilias* who practiced law and entertained Tennyson and Browning in his parlor, and a mother who looked after the running of the household and did good works for charity. Mary Coleridge's own life departed little from Victorian modes. She acquired an excellent education in languages and, as she grew older, had many literary friends, most of them women, who formed small groups for the purpose of discussing literature and culture. She never lived outside the family home. Several successful novels were published in her lifetime, but the poetry remained hidden. The few poems she did allow to be published appeared anonymously or were signed with a Greek pseudonym that meant "The Wanderer."

THE OTHER SIDE OF A MIRROR

I sat before my glass one day,
   And conjured up a vision bare,
Unlike the aspects glad and gay,
   That erst were found reflected there—
The vision of a woman, wild
   With more than womanly despair.

Her hair stood back on either side
   A face bereft of loveliness.
It had no envy now to hide
   What once no man on earth could guess.
It formed the thorny aureole
   Of hard unsanctified distress.

Her lips were open—not a sound
   Came through the parted lines of red.
Whate'er it was, the hideous wound
   In silence and in secret bled.
No sigh relieved her speechless woe,
   She had no voice to speak her dread.

And in her lurid eyes there shone
   The dying flame of life's desire,
Made mad because its hope was gone,
   And kindled at the leaping fire
Of jealousy, and fierce revenge,
   And strength that could not change nor tire.

Shade of a shadow in the glass,
   O set the crystal surface free!
Pass—as the fairer visions pass—
   Nor ever more return, to be
The ghost of a distracted hour,
   That heard me whisper, "I am she!"

MORTAL COMBAT

It is because you were my friend,
  I fought you as the devil fights.
Whatever fortune God may send,
  For once I set the world to rights.

And that was when I thrust you down,
  And stabbed you twice and twice again,
Because you dared take off your crown,
  And be a man like other men.

EYES

Eyes, what are they? Coloured glass,
Where reflections come and pass.

Open windows—by them sit
Beauty, Learning, Love, and Wit.

Searching cross-examiners;
Comfort holy ministers.

Starry silences of soul,
Music past the lips' control.

Fountains of unearthly light;
Prisons of the infinite.

THE WITCH

I have walked a great while over the snow,
And I am not tall nor strong.
My clothes are wet, and my teeth are set,
And the way was hard and long.
I have wandered over the fruitful earth,
But I never came here before.
Oh, lift me over the threshold, and let me in at the door!

The cutting wind is a cruel foe.
I dare not stand in the blast.
My hands are stone, and my voice a groan,

And the worst of death is past.
I am but a little maiden still,
My little white feet are sore.
Oh, lift me over the threshold, and let me in at the door!

Her voice was the voice that women have,
Who plead for their heart's desire.
She came—she came—and the quivering flame
Sank and died in the fire.
It never was lit again on my hearth
Since I hurried across the floor,
To lift her over the threshold, and let her in at the door!

REGINA

My Queen her sceptre did lay down,
She took from her head the golden crown
Worn by right of her royal birth.
Her purple robe she cast aside,
And the scarlet vestures of her pride,
That was the pride of the earth.
In her nakedness was she
Queen of the world, herself and me.

My Queen took up her sceptre bright,
Her crown more radiant than the light,
The rubies gleaming out of the gold.
She donned her robe of purple rare,
And did a deed that none may dare,
That makes the blood run cold.
And in her bravery is she
Queen of herself, the world and me.

HORROR

Thy body is no more thy house,
    It is become thy sepulchre.
I cannot any more arouse
    The spirit that did inhabit there.

The brain's asleep before its time.
   I would that thou hadst died outright,
And I had seen thee, in thy prime,
   Go half to darkness, half to light!

ALICE MEYNELL
(1847-1922)

Alice Thompson's family encouraged the artistic bent
of their daughters. Her sister became a painter who
shocked the art world by painting military scenes,
considered a bizarre subject for a woman. Alice
Thompson's first book of poems was published in
1875. She married Wilfred Meynell and with him became one of the leading figures of the Catholic Literary Revival. She had, in the course of her marriage,
eight children; the periods of intense poetry-writing
came before all the children and then in the last
decade of her life. She was extremely famous, particularly in the 1890s, as an essayist and literary journalist. She wrote "women's columns" for newspapers
and raised that form from chit-chat to serious consideration of literary and political issues concerning
women. The poet Coventry Patmore once wrote that
Alice Meynell was the only woman of recent times to
achieve distinction of style. As a reply Meynell
promptly sent him Sonnets from the Portuguese and
Wuthering Heights. She was an active feminist and
socialist. Her poetry was so well known that, it is
said, shop girls would stop Wilfred Meynell and ask
if he was related to her. She was seriously considered
for the honor of Poet Laureate.

PARENTAGE

"When Augustus Caesar legislated against the unmarried citizens of Rome, he declared them to be, in some sort, slayers of the people."

Ah no! not these!
These, who were childless, are not they who gave
So many dead unto the journeying wave,
The helpless nurslings of the cradling seas;
Not they who doomed by infallible decrees
Unnumbered man to the innumerable grave.

But those who slay
Are fathers. Theirs are armies. Death is theirs—
The death of innocences and despairs;
The dying of the golden and the grey.
The sentence, when these speak it, has no Nay.
And she who slays is she who bears, who bears.

SAINT CATHERINE OF SIENA

Written for Strephon, who said that a woman must lean, or she should not have his chivalry

The light young man who was to die,
    Stopped in his frolic by the State,
Aghast, beheld the world go by;
    But Catherine crossed his dungeon gate.

She found his lyric courage dumb,
    His stripling beauties strewn in wrecks,
His modish bravery overcome;
    Small profit had he of his sex.

On any old wife's level he,
    For once—for all. But he alone—
Man—must not fear the mystery,
    The pang, the passage, the unknown:

Death: He did fear it, in his cell,
　　Darkling amid the Tuscan sun;
And, weeping, at her feet he fell,
　　The sacred, young, provincial nun.

She prayed, she preached him innocent;
　　She gave him to the Sacrificed;
On her courageous breast he leant,
　　The breast where beat the heart of Christ.

He left it for the block, with cries
　　Of victory on his severed breath.
That crimson head she clasped, her eyes
　　Blind with the splendour of his death.

And will the man of modern years
　　—Stern on the Vote—withhold from thee,
Thou prop, thou cross, erect, in tears,
　　Catherine, the service of his knee?

MATERNITY

One wept whose only child was dead,
　　New-born, ten years ago.
"Weep not; he is in bliss," they said.
　　She answered, "Even so,

"Ten years ago was born in pain
　　A child, not now forlorn.
But oh, ten years ago, in vain,
　　A mother, a mother was born."

EASTER NIGHT

All night had shout of men and cry
　　　　Of woeful women filled His way;
Until that noon of sombre sky
　　　　On Friday, clamour and display
Smote Him; no solitude had He,
No silence, since Gethsemane.

Public was Death; but Power, but Might,
    But Life again, but Victory,
Were hushed within the dead of night,
    The shutter'd dark, the secrecy.
And all alone, alone, alone,
He rose again behind the stone.

A FATHER OF WOMEN:
AD SOROREM E.B.

"Thy father was transfused into thy blood."
           Dryden: *Ode to Mrs. Anne Killigrew.*

Our father works in us,
The daughters of his manhood. Not undone
Is he, not wasted, thou transmuted thus,
    And though he left no son.

    Therefore on him I cry
To arm me: "For my delicate mind a casque,
A breastplate for my heart, courage to die,
    Of thee, captain, I ask.

    "Nor strengthen only; press
A finger on this violent blood and pale,
Over this rash will let thy tenderness
    A while pause, and prevail.

    "And shepherd-father, thou
Whose staff folded my thoughts before my birth,
Control them now I am of earth, and now
    Thou art no more of earth.

    "O liberal, constant, dear,
Crush in my nature the ungenerous art
Of the inferior; set me high, and here,
    Here garner up thy heart!"

Like to him now are they,
The million living fathers of the War—
Mourning the crippled world, the bitter day—
Whose striplings are no more.

The crippled world! Come then,
Fathers of women with your honour in trust,
Approve, accept, know them daughters of men,
Now that your sons are dust.

THE SUNDERLAND CHILDREN

On the 183 Sunderland children who lost their lives in a panic at the Victoria Hall, 16th June, 1883

This was the surplus childhood, held as cheap!
    Not worth the care which shields
The lambs that are to stay, the corn to reap—
    The promise of the fields.

The nation guards her future. Fruits and grass
    And vegetable life
Are fostered league by league. But oh, the mass
    Of childhood over-rife!

O mass, O units! Oh, the separate story
    Planned for each breather of breath!
This futile young mankind, and transitory,
    Is left to stray to Death.

O promise, presage, menace! Upon these
    A certain seal is laid.
Unkept, unbroken, are the auguries
    These little children made.

For threat is bound with promise; and the nation
    Holds festival of regret
Over these dead—dead in their isolation—
    Wisely. She feared their threat.

IN TIME OF WAR

"Lord, I owe Thee a Death"—Richard Hooker

Man pays that debt with new munificence,
  Not piecemeal now, not slowly, by the old:
Not grudgingly, by the effaced thin pence,
  But greatly and in gold.

TO CONSCRIPTS

"Compel them to come in"—St. Luke's Gospel

You "made a virtue of necessity"
  By divine sanction; you, the loath, the grey,
The random, gentle, unconvinced; oh, be
  The crowned!—you may, you may.

You, the compelled, be feasted! You, the caught,
  Be freemen of the gates that word unlocks!
Accept your victory from that unsought,
  That heavenly, paradox.

RACHEL ANNAND TAYLOR (1876–?)

Rachel Taylor is the author of a pioneering book called *Aspects of the Italian Renaissance,* written in 1923 and recently brought out in a modern edition. Her interest in that period and in art history and aesthetics continued; she wrote *Leonardo the Florentine: A Study in Personality* several years afterward. Her poetry belongs mostly to an early period in her life and in 1910 was the subject of a paper given at a literary society by D. H. Lawrence.

ART AND WOMEN

The triumph of Art compels few womenkind;
   And these are yoked like slaves to Eros' car,—
No victors they! Yet ours the Dream behind,
   Who are nearer to the gods than poets are.
For with the silver moons we wax and wane,
   And with the roses love most woundingly,
And, wrought from flower to fruit with dim rich pain,
   The Orchard of the Pomegranates are we.
For with Demeter still we seek the Spring,
   With Dionysus tread the sacred Vine,
Our broken bodies still imagining
   The mournful Mystery of the Bread and Wine.—
And Art, that fierce confessor of the flowers,
Desires the secret spice of those veiled hours.

POEMS FROM HOLLOWAY PRISON

Holloway was the notorious prison for militant suffragists, the place where they suffered the most bar-
baric treatment, including force-feeding. Emmeline
Pankhurst was but one of its famous prisoners. The
following poems were written during a hunger strike
in the spring of 1912.

There was a small woman called G,
Who smashed two big windows at B—
They sent her to jail, her fate to bewail,
For Votes must be kept, must be kept for the male.

They asked that small woman called G,
Why she smashed those big windows at B—
She made a long speech, then made her defence,

But it wasn't no use, their heads were so dense;
They just hummed the refrain, altho' it is stale—
Votes must be kept, must be kept for the male.

They sent her to H for six months and a day,
In the coach Black Maria she went sadly away;
But she sang in this strain, as it jolted and rumbled,
We will have the Vote, we will not be humbled.
We must have the vote by hill and by dale,
Votes shall not alone be kept for the male.

—Anonymous

There's a strange sort of college,
    And the scholars are unique,
Yet the lessons are important which they learn;
    They fit them for the fight,
    For all that's true and right,
And for liberty and justice make them burn.

There the scholars are the teachers,
    And the staff they are the taught,
Though they sometimes try to get the upper hand;
    But their rules they are too grim,
    So they find they must give in
To that gallant, honour-loving little band.

It is there you grow quite knowing,
    If you ever have been dull,
For the things you see and hear they make you wise;
    There we take our F. H. G.,
    A very high degree,
And the hand-grip of true friendship—that's the prize.

There the terms they often vary,
    Some are long and some are short,
But the rules they never alter in the least;
    They go on from day to day,
    In the same old prosy way,
And the food you get there isn't quite a feast.

Just watch those scholars' faces,
It's truth on them you'll find,
Hear their laughter ringing out so clear and bright;
"Unto others you must do
As you'd have them do to you,"
Is their motto, and you know that they are right.

When you're singing "Rule, Britannia,"
Britons never shall be slaves,
Remember it's not words which tell but deeds;
'Tis actions brave and strong
Which always right the wrong,
For justice unto freedom always leads.

Hark to the trumpet calling!
Come out and take your place
'Neath the standard of the purple, white, and green;
True courage must prevail,
For the tyrants we assail,
It's the grandest fight the world has ever seen.

The students and the college
Are known throughout the world,
Of God's truth the light upon them never sets;
'Tis the prison, cold and grey,
Of noted Holloway,
And the scholars are my colleague Suffragettes.

—*Edith Aubrey Wingrove*

Before I came to Holloway,
It was not cold nor illness,
Nor harshness that I feared, oh stay!
It was the deathly stillness.

Inside, it's bang with supper, or
It's dinner or "your apple;"
Or "pass out, please, to exercise,"
Or "pass along to chapel."

'Tis "close your door there," "pass out, please,"
  It's clattering with the rations,
"Baths," turning locks, and clinking keys,
  And "any applications?"

All day it's "have you got those?" Oh,
  Bells, bangings, people larking;
"You cleaners there," "Miss So-and-so,"
  Or "are you there, Miss Sharky?"

And if you think you're safely in,
  They must have done their caperin',
Then "governor," "visiting magistrates,"
  "The chaplain," "doctor," "matron."

At night, quite late, at nearly six,
  "Haven't they finished speaking?"
Your mattress like the whole D x
  Is simmering and creaking.

You hear them chopping, stoking too,
  And really all their clamour .
Breaks up the peace far more than you
  Or I, with stone and hammer.

Before I came to Holloway
  It was not cold nor illness,
Nor harshness that I feared, oh stay!
  It was the deathly stillness.

                                    —M. C. R.

Beyond the bars I see her move,
  A mystery of blue and green,
As though across the prison yard
  The spirit of the spring had been.
And as she lifts her hands to press
  The happy sunshine of her hair,
From the grey ground the pigeons rise,
  And rustle upwards in the air,

As though her two hands held a key
    To set imprisoned spirits free.

—*Laura Grey*

Newington Butts were lively,
    When session's time fell due,
For there sat Justice Lawrie,
    With twelve good men and true:
And sat to sentence me—
    And except for Justice Lawrie,
I'd be far away and free.

The lies piled up like snow drifts,
    The women's case looked wan;
Their answers were the bravest
    That e'er a judge frowned on:
And a biassed judge was he—
    And except for Justice Lawrie,
I'd be far away and free.

Hear the Jew as witness lying,
    Measuring damages in feet;
And to hear the owner sighing,
    When it proves too much, is sweet.
And all the world can see,
    That except for Justice Lawrie,
I'd be far away and free.

—*Dr. Alice Ker*

SYLVIA PANKHURST (1882–1960)

This "Fighting Pankhurst" is a well-known figure in the political history of the Woman Movement, but

she is relatively unknown as a writer. Unlike her
mother and sister, she devoted her life to linking the
women's cause to that of the working class. She was
often imprisoned and, following the model of other
English Suffragists, went on hunger strikes and had
to be force-fed. She wrote a history of the women's
militant suffrage movement, a biography of her
mother (Emmeline Pankhurst), and books about Rus-
sia and India. These poems are about her experiences
and observations in jail. The book from which they
are taken, *Writ on Cold Slate*, was published in 1922.

THE MOTHERS

O pregnant womanhood that scarce can drag
thy weary ripeness round the allotted track,
and soon would rest thee on unkindly bench,
closely foregathering like affrighted sheep;

In these thy days of fruitfulness thou'rt robbed
of those dear joys that should thy state enrich,
making thy presence blossom like thy womb
and with a sweet expectancy thy thoughts to leap;
a changeless sadness girdles thee about;
each sister whispers faltering unto each
and with wan smiles and pleading arms outstretched,
thou turn'st towards youngling babes, born 'twixt these
    walls,
pledges to thee that thy regretful fruit
will not be monstrous though in prison grown.

IN LOFTY SCORN

With frowning brows and pouting lips she sate,
the fair young woman with her milk white flesh
sweet flushed with rose, by gentle sunshine kissed,
and splendid limbs, and hair of fine pale gold,

like to a Titian maiden on a Venice wall:
a proud sad queen gazing on distant heights.

In lofty scorn she bore her pregnant state,
which marred her beauty not, but seemed to add,
as though Demeter, big with fruits of life
and wealth of hopeful harvests, did increase,
or Flora, with an apron full of flowers,
brooded through Winter's adverse days till Spring.

Yet sombrely she dwelt nor ever smiled;
musing aloof in dreary prison yard.

ANNA WICKHAM
(1884-1947)

Until she began writing poetry, Anna Wickham had
been preparing herself for a career as an opera singer.
Her background was quite different from that of her
English contemporaries, for she had been brought up
in Australia under freer conditions than late Victorian
England allowed its girls. She married and was considered a "rebellious" wife, a woman who lived by her
own rules. She had no higher education and no training as a poet, but she had a burst of creative energy
in the years just after the First World War and produced nine hundred poems in four years. Her first
poems were privately printed in 1911; four years later,
the Poetry Bookshop, under the direction of Alida
Monro, brought out *The Contemplative Quarry*. She
was quite well known in London, particularly in its
Bohemian circle, where her friends included T. E.
Hulme, Henri Gaudier-Brzeska, Jacob Epstein and
D. H. Lawrence. No one has recorded her friendships

with women in that circle, nor her connection with the Woman Movement which, considering the subject matter of her poems, must have had great impact upon her. After the twenties, her work was virtually forgotten and she is surprisingly, lamentably, unknown to this generation of readers.

GIFT TO A JADE

For love he offered me his perfect world.
This world was so constricted, and so small,
It had no sort of loveliness at all,
And I flung back the little silly ball.
At that cold moralist I hotly hurled,
His perfect, pure, symmetrical, small world.

DIVORCE

A voice from the dark is calling me.
In the close house I nurse a fire.
Out in the dark, cold winds rush free,
To the rock heights of my desire.
I smother in the house in the valley below,
Let me out to the night, let me go, let me go!

Spirits that ride the sweeping blast,
Frozen in rigid tenderness,
Wait! For I leave the fire at last,
My little-love's warm loneliness.
I smother in the house in the valley below,
Let me out to the night, let me go, let me go!

High on the hills are beating drums.
Clear from a line of marching men
To the rock's edge the hero comes.
He calls me, and he calls again.
On the hill there is fighting, victory, or quick death,
In the house is the fire, which I fan with sick breath.

I smother in the house in the valley below,
Let me out to the dark, let me go, let me go!

NERVOUS PROSTRATION

I married a man of the Croydon class
When I was twenty-two.
And I vex him, and he bores me
Till we don't know what to do!
It isn't good form in the Croydon class
To say you love your wife,
So I spend my days with the tradesmen's books
And pray for the end of life.

In green fields are blossoming trees
And a golden wealth of gorse,
And young birds sing for joy of worms:
It's perfectly clear, of course,
That it wouldn't be taste in the Croydon class
To sing over dinner or tea:
But I sometimes wish the gentleman
Would turn and talk to me!

But every man of the Croydon class
Lives in terror of joy and speech.
"Words are betrayers," "Joys are brief"—
The maxims their wise ones teach—
And for all my labour of love and life
I shall be clothed and fed,
And they'll give me an orderly funeral
When I'm still enough to be dead.

THE ECONOMIST

It must be true I love you well
Since your light words are whips of Hell.
But who has pain has songs to sell.
My profitable Friends, farewell!

INSPIRATION

I tried to build Perfection with my hands
And failed.
Then with my will's most strict commands,
And naught availed.
What shall he gain but some poor miser's pelf,
Who thinks for ever of his silly self?
Then to the Stars I flung my trust,
Scorning the menace of my coward dust;
Freed from my little will's control
To a good purpose marched my soul;
In nameless, shapeless God found I my rest,
Though for my solace I built God a breast

CHARLOTTE MEW (1870–1928)

Charlotte Mew left no record of her life in Bloomsbury. All that is known of her comes from a slim memoir published by Alida Monro, who first printed these extraordinary poems. She is described as being "passionately attached to another woman" and the photograph in her *Collected Poems* shows her dressed in "masculine" clothes. What remains of her poetry is a small portion of what she wrote, for the poet destroyed much of her work in fits of self-criticism. She wrote occasional fiction and was published in *The Yellow Book*. In 1928, poor and un-attended, in spite of a last-ditch effort by Hardy, De La Mare and Masefield that got her a civil list pension, she committed suicide by drinking a bottle of Lysol.

FAME

Sometimes in the over-heated house, but not for long,
  Smirking and speaking rather loud,
  I see myself among the crowd,
Where no one fits the singer to his song,
Or sifts the unpainted from the painted faces
Of the people who are always on my stair;
They were not with me when I walked in heavenly
      places;
      But could I spare
In the blind Earth's great silences and spaces,
  The din, the scuffle, the long stare
  If I went back and it was not there?
Back to the old known things that are the new,
The folded glory of the gorse, the sweet-briar air,
To the larks that cannot praise us, knowing nothing of
      what we do
  And the divine, wise trees that do not care
Yet, to leave Fame, still with such eyes and that bright
      hair!
God! If I might! And before I go hence
      Take in her stead
      To our tossed bed,
One little dream, no matter how small, how wild.
Just now, I think I found it in a field, under a fence—
A frail, dead, new-born lamb, ghostly and pitiful and
      white,
      A blot upon the night,
      The moon's dropped child!

DOMUS CAEDET ARBOREM

Ever since the great planes were murdered at the end of
      the gardens
The city, to me, at night has the look of a Spirit
      brooding crime;

As if the dark houses watching the trees from dark
windows
Were simply biding their time.

HERE LIES A PRISONER

Leave him: he's quiet enough: and what matter
Out of his body or in, you can scatter
The frozen breath of his silenced soul, of his outraged
soul to the winds that rave:
Quieter now than he used to be, but listening still to
the magpie chatter
Over his grave.

AGAIN

One day, not here, you will find a hand
Stretched out to you as you walk down some heavenly
street;
You will see a stranger scarred from head to feet;
But when he speaks to you you will not understand,
Nor yet who wounded him nor why his wounds are
sweet.
And saying nothing, letting go his hand,
And you will leave him in the heavenly street—
So we shall meet!

ROOMS

I remember rooms that have had their part
In the steady slowing down of the heart.
The room in Paris, the room at Geneva,
The little damp room with the seaweed smell,
And that ceaseless maddening sound of the tide—
Rooms where for good or for ill—things died.
But there is the room where we (two) lie dead,
Though every morning we seem to wake and might
just as well seem to sleep again

As we shall somewhere in the other quieter,
    dustier bed
Out there in the sun—in the rain.

EDITH SITWELL
(1887–1964)

The second chapter of Edith Sitwell's autobiography is called "In Disgrace For Being A Female" and in it the poet describes her early childhood:

> . . . unpopular with my parents from the moment of my birth and throughout childhood and youth. I was in disgrace for being a female and, worse, as I grew older it was obvious that I was not going to conform to my father's standard of feminine beauty. . . . My eighteen year old mother had thought she was being endowed with a new doll . . . I was unsatisfactory in those ways, as in every other.

Sitwell lived on the ancient family estate amid abundant wealth and aristocratic heritage until, in 1914, she moved to London and became involved in her own poetry and some small part of the literary life of that city at that time. She knew, but was not part of, the Bloomsbury circle. Her own work was experimental and she edited an important poetry anthology, *Wheels*, for six years. Her most "outrageous" (to critics at the time) public notice was the performance in 1923 of her "entertainment in verse," "Façade," accompanied by the music of Sir William Walton and recited by Sitwell through a megaphone. Her later work achieved more recognition and she became, by the forties, a grande dame of English letters, and author of some of the most prophetic poems written about the Second World War as well as extensive literary criticism, biographies and journals.

ANNE BOLEYN'S SONG

to Minnie Astor

"After the terrible rain, the Annunciation"—
The bird-blood in the veins that has changed to emeralds
Answered the bird-call. . . .
In the neoteric Spring the winter coldness
Will be forgotten
As I forget the coldness of my last lover,

The great gray King
Who lies upon my breast
And rules the bird-blood in my veins that shrieked
    with laughter
—A sound like fear—
When my step light and high
Spurned my sun down from the sky
In my heedless headless dance—
O, many a year ago, my dear,
My living lass!

In the nights of Spring, the bird, the Angel of the
    Annunciation,
Broods over his heaven of wings and of green wild-fire
That each in its own world, each in its egg
Like Fate is lying.

He sang to my blood, as Henry, my first King,
My terrible sun,
Came like the Ethos of Spring, the first green streak,
And to me cried,
"Your veins are the branches where the first blossom
    begins

After the winter rains—
Your eyes are black and deep
As the prenatal sleep,
And your arms and your breasts are my Rivers of Life
While a new world grows in your side."

Men said I was the primal Fall,
That I gave him the world of spring and of youth like
    an apple
And the orchards' emerald lore—
And sin lay at the core.

But Henry thought me winter-cold
When to keep his love I turned from him as the world
Turns from the sun . . . and then the world grew old.

But I who grew in the heart as the bird-song
Grows in the heart of Spring . . . I, terrible Angel
Of the emeralds in the blood of man and tree,
How could I know how cold the nights of Spring
    would be

When my gray glittering King—
Old amorous Death—grew acclimatized to my
    coldness:
His age sleeps on my breast,
My veins, like branches where the first peach-blossom
Trembles, bring the Spring's warmth to his grayness.

MARY STUART TO JAMES BOTHWELL

Casket Letter No. 2

O you who are my heavenly pain of Hell,
My element, my Paradise of the First Man
That knows not sin—the eternity wherein I dwell!
Before the Flood were you not my primeval clay?
Did you not shape me from that chaos to the form
Of that which *men* call Murder—*I*, the light of the First
    Day?

Leaving you, I was sundered like the Sea!
Departed from the place where I left my heart
I was as small as any body may be
Whose heart is gone—small as the shade of Spring
That has no heart.

                        My mate, the leper-King,

White as a man of diamonds, spotted over
With the ermines of God's wrath for a kingly robe—
My leper-stick of bone

Covered with melting snows, to which I am crucified—
Saw not Death gape wide
Wearing my smile, and bade me come again as his lover.

I was the thunder of the seas within man's blood, and
    the world's wonder!
But he sold my kiss for that of the fair-skinned Sickness
Who melted him away like the spring snows:
The bite of the bright-spotted leopard from Hell's
    thickets—this he chose!
She devoured his bones like fire . . . the bite that tore
    him asunder
Hidden behind the mouth of the ultimate Rose.

I lodged him in a beggar's house, Death-low
And ragged as a leper's flesh. . . . Then, weeping like
    the Spring
From amid his melting snow,
He begged me watch by him, night long. Did I not know
His heart is wax,
While mine is diamond that no blow can break—
But only the touch of your hand—I had pitied those
    lidless eyes that must wake
Until Death seal them, mimicking my kiss.

But how should Pity stand between you and me!
The Devil sunder us from our mates, and God
Knit us together

Until nor man nor devil could tell lover from lover
In our heaven of damnation! Could these sunder our
  clay
Or the seas of our blood? As well might they part
  the fires
That would burn to the bottom of Hell. . . . But there
  is no Hell—
We have kissed it away.

DOROTHY WELLESLEY (1891–1956)

Dorothy Wellesley was an aristocrat. As a child, she was educated by governesses and when she married, it was to a man who became the Duke of Wellington. She began to write and publish poetry before the First World War and continued until just before her death. She had, in the thirties, a considerable reputation in literary circles, largely because William Butler Yeats "discovered" her. Yeats became her friend, wrote an introduction to her *Selected Poems,* and devoted a lot of space to her work when he edited *The Oxford Book of Modern Verse.* In her correspondence with Yeats, Dorothy Wellesley revealed the difficulty of being a woman poet, in spite of her comfortable circumstances: "If I were a man, and had a wife to take practical life off my shoulders, I might start the inner life again."

DEMETER IN SICILY

Grain-mother, thou art still our mother: now
These men thy servants still

Push between stones the small and wooden plough,
And to and from the rock-face on the hill
Go grating with a harsh ungodly scream
The ravens of the rock that waste the corn;
Here was thy daughter born,
And here amid the music of water the sun
Lights the lost genius of Enna's stream,
And the young poplars thicken into gold
In stony river-beds.
                              Here comes thy kid, thy flossy one,
White goats stream down the dark, the rocky walls,
Wavering like water, like the waterfalls.

Demeter! I have seen
Thee throned in rock, thy stallion beside,
Gazing in weeping over uplands wide;
In the right hand a dolphin, left a dove—
Dolphin to swim to heaven on, bird for love—
And I have travelled to the far serene
Pale temples spring from the plains of green,
Where wind the sacred ways around the hills.

Earth-Mother, I know through these thy mysteries
In orchards spare of trees,
Thy body thou gavest in the fields of Greece.
Oft ploughed wert thou as this unkindly field
That now no sun-split apricot can yield,
Anemones, or wheat.

Hearken, my mother! In this early morn
I kneel to thee among narcissus flower,
For thy child Persephone at edge of dawn
Stole these to star the dark of Hades' bower,
To star the shadowy beauty of a kiss
Within the dear and dreadful arms of Dis.

For these things were we born.

The rocky rivers have for long been dry,
The stony streams are waterless this year,

The cottage marigold
Savours the sites of the old Grecian graves,
And here the wildling plum
Breaks into bloom above sweet alyssum;
And squat and frail blue iris here
Grows by the sea among the temple stones;
And now persimmon leans above the waves.

Cease weeping: now for thee the almond springs.
Stay sighing then,
Demeter, goddess still.
For in this strange, this iris-region wild
I dream that dreadful things
For ever hold thy child.

How shall I know
If these thy worshippers remember thee?
As I, these lighted days,
Who may not push the plough about the tree
Nor break the favoured bough
To deck an altar by a sighing sea,
Where comes bright foam to little coloured bays.

VIRGINIA MOORE
(1903-   )

Virginia Moore is one of the first women to write
systematically about women writers. In 1934, six years
after the publication of her own book of poems from
which this selection is made, she published *Distinguished Women Writers*, a study in which she ex-
amines such seemingly disparate women as Saint
Theresa, Sappho, Dorothy Wordsworth and George

Sand. Moore wrote a very early biography of Emily Brontë and, later in her life, became a Yeats scholar.

AVOWAL

Once and for all, I go my chosen way,
Once and for all, neglect to interfere.
Upon the very forehead of the day
I set my seal, and dare to persevere
In making pit and pinnacle my own,
In staying—at what cost!—natively free;
In meeting, unmolested and alone,
What is, and was, and presently will be.

Through this ungovernable air between the dark
Of comets' paths, I cut a glittering arc,
Dying as I was born, an original spark,
Orbitless, golden, answering to none,
Conditioned in myself, ended, begun
And ended, with the shrivelling of the sun.

"IN DEJECTION NEAR NAPLES"

I must be calm. What if he did? What if he does?
Nothing can make me less than the woman I was.
Now is the time, if ever, to look at the birds,
Think quiet thoughts, say only peaceful words,
Hold fast to something: insubstantial air
Is better than a fistful of despair.
What does it matter? The poplar-tree's unbent,
The waves of the sea are troubled but never spent,
And cruelty in elemental form
Sustains the rock that strengthens with the storm.
I must be calm and watch this Roman bay
Where generations flourished to decay,
Where men were strong and women for their sake
Asked nothing better than a slow heartache.
People and promises: they come, they go,

And I must not remember what I know,
But learn some wisdom from the stone Fratelli
And calm Vesuvius—with fire in her belly.

NOT AN APOLOGY

This I am: fretful as wind, perverse,
Not worth your loving, worthy of my lot
Of weeping for perfection I have not;
Too much a child, a woman with a curse
Which foe or friend would suffer to rehearse;
Too full of wishes, caring not a jot
Whether convention's kept or groceries got:
A bit of cloud that changing winds coerce.
No, love, for truth's unshaken by a mood,
The soul is greater than its garments are,
Faults are the devil's promptings and his brood,
And what I am eludes a net of lies.
You knew it that first night when, under a star,
Our lips were sealed. You saw it in my eyes.

ELIZABETH DARYUSH (1891?–?)

By the time a small edition of Elizabeth Daryush's work was brought out in America, in 1948, she had published nine significant volumes of poetry in England. Most of her work was done in the thirties, when a new book of poems came out every other year. The poet is the daughter of Robert Bridges and shares with her father an intellectual as well as practicing interest in linguistics and metrics.

SONG: AH, THIS IS NOT ENOUGH, I CRY—

Ah, this is not enough, I cry—
A captive on thought's tower to lie,
    To rest while others roam:
I too on action's stormy sea
Am fain to fight and further me,
    To make that heaven my home.

'Tis not enough that I should dwell
In cold imagination's cell,
    Nor range love's sunny land:
Of paradise's every tree
I too would taste, to ecstasy
    Would thrust at will my hand.

Nor can it calm me to behold
Bonds turned to beauty, needs out-told
    As art immortal: I,
I too from prisoning, starving fate
Would free, full, perfect truth create—
    'Tis not enough, I cry.

YOU MUST BREAK THROUGH OLD THOUGHT

You must break through old thought
    As a seed through its rind,
You must be bound by naught
    Beyond your own young mind;

You must pierce old language
    As a fresh shoot pierces
Fallen leaves of an age
    That was, to one that is;

You must know your own need,
    You must nakedly dare,
To form a perfect deed,
    To fruit a spirit fair.

CHILDREN OF WEALTH
IN YOUR WARM NURSERY

Children of wealth in your warm nursery,
Set in the cushioned window-seat to watch
The volleying snow, guarded invisibly
By the clear double pane through which no touch
Untimely penetrates, you cannot tell
What winter means; its cruel truths to you
Are only sound and sight; your citadel
Is safe from feeling, and from knowledge too.

Go down, go out to elemental wrong,
Waste your too round limbs, tan your skin too white;
The glass of comfort, ignorance, seems strong
To-day, and yet perhaps this very night

You'll wake to horror's wrecking fire—your home
Is wired within for this, in every room.

THIS IS THE SWORD

This is the sword
That you shall wield for me (says the world-lord)

Not that soiled arm
The scimitar of vengeance, bent for harm,

Not what relies
On a cross-hilt held up to exorcize,

No, the soul-pain
That you shall wield has clean sharp edges twain. . . .

Wound, grieve all men,
Scourge the unworthy in earth's temple, then

Say (grieving too)
'Forgive them, for they know not what they do'.

RUTH PITTER
(1897–   )

Her parents "loved poetry and were determined to impart it to their children," according to Ruth Pitter. She has been writing poetry since "about five," but there was nothing she thought worth keeping until she was thirty years old. Others thought her work "worth keeping" too, and she was first published in *The New Age* and other experimental English reviews. Pitter has "earned a living somehow," which has included a job at the War Office and making several kinds of handicrafts (hand-painted trays, woodworking), which she has sold. She is "not a professional writer, just a poet." Her work has had no popular success, but since the first volume appeared in 1920, has been constantly acclaimed by other poets. The following selections are largely from what Pitter published in the thirties. An "uncongenial mental climate" at the time has been blamed for their failure to find a wider audience.

THE OLD WOMAN

She reigns in the tarred cottage in the corn,
Clothed on with power, where her docile mate
Haunts rather than inhabits. To her state
Come suppliant both the dead and the unborn,
And village lovers of their loves forlorn;
And there sit down the aimless desolate.
These she delivers, these lays clean and straight,
These does she counsel, smiling without scorn:
And for these wretched, from her look severe
And winter-bright shines forth Philosophy,
A mind still satisfied with what must be,

Nobility of faith, and quiet breath.
They live, they sleep, take comfort, knowing her
Handmaid to love, priestess of life and death.

TO J. S. COLLIS

Live unlamenting though obscure remaining:
be as the bird that in the desolate places
feeds her two young, and man-unheard is heard still
    to her God crying.

Die unaccursed though the universal
curse be abroad: for of her God remembered
though the world burn, the spirit as a bird shall
    flee to her mountain.

THE SPARROW'S SKULL

Memento Mori. Written at the Fall of France.

The kingdoms fall in sequence, like the waves on the
    shore.
All save divine and desperate hopes go down, they are
    no more.
Solitary is our place, the castle in the sea,
And I muse on those I have loved, and on those who
    have loved me.

I gather up my loves, and keep them all warm,
While above our heads blows the bitter storm:
The blessed natural loves, of life-supporting flame,
And those whose name is Wonder, which have no
    other name.

The skull is in my hand, the minute cup of bone,
And I remember her, the tame, the loving one,
Who came in at the window, and seemed to have a mind
More towards sorrowful man than to those of her own
    kind.

She came for a long time, but at length she grew old;
And on her death-day she came, so feeble and so bold;
And all day, as if knowing what the day would bring,
She waited by the window, with her head beneath her
wing.

And I will keep the skull, for in the hollow here
Lodged the minute brain that had outgrown a fear;
Transcended an old terror, and found a new love,
And entered a strange life, a world it was not of.

Even so, dread God! even so, my Lord!
The fire is at my feet, and at my breast the sword:
And I must gather up my soul, and clap my wings, and
flee
Into the heart of terror, to find myself in thee.

THE IRISH PATRIARCH

He bathes his soul in women's wrath;
His whiskers twinkle, and it seems
As if he trod some airy path
In that young land of warriors' dreams;
As if he took a needle-bath
In mountain falls, in tingling streams.

The man whom nagging drives to drink
Should learn from him, whom female rage
Seems but to make a precious link
With some sweet ancient heritage,
With women saying—huh!—what they think!
To the amusement of the sage.

O women, what a boon it is,
With workday worries at their worst,
When hordes of little miseries
Force us to speak our mind or burst,
To be Rich-angered Mistresses,
Not Shrews and Vixens, Cross and Curst!

MATERNAL LOVE TRIUMPHANT

or, SONG OF THE VIRTUOUS FEMALE SPIDER

Time was I had a tender heart,
But time hath proved its foe;
That tenderness did all depart,
And it is better so;
For if it tender did remain
How could I play my part,
That must so many young sustain?
Farewell the tender heart!

A swain had I, a loving swain,
A spider neat and trim,
Who used no little careful pain
To make me dote on him.
The fairest flies he brought to me,
And first I showed disdain;
For lofty we must ever be
To fix a loving swain.

But soon I bowed to nature's ends
And soon did wed may dear,
For all at last to nature bends;
So in a corner near
We fixed our web, and thought that love
For toil would make amends;
For so all creatures hope to prove
Who bow to nature's ends.

Ere long the sorry scrawny flies
For me could not suffice,
So I prepared with streaming eyes
My love to sacrifice.
I ate him, and could not but feel
That I had been most wise;
An hopeful mother needs a meal
Of better meat than flies.

My eggs I laid, and soon my young
Did from the same creep out:
Like little cupids there they hung
Or trundled round about;
And when alarmed, like a soft ball
They all together clung;
Ah mothers! we are paid for all
Who watch our pretty young.

For their sweet sake I do pursue
And slay whate'er I see;
Nothing's too much for me to do
To feed my progeny;
They'll do the same for me some day—
(Did someone say *Says You?*)
So still I leap upon the prey
And everything pursue.

Two bluebottles that loved so dear
Fell in my web together;
They prayed full fast and wept for fear,
But I cared not a feather;
Food I must have, and plenty too,
That would my darlings rear,
So, thanking Heaven, I killed and slew
The pair that loved so dear.

But most do I delight to kill
Those pretty silly things
That do themselves with nectar fill
And wag their pointed wings;
For I above all folly hate
That vain and wasted skill
Which idle flowers would emulate;
And so the fools I kill.

Confess I may some virtue claim,
For all that I desire
Is first an honest matron's name,
Than which there is none higher;

And then my pretty children's good—
A wish that bears no blame;
These in my lonely widowhood
As virtues I may claim.

I look not here for my reward,
But recompense shall come
When from this toilsome life and hard
I seek a heavenly home;
Where in the mansions of the blest,
By earthly ills unmarred,
I'll meet again my Love, my best
And sole desired reward.

LILIAN BOWES LYON
(1855–1949)

With an aristocratic lineage that included a relationship to the royal family, and a vast fortune, Lilian
Bowes Lyon lived partly in the hills of Northumbria,
a life of peaceful country serenity, and partly in London, a life of social concern and activity as head of
Women's Voluntary Services. During the Second
World War, she lived in the East End of London,
working with the people during the nightly horrors of
the blitz. She was wounded, refused to go to a hospital
and, eventually, contracted gangrene and had to have
both legs amputated. The end of her life was lived in
circumstances which C. Day Lewis said "would have
silenced most poets." She suffered violently from
arthritis and diabetes as well as the war wounds. Part
of her fortune was left to provide play centers for
slum children. During her lifetime she published six
small volumes of poems.

LEDA

Remember still the first, impetuous form
His person took, when like a pool your mind
Contained the sun, though furious the storm
That struck your reed-bed of a body blind.

Revive your wonder that his thrashing breath
Was every violet's, yet an outlaw wind's.
So strong the river rolls; not even death
Can stop it rippling over rush-lit hands.

Love, you were more than rover, robber, ranger;
More than a serpent throat, or silvered thighs.
Alas! We lose the fiery fellow-stranger
Light on the water hurts our human eyes.

HELEN MEDITATES BEFORE HER PORTRAIT AS A WOMAN

They still woo me there, and none miss me;
    In their eyes, that were my prison, dead I live.
Foolish are men, that in a fleeting image would embrace
    me.
    My bright Ghost to whom shall I give?

A SHEPHERD'S COAT

I woke from death and dreaming.
His absence be the child I carry,
All days, and all years.
Eternally and this night he will deliver me.
Come peace. For he is coming.

Time tells a marginal story;
Dilates with midsummer that less than leaf
A mute heart, light heart, blown along the pavement;
Then mortally wintry, sears
The implicit glade—oh universe enough

Orchard in bloom bereaved beyond bereavement
Yet peace! For now it is gloaming,
Simple and provident, folding the numbered lambs.

No spatial streams, no tears
Can melt the insensate piety of grief.
Adore instead the untold event still happening;
That miracle be the child I carry,
All days, and all years.
Come other south, come wise and holier thaws,
Enlarge me to inhale so ample a breath;
Come peace for he is coming.
Between the lily in bud and the lily opening
Love is, and love redeems.
Come haven, come your hush, horizoning arms.

I shall not want, I wake renewed by death,
A shepherd's coat drawn over me.

ALISON BOODSON
(1925-   )

This poem was published in a 1944 anthology called
Poetry London X. Alison Boodson, who describes herself as having received "the usual English liberal education," became a physician at University College
hospital in London and her poems appear in rare
anthologies, but there has never been a collection.

I DO NOT WANT TO BE
YOUR WEEPING WOMAN

I do no want to be your weeping woman
holding you to me with a chain of grief.

I could more easily bear the flame of your anger
than the frost of your kisses empty of desire:

I do not want to be your gentle lover
dragging you to me on a rope of pity.

Sooner that you never touched me than that you ever
should touch me from a distance made of mercy:

I do not want to be your silent mother
always forgiving and smiling and never loving.

If you forget me, forget me utterly. Never
come to my arms without interest. I shall know it:

I do not want to be your weeping woman
pinning you to me with a sword of tears.

I do not want to be your weeping woman.

KATHLEEN RAINE
(1908-   )

Kathleen Raine grew up in Northumberland and always described her poetic roots as being in that "wild"
region. She was very well educated. Her father was a
schoolmaster and Kathleen Raine went to Cambridge,
where she took an M.A. in Natural Sciences. She was
the youngest member and only woman associated
with the group called The Cambridge Poets: William
Empson, Charles Madge, John Cornford, Julian Bell.
Her first poems were published by Empson in his
magazine, *Experiment,* but she did not feel her work
was ready to be published as a book until 1943, when
Stone and Flower appeared. Her conversion to Ca-
tholicism came the following year. Raine describes

herself as being "in the tradition of Spenser, Vaughan
and Traherne, Coleridge, Shelley and Yeats, a Platon-
ist." In addition to poetry, she has written several
studies of Blake, edited the letters of Coleridge and
translated Balzac.

INVOCATION

There is a poem on the way,
there is a poem all round me,
the poem is in the near future,
the poem is in the upper air
above the foggy atmosphere
it hovers, a spirit
that I would make incarnate.
Let my body sweat
let snakes torment my breast
my eyes be blind, ears deaf, hands distraught
mouth parched, uterus cut out,
belly slashed, back lashed,
tongue slivered into thongs of leather
rain stones inserted in my breasts,
head severed,

if only the lips may speak,
if only the god will come.

MATERNAL GRIEF

I am not human,
I am not human,
Nor am I divine.

To whom,
to whom can I cry,
'I am thine'?

I have picked my grandsire's corpse to the bone,
I have found no ghost in brisket or chine.

I have shed the blood of my female kin,
but they never return to speak again.

I am not human,
I am not human,
How shall I feed my hungry children?

I make the porridge of meal and wine
and pour it out in the troughs for swine.

The ghosts are hungry, the ghosts are divine,
but the pigs eat the meal, and the priests drink the wine.

THE TRANSIT OF THE GODS

Strange that the self's continuum should outlast
The Virgin, Aphrodite, and the Mourning Mother,
All loves and griefs, successive deities
That hold their kingdom in the human breast.

Abandoned by the gods, woman with an ageing body
That half remembers the Annunciation
The passion and the travail and the grief
That wore the mask of my humanity,

I marvel at the soul's indifference.
For in her theatre the play is done,
The tears are shed; the actors, the immortals
In their ceaseless manifestation, elsewhere gone,

And I who have been Virgin and Aphrodite,
The mourning Isis and the queen of corn
Wait for the last mummer, dread Persephone
To dance my dust at last into the tomb.

STORM

God in me is the fury on the bare heath
God in me shakes the interior kingdom of my heaven.
God in me is the fire wherein I burn.

God in me swirling cloud and driving rain
God in me cries a lonely nameless bird
God in me beats my head upon a stone.

God in me the four elements of storm
Raging in the shelterless landscape of the mind
Outside the barred doors of my Goneril heart.

THE PYTHONESS

(*For John Hayward*)

I am that serpent-haunted cave
Whose navel breeds the fates of men.
All wisdom issues from a hole in the earth:
The gods form in my darkness, and dissolve again.

From my blind womb all kingdoms come,
And from my grave seven sleepers prophesy.
No babe unborn but wakens to my dream,
No lover but at last entombed in me shall lie.

I am that feared and longed-for burning place
Where man and phoenix are consumed away,
And from my low polluted bed arise
New sons, new suns, new skies.

THE CLUE

Only the virgin knows the life story,
The myth implicit in the silk-spun bud
Whose leaves are the unopened pages of the heart.

The gossamer of her dream floats out across the night;
Its fragile thread upholds the somnambulist—
(Let none awaken my beloved, or she is lost)

When the angel came, she knew his face
And to the stranger asking a strange thing
Gave the answer predestined before time.

Young spiders weave at first their perfect webs,
Later, less certain, they weave worse.
Old age spins tattered cobwebs, rags and shreds.

Mater Dolorosa, at the end of a spent myth,
Remembering the past, but not the future,
Has lost her clue, like an old spider,

For time undoes us, darkness defaces
The figures of Penelope's night loom.
Revolving stars wind up the tenuous threads of
    day-dream
And the old spinner ravels skeins of death.

ANNE RIDLER
(1912–   )

Anne Ridler was born in Warwickshire and educated
at London University, where she took a diploma in
journalism. She worked as a secretary to T. S. Eliot,
who, it is said, influenced her work. In addition to her
books of poetry, Anne Ridler has published five plays
and a scholarly edition of the poems of Thomas
Traherne.

A DREAM OBSERVED

Out from his bed the breaking seas
    By waking eyes unseen
Now fall, aquatic creatures whirl
    And he whirls through the ambient green.

The sea lion and the scolpendra
    Lolling in sleep he sees
Strange in their ways, and the swift changes
    Their landscape makes, from shells to trees.

Down English lanes a camel walks,
    Or untrammelled flies.
But I, wakeful and watching, see
    How chilly out of the clothes he lies.

Easy an act to cover him warm:
    Such a lover's small success
Like the heaped mind so humble in sleep
    But points our actual powerlessness.

Monsters in dreams he sees, yet lies
    At peace in his curling bed;
Blessings that outdo all distress
    Implicit in his sleeping head.

JUANITA PEIRSE

This poem appeared in a small English anthology in
the early fifties. Little is known about the author or
her work.

LAMENT FOR A DICTATOR

He dreamed that he bestrode the sun.
His opulent loins gave forth new worlds
To brighten chaos. He saw them spun
From his own life-stuff:
From thighs that coaxed his sky-high steed
To dark obedience at his need.

Thrusting to that flaming core,
His self was doomed, his golden manhood quenched
With trivial hiss. Too faint the sound that tore
His power away:
Too shrill the voice that urged him then,
'Beget a paradise for men!'

Like toy balloons the bright worlds dropped;
—His hybrid by-blows of the sun!—
The pretty trifles danced a jig, till popped
By Jovian hailstones.
His blackened burnt-out body fell
In No-man's-land 'twixt heaven and hell.

MARJORIE BATTCOCK

Marjorie Battcock says that poetry and painting are
her recreations and that her major concerns are "the
architectural future of London, regarding developers
as a modern species of Brontossaurus." She is involved
in social concerns such as the natives in South Africa
and overpopulation. Most of her poems, written in
the fifties, are unpublished.

THE REFUGEE

Mud dark above the stream the factory's finger
Points through the rain towards a sodden sky,
Setting and cold crush her desire to linger,
Barred shops and shuttered windows mute the street,
The scene's decay is like an ugly cry.

She turns towards her home, a furnished room,
Its paint beer-brown, its three-piece, saxe-blue plush,
Where a bald light diminishes the gloom,
But leaves her chilled, and turns her thoughts towards,
The foreign city that was once her home, lush

In the summer with grape-green linden trees;
Evenings of music, cafés, interchange
Of differing views; all this she sees,

Vivid in retrospect, each richly-textured day
Ended with war; instead the pinchbeck range

Of work's monotony, that dims her pride
In memories. But for this isolation
She blames herself—friends have been tortured, died,
She, rootless, without future, should be glad,
And being so, deny her desolation.

THE POETS OF
AMERICA

ANNE BRADSTREET (1612?–1672)

Anne Dudley spent the first sixteen years of her life on the estate of the Earl of Lincoln in Lincolnshire, England, where her father served as steward of the Earl's estates, a prestigious position. Those years were spent in an atmosphere of noncomformist thinking in which she was given a good education by tutors and access to the Earl's library. Two years after she married Simon Bradstreet, she sailed on the *Arabella* for the New World. Her father and her husband became prominent leaders of the Massachusetts Bay Company; the Bradstreets eventually settled at North Andover. Anne had eight children. She was frequently sick, which was not uncommon considering the difficult life-circumstances of the time. Her illness has been diagnosed by contemporary scholars as tuberculosis, which grew progressively worse as she grew older. In 1650, a book of poems appeared in London under the title *The Tenth Muse Lately Sprung Up in America. Or Severall Poems, Compiled With Great Variety of Wit and Learning, Full of Delight . . . By a Gentlewoman of Those Parts*. These were her earliest poems, taken to London by her brother-in-law, John Woodbridge, and published without, it is said, her knowledge or consent. Around 1666, she began to revise the poems that had been printed and to work on most of the poems that are directly personal, autobiographical, reflections of her life in New England. She did not live to see the authorized edition, which was published in 1678. Although her roots were English, she is America's first poet.

THE PROLOGUE

To sing of wars, of captains, and of kings,
Of cities founded, commonwealths begun,
For my mean pen are too superior things:
Or how they all, or each their dares have run
Let poets and historians set these forth,
My obscure lines shall not so dim their worth.

But when my wond'ring eyes and envious heart
Great Bartas' sugared lines do but read o'er,
Fool I do grudge the Muses did not part
'Twixt him and me that overfluent store;
A Bartas can do what a Bartas will
But simple I according to my skill.

From schoolboy's tongue no rhet'ric we expect,
Nor yet a sweet consort from broken strings,
Nor perfect beauty where's a main defect:
My foolish, broken, blemished Muse so sings,
And this to mend, alas, no art is able,
'Cause nature made it so irreparable.

Nor can I, like that fluent sweet tongued Greek
Who lisped at first, in future times speak plain.
By art he glady found what he did seek,
A full requital of his striving pain.
Art can do much, but this maxim's most sure:
A weak or wounded brain admits no cure.

I am obnoxious to each carping tongue
Who says my hand a needle better fits,
A poet's pen all scorn I should thus wrong,
For such despite they cast on female wits:
If what I do prove well, it won't advance,
They'll say it's stol'n, or else it was by chance.

But sure the antique Greeks were far more mild
Else of our sex, why feigned they those nine
And poesy made Calliope's own child;

So 'mongst the rest they placed the arts divine.
But this weak knot they will full soon untie,
The Greeks did nought, but play the fools and lie.

Let Greeks be Greeks, and women what they are
Men have precedency and still excel,
It is but vain unjustly to wage war;
Men can do best, and women know it well.
Preeminence in all and each is yours;
Yet grant some small acknowledgement of ours.

And oh ye high flown quills that soar the skies,
And ever with your prey still catch your praise,
If e'er you deign these lowly lines your eyes,
Give thyme or parsley wreath, I ask no bays;
This mean and unrefined ore of mine
Will make your glist'ring gold but more to shine.

THE FLESH AND THE SPIRIT

In secret place where once I stood
Close by the banks of Lacrim flood,
I heard two sisters reason on
Things that are past and things to come;
One flesh was called, who had her eye
On worldly wealth and vanity;
The other Spirit, who did rear
Her thoughts unto a higher sphere:
Sister, quoth Flesh, what liv'st thou on,
Nothing but meditation?
Doth contemplation feed thee so
Regardlessly to let earth go?
Can speculation satisfy
Notion without reality?
Dost dream of things beyond the moon,
And dost thou hope to dwell there soon?
Hast treasures there laid up in store
That all in th' world thou count'st but poor?
Art fancy sick, or turned a sot

To catch at shadows which are not?
Come, come, I'll show unto thy sense,
Industry hath its recompense.
What canst desire, but thou may'st see
True substance in variety?
Dost honour like? Acquire the same,
As some to their immortal fame,
And trophies to thy name erect
Which wearing time shall ne'er deject.
For riches doth thou long full sore?
Behold enough of precious store.
Earth hath more silver, pearls, and gold,
Than eyes can see or hands can hold.
Affect's thou pleasure? Take thy fill,
Earth hath enough of what you will.
Then let not go, what thou may'st find
For things unknown, only in mind.
Spir. Be still thou unregenerate part,
Disturb no more my settled heart,
For I have vowed (and so will do)
Thee as a foe still to pursue.
And combat with thee will and must,
Until I see thee laid in th' dust.
Sisters we are, yea, twins we be,
Yet deadly feud 'twixt thee and me;
For from one father are we not,
Thou by old Adam wast begot,
But my arise is from above,
Whence my dead Father I do love.
Thou speak'st me fair, but hat'st me sore,
Thy flatt'ring shows I'll trust no more.
How oft thy slave, hast thou me made,
When I believed what thou hast said,
And never had more cause of woe
Than when I did what thou bad'st do.
I'll stop mine ears at these thy charms,
And count them for my deadly harms.
Thy sinful pleasures I do hate,

Thy riches are to me no bait,
Thine honours do, nor will I love;
For my ambition lies above.
My greatest honour it shall be
When I am victor over thee,
And triumph shall with laurel head,
When thou my captive shalt be led,
How I do live, thou need'st not scoff,
For I have meat thou know'st not of;
The hidden manna I do eat,
The word of life it is my meat.
My thoughts do yield me more content
Than can thy hours in pleasure spent.
Nor are they shadows which I catch,
Nor fancies vain at which I snatch,
But reach at things that are so high,
Beyond thy dull capacity;
Eternal substance I do see,
With which enriched I would be.
Mine eye doth pierce the heavens and see
What is invisible to thee.
My garments are not silk nor gold,
Nor such like trash which earth doth hold,
But royal robes I shall have on,
More glorious than the glist'ring sun;
My crown not diamonds, pearls, and gold,
But such as angels' heads enfold.
The city where I hope to dwell,
There's none on earth can parallel;
The stately walls both high and strong,
Are made of precious jasper stone;
The gates of pearl, both rich and clear,
And angels are for porters there;
The streets thereof transparent gold,
Such as no eye did e'er behold;
A crystal river there doth run,
Which doth proceed from the Lamb's throne.
Of life, there are the waters sure,

Which shall remain forever pure,
Nor sun, nor moon, they have no need,
For glory doth from God proceed.
No candle there, nor yet torchlight,
For there shall be no darksome night.
From sickness and infirmity
For evermore they shall be free;
Nor withering age shall e'er come there,
But beauty shall be bright and clear;
This city pure is not for thee,
For things unclean there shall not be.
If I of heaven may have my fill,
Take thou the world and all that will.

BEFORE THE BIRTH OF ONE OF HER CHILDREN

All things within this fading world hath end,
Adversity doth still our joys attend;
No ties so strong, no friends so dear and sweet,
But with death's parting blow is sure to meet.
The sentence past is most irrevocable,
A common thing, yet oh, inevitable.
How soon, my Dear, death may my steps attend,
How soon't may be thy lot to lose thy friend,
We both are ignorant, yet love bids me
These farewell lines to recommend to thee,
That when that knot's untied that made us one,
I may seem thine, who in effect am none.
And if I see not half my days that's due,
What nature would, God grant to yours and you;
The many faults that well you know I have
Let be interred in my oblivious grave;
If any worth or virtue were in me,
Let that live freshly in thy memory
And when thou feel'st no grief, as I no harms,
Yet love thy dead, who long lay in thine arms.
And when thy loss shall be repaid with gains

Look to my little babes, my dear remains.
And if thou love thyself, or loved'st me,
These O protect from step-dame's injury.
And if chance to thine eyes shall bring this verse,
With some sad sighs honour my absent hearse;
And kiss this paper for thy love's dear sake,
Who with salt tears this last farewell did take.

SOME VERSES UPON THE BURNING OF OUR HOUSE JULY 10TH, 1666

In silent night when rest I took
For sorrow near I did not look
I wakened was with thund'ring noise
And piteous shrieks of dreadful voice.
That fearful sound of "Fire!" and "Fire!"
Let no man know is my desire.
I, starting up, the light did spy,
And to my God my heart did cry
To strengthen me in my distress
And not to leave me succorless.
Then, coming out, beheld a space
The flame consume my dwelling place.
And when I could no longer look,
I blest His name that gave and took,
That laid my goods now in the dust.
Yea, so it was, and so 'twas just.
It was His own, it was not mine,
Far be it that I should repine;
He might of all justly bereft
But yet sufficient for us left.
When by the ruins oft I past
My sorrowing eyes aside did cast,
And here and there the places spy
Where oft I sat and long did lie:
Here stood that trunk, and there that chest,
There lay that store I counted best.
My pleasant things in ashes lie,

And them behold no more shall I.
Under thy roof no guest shall sit,
Nor at thy table eat a bit.
No pleasant tale shall e'er be told,
Nor things recounted done of old.
No candle e'er shall shine in thee,
Nor bridegroom's voice e'er heard shall be.
In silence ever shall thou lie,
Adieu, Adieu, all's vanity.
Then straight I 'gin my heart to chide,
And did thy wealth on earth abide?
Didst fix thy hope on mold'ring dust?
The arm of flesh didst make thy trust?
Raise up thy thoughts above the sky
That dunghill mists away may fly.
Thou hast an house on high erect,
Framed by that mighty Architect,
With glory richly furnished,
Stands permanent though this be fled.
It's purchased and paid for too
By Him who hath enough to do.
A price so vast as is unknown
Yet by His gift is made thine own;
There's wealth enough, I need no more,
Farewell, my pelf, farewell my store.
The world no longer let me love,
My hope and treasure lies above.

IN HONOUR OF THAT HIGH AND MIGHTY PRINCESS QUEEN ELIZABETH OF HAPPY MEMORY

No Phoenix pen, nor Spenser's poetry,
No Speed's nor Camden's learned history,
Eliza's works wars, praise, can e'er compact;
The world's the theatre where she did act.
No memories nor volumes can contain

The 'leven Olympiads of her happy reign.
Who was so good, so just, so learn'd, so wise,
From all the kings on earth she won the prize.
Nor say I more than duly is her due,
Millions will testify that this is true.
She hath wiped off th' apersion of her sex,
That women wisdom lack to play the rex.
Spain's monarch, says not so, nor yet his host;
She taught them better manners, to their cost.
The Salic law, in force now had not been,
If France had ever hoped for such a queen.
But can you, doctors, now this point dispute,
She's argument enough to make you mute.
Since first the Sun did run his ne'er run race,
And earth had, once a year, a new old face,
Since time was time, and man unmanly man,
Come show me such a Phoenix if you can.
Was ever people better ruled than hers?
Was ever land more happy freed from stirs?
Did ever wealth in England more abound?
Her victories in foreign coasts resound;
Ships more invincible than Spain's, her foe,
She wracked, she sacked, she sunk his Armado;
Her stately troops advanced to Lisbon's wall,
Don Anthony in's right there to install.
She frankly helped Frank's brave distressed king;
The states united now her fame do sing.
She their protectrix was; they well do know
Unto our dread virago, what they owe.
Her nobles sacrificed their noble blood,
Nor men nor coin she spared to do them good.
The rude untamed Irish, she did quell,
Before her picture the proud Tyrone fell.
Had ever prince such counsellors as she?
Herself Minerva caused them so to be.
Such captains and such soldiers never seen,
As were the subjects of our Pallas queen.
Her seamen through all straits the world did round;

Terra incognita might know the sound.
Her Drake came laden home with Spanish gold;
Her Essex took Cadiz, their Herculean hold.
But time would fail me, so my tongue would too,
To tell of half she did, or she could do.
Semiramis to her is but obscure,
More infamy than fame she did procure.
She built her glory but on Babel's walls,
World's wonder for a while, but yet it falls.
Fierce Tomris (Cyrus' headsman) Scythians' queen,
Had put her harness off, had she but seen
Our Amazon in th' Camp of Tilbury,
Judging all valour and all majesty
Within that princess to have residence,
And prostrate yielded to her excellence.
Dido, first foundress of proud Carthage walls
(Who living consummates her funerals),
A great Eliza, but compared with ours,
How vanisheth her glory, wealth, and powers.
Profuse, proud Cleopatra, whose wrong name,
Instead of glory, proved her country's shame,
Of her what worth in stories to be seen,
But that she was a rich Egyptian queen.
Zenobya, potent empress of the East,
And of all these without compare the best,
Whom none but great Aurelius could quell;
Yet for our Queen is no fit parallel.
She was a Phoenix queen, so shall she be,
Her ashes not revived, more Phoenix she.
Her personal perfections, who would tell
Must dip his pen in th' Heleconian well,
Which I may not, my pride doth but aspire
To read what others write and so admire.
Now say, have women worth? or have they none?
Or had they some, but with our Queen is't gone?
Nay masculines, you have thus taxed us long,
But she, though dead, will vindicate our wrong.
Let such as say our sex is void of reason,

Know 'tis a slander now but once was treason.
But happy England which had such a queen;
Yea happy, happy, had those days still been.
But happiness lies in a higher sphere,
Then wonder not Eliza moves not here.
Full fraught with honour, riches and with days
She set, she set, like Titan in his rays.
No more shall rise or set so glorious sun
Until the heaven's great revolution;
If then new things their old forms shall retain,
Eliza shall rule Albion once again.

PHYLLIS WHEATLEY (1753?–1784)

The first black poet to be "preserved" in American literary history arrived in Boston harbor on a slave ship in 1761. The girl, approximately seven years old, said to have been born on the western coast of Africa, was promptly sold to the family of John Wheatley, a tailor. Phyllis (sometimes spelled "Phillis"), as she was called, received rather unusual treatment in the Wheatley household: the wife and daughter of John Wheatley taught her to read and write. It is said that within two years, she had learned not only the English language, but Latin. Somehow, she began to write poetry and it became a focus for the anti-slavery forces; a pamphlet of her work was issued in Boston and, in 1773, a book was published in England. That book, *Poems on Various Subjects, Religious and Moral,* contained a pronouncement in which "the most respectable characters in Boston" attested to the authenticity of the work. A "Negro servant" had, indeed, written the poems. Phyllis Wheatley was invited to visit England as the guest of the Countess of Huntingdon, to whom the book was dedicated. The Countess acted as her patron for what were probably political reasons. One year later, Mrs. Susannah Wheatley was reported to be dying in Boston; the then-celebrated poet returned to be with her "mistriss." Four years later, Phyllis Wheatley married and disappeared from public view. Reports of the last years of her life are a grim tale of poverty and illness somewhere in the South. There is no mention of her writing poetry. Little attention was paid to Phyllis Wheatley's works for half a century after her death. The reawakening of interest came with the large-scale stirring of abolitionist activity in the 1830s.

ON BEING BROUGHT FROM AFRICA TO AMERICA

'Twas mercy brought me from my Pagan land,
　　Taught my benighted soul to understand
　　That there's a God, that there's a Saviour too.
Once I redemption neither sought nor knew.
Some view our sable race with scornful eye;
"Their colour is a diabolic dye."
Remember, Christians, Negroes, black as Cain,
May be refined, and join the angelic train.

TO THE RIGHT HONORABLE WILLIAM, EARL OF DARTMOUTH

Hail, happy day, when, smiling like the morn,
Fair Freedom rose New England to adorn:
The northern clime beneath her genial ray,
Dartmouth, congratulates thy blissful sway:
Elate with hope her race no longer mourns,
Each soul expands, each grateful bosom burns,

While in thine hand with pleasure we behold
The silken reins, and Freedom's charms unfold.
Long lost to realms beneath the northern skies
She shines supreme, while hated faction dies:
Soon as appear'd the Goddess long desir'd,
Sick as the view, she languish'd and expir'd;
Thus from the splendors of the morning light
The owl in sadness seeks the caves of night.

  No more America in mournful strain
Of wrongs, and grievance unredress'd complain,
No longer shalt thou dread the iron chain,
Which wanton Tyranny with lawless hand
Had made, and which it meant t' enslave the land.

  Should you, my lord, while you peruse my song,
Wonder from whence my love of Freedom sprung,
Whence flow these wishes for the common good,
By feeling hearts alone best understood,
I, young in life, by seeming cruel fate
Was snatch'd from Afric's fancy'd happy seat:
What pangs excruciating must molest,
What sorrows labour in my parent's breast!
Steel'd was the soul and by no misery mov'd
That from a father seiz'd his babe belov'd.
Such, such my case. And can I then but pray
Others may never feel tyrannic sway?
  For favours past, great Sir, our thanks are due,
And thee we ask thy favours to renew,
Since in thy pow'r, as in thy will before,
To sooth the griefs, which thou did'st once deplore.
May heav'nly grace the sacred sanction give
To all thy works, and thou for ever live
Not only on the wings of fleeting Fame,
Though praise immortal crowns the patriot's name,
But to conduct to heav'n's refulgent fane,
May fiery courses sweep th' ethereal plain,
And bear thee upwards to that blest abode,
Where, like prophet, thou shalt find thy God.

LUCY LARCOM
(1824–1893)

Lucy Larcom was born in Beverly, Massachusetts, one
of ten children of a sea captain father who died soon
after her birth. Her mother took the family to the
town of Lowell, where at the textile mill she became
supervisor of one of the company dormitories for
mill girls. Lucy went to work at various mill jobs. She
worked in the mills for ten years and during that time
contributed poems and prose to *The Lowell Offering*
and other mill publications. Finally drawing considerable literary attention to herself, she left the mill for
a job as a seminary teacher. The four volumes of
poetry she published in her lifetime, as well as the
work she published at Lowell, express no sympathy
for the suffragettes or any other reform movement.

WEAVING

All day she stands before her loom;
  The flying shuttles come and go:
By grassy fields, and trees in bloom,
  She sees the winding river flow:
And fancy's shuttle flieth wide,
And faster than the waters glide.

Is she entangled in her dreams,
  Like that fair weaver of Shalott,
Who left her mystic mirror's gleams,
  To gaze on light Sir Lancelot?
Her heart, a mirror sadly true,
Brings gloomier visions into view.

"I weave, and weave, the livelong day:
  The woof is strong, the warp is good:

I weave, to be my mother's stay;
   I weave, to win my daily food:
But ever as I weave," saith she,
"The world of women haunteth me.

"The river glides along, one thread
   In nature's mesh, so beautiful!
The stars are woven in; the red
   Of sunrise; and the rain-cloud dull.
Each seems a separate wonder wrought;
Each blends with some more wondrous thought.

"So, at the loom of life, we weave
   Our separate shreds, that varying fall,
Some stained, some fair; and, passing, leave
   To God the gathering up of all,
In that full pattern, wherein man
Works blindly out the eternal plan.

"In his vast work, for good or ill,
   The undone and the done he blends:
With whatsoever woof we fill,
   To our weak hands His might He lends,
And gives the threads beneath His eye
The texture of eternity.

"Wind on, by willow and by pine,
   Thou blue, untroubled Merrimack!
Afar, by sunnier streams than thine,
   My sisters toil, with foreheads black;
And water with their blood this root,
Whereof we gather bounteous fruit.

"I think of women sad and poor;
   Women who walk in garments soiled:
Their shame, their sorrow, I endure;
   By their defect my hope is foiled:
The blot they bear is on my name;
Who sins, and I am not to blame?

"And how much of your wrong is mine,
   Dark women slaving at the South?
Of your stolen grapes I quaff the wine;
   The bread you starve for fills my mouth:
The beam unwinds, but every thread
With blood of strangled souls is red.

"If this be so, we win and wear
   A Nessus-robe of poisoned cloth;
Or weave them shrouds they may not wear,—
   Fathers and brothers falling both
On ghastly, death-sown fields, that lie
Beneath the tearless Southern sky.

"Alas! the weft has lost its white.
   It grows a hideous tapestry,
That pictures war's abhorrent sight:
   Unroll not, web of destiny!
Be the dark volume left unread,
The tale untold, the curse unsaid!"

So up and down before her loom
   She paces on, and to and fro,
Till sunset fills the dusty room,
   And makes the water redly glow,
As if the Merrimack's calm flood
Were changed into a stream of blood.

Too soon fulfilled, and all too true
   The words she murmured as she wrought:
But, weary weaver, not to you
   Alone was war's stern message brought:
"Woman!" it knelled from heart to heart,
"Thy sister's keeper know thou art!"

MARIA WHITE LOWELL (1821–1853)

Maria White was a New England aristocrat. She was given an unusually decent education, first by governesses and then in an Ursuline convent. Her brother, William, had a more decent education; he studied at Harvard College. With William and his friends and the sisters of his friends, Maria White belonged to a literary and progressive group that called themselves "The Band." When Margaret Fuller initiated her weekly "Conversations" in Boston, Maria White became a member of that circle along with the wives of Emerson and Hawthorne. In 1844, she married James Russell Lowell and converted him from his conservative politics to a rabid abolitionist. In the nine years of her marriage, she had four children, three of whom died. She was almost constantly ill, but the nature of her illness remains unclear. She wrote a great deal of poetry, published little, and it was not until after her death that James Russell Lowell issued a small edition revealing his wife's strange and uneven poetic gift.

AN OPIUM FANTASY

Soft hangs the opiate in the brain,
And lulling soothes the edge of pain,
Till harshest sound, far off or near,
Sings floating in its mellow sphere.

What wakes me from my heavy dream?
    Or am I still asleep?
Those long and soft vibrations seem
    A slumberous charm to keep.

The graceful play, a moment stopped,
    Distance again unrolls,
Like silver balls, that, softly dropped,
    Ring into golden bowls.

I question of the poppies red,
    The fairy flaunting band,
While I a weed, with drooping head,
    Within their phalanx stand.

"Some airy one, with scarlet cap,
    The name unfold to me
Of this new minstrel, who can lap
    Sleep in his melody?"

Bright grew their scarlet-kerchiefed heads,
    As freshening winds had blown,
And from their gently swaying beds
    They sang in undertone,

"Oh, he is but a little owl,
    The smallest of his kin,
Who sits beneath the midnight's cowl,
    And makes this airy din."

"Deceitful tongues, of fiery tints,
    Far more than this you know,—
That he is your enchanted prince,
    Doomed as an owl to go;

"Nor his fond play for years hath stopped,
    But nightly he unrolls
His silver balls, that, softly dropped,
    Ring into golden bowls."

EMILY DICKINSON
(1830-1886)

Emily Dickinson was born in, spent her entire life in, and died in Amherst, Massachusetts. Her father, Edward Dickinson, was a prominent lawyer and legislator, a tyrannical head of the family. She went to school at the Amherst Academy and spent a year at the Female Seminary in South Hadley, Massachusetts. She acquiesced in her father's decision that she not return there and afterwards spent her time at home, being a dutiful daughter except that she would not profess herself a Christian. Her poetry was written secretly, painstakingly, in the bedroom of the Dickinson house. Her brother Austin and his wife Sue, who lived a few yards away, were often sent copies of the poems. The period of greatest productivity in her work seems to be the decade of the sixties.

In 1862, Emily Dickinson wrote to Thomas Wentworth Higginson, essayist, critic and editor of the *Atlantic* magazine, enclosing some poems and asking his opinion. Higginson, whose taste was quite orthodox, hardly understood her work and encouraged her to make it more "regular." They corresponded for several years and Higginson came twice to visit her in Amherst, for she refused to go to Boston. Sue Dickinson, Emily's sister-in-law, served as a source of emotional support to the poet. Only seven poems were published while Dickinson was still alive, one of them, "Success is counted sweetest," at the urging of Helen Hunt Jackson, a childhood friend. In response to a publisher who begged to bring out an edition of her poems, Emily Dickinson sent a volume of the

Brontë sisters' poetry. After her death, of what was diagnosed as Bright's disease, 1,775 poems were discovered in a dresser drawer in her bedroom. It was not until 1958, however, that the complete texts, exactly as the poet wished them to be seen, particularly with their "unorthodox" punctuation, were made available to readers.

NO RACK CAN TORTURE ME—

No Rack can torture me—
My Soul—at Liberty—
Behind this mortal Bone
There knits a bolder One—

You Cannot prick with saw—
Nor pierce with Cimitar—
Two Bodies—therefore be—
Bind One—The Other fly—

The Eagle of his Nest
No easier divest—
And gain the Sky
Than mayest Thou—

Except Thyself may be
Thine Enemy—
Captivity is Consciousness—
So's Liberty.

HE FUMBLES AT YOUR SOUL

He fumbles at your Soul
As Players at the Keys
Before they drop full Music on—
He stuns you by degrees—
Prepares your brittle Nature
For the Etherial Blow
By fainter Hammers—further heard—

Then nearer—Then so slow
Your Breath has time to straighten—
Your Brain—to bubble Cool—
Deals—One—imperial—Thunderbolt—
That scalps your naked Soul—

When Winds take Forests in their Paws—
The Universe—is still—

I'M CEDED—I'VE STOPPED BEING THEIR'S—

I'm ceded—I've stopped being Their's—
The name They dropped upon my face
With water, in the country church
Is finished using, now,
And They can put it with my Dolls,
My childhood, and the string of spools,
I've finished threading—too—

Baptized, before, without the choice,
But this time, consciously, of Grace—
Unto supremest name—
Called to my Full—The Crescent dropped—
Existence's whole Arc, filled up,
With one small Diadem.

My second Rank—too small the first—
Crowned—Crowing—on my Father's breast—
A half unconscious Queen—
But this time—Adequate—Erect,
With Will to choose, or to reject,
And I choose, just a Crown—

TITLE DIVINE—IS MINE!

Title divine—is mine!
The Wife—without the Sign!
Acute Degree—conferred on me—
Empress of Calvary!

Royal—all but the Crown!
Betrothed—without the swoon
God sends us Women—
When you—hold—Garnet to Garnet—
Gold—to Gold—
Born—Bridalled—Shrouded—
In a Day—
"My Husband"—women say—
Stroking the Melody—
Is *this*—the way?

WITCHCRAFT WAS HUNG, IN HISTORY

Witchcraft was hung, in History,
But History and I
Find all the Witchcraft that we need
Around us, every Day—

I THINK I WAS ENCHANTED

I think I was enchanted
When first a sombre Girl—
I read that Foreign Lady—
The Dark—felt beautiful—

And whether it was noon at night—
Or only Heaven—at Noon—
For very Lunacy of Light
I had not power to tell—

The Bees—became as Butterflies—
The Butterflies—as Swans—
Approached—and spurned the narrow Grass—
And just the meanest Tunes

That Nature murmured to herself
To keep herself in Cheer—
I took for Giants—practising
Titanic Opera—

The Days—to Mighty Metres stept—
The Homeliest—adorned
As if unto a Jubilee
'Twere suddenly confirmed—

I could not have defined the change—
Conversion of the Mind
Like Sanctifying in the Soul—
Is witnessed—not explained—

'Twas a Divine Insanity—
The Danger to be Sane
Should I again experience—
'Tis Antidote to turn—

To Tomes of solid Witchcraft—
Magicians be asleep—
But Magic—hath an Element
Like Deity—to keep—

HER—"LAST POEMS"—

Her—"last Poems"—
Poets—ended—
Silver—perished—with her Tongue—
Not on Record—bubbled other,
Flute—or Woman—
So divine—
Not until it's Summer—Morning
Robin—uttered Half the Tune—
Gushed too free for the Adoring—
From the Anglo-Florentine—
Late—the Praise—
'Tis dull—conferring
On the Head too High to Crown—
Diadem—or Ducal Showing—
Be it's Grave—sufficient sign—
Nought—that We—No Poet's Kinsman—
Suffocate—with easy wo—

What, and if, Ourself a Bridegroom—
Put Her down—in Italy?

I WENT TO THANK HER—

I went to thank Her—
But She Slept—
Her Bed—a funneled Stone—
With Nosegays at the Head and Foot—
That Travellers—had thrown

Who went to thank Her—
But She Slept—
'Twas Short—to cross the Sea—
To look upon Her like—alive—
But turning back—'twas slow—

PUBLICATION—IS THE AUCTION

Publication—is the Auction
Of the Mind of Man—
Poverty—be justifying
For so foul a thing

Possibly—but We—would rather
From Our Garret go
White—Unto the White Creator—
Than invest—Our Snow—

Thought belong to Him who gave it—
Then—to Him Who bear
It's Corporeal illustration—Sell
The Royal Air—

In the Parcel—Be the Merchant
Of the Heavenly Grace—
But reduce no Human Spirit
To Disgrace of Price—

HELEN HUNT JACKSON (1830–1885)

Helen Hunt Jackson began writing when she was thirty-five years old, publishing much of her work unsigned because she felt publicity and fame were indecorous for women. In 1881, however, she created a public sensation by publishing, bound in blood-red covers, *A Century of Dishonor*, a book attacking the federal government for its treatment of Indians. Three years later, she published *Ramona*, a protest novel about the American Indian. Emerson considered her the best woman poet in America at the time. She was a schoolmate and friend of Emily Dickinson, and later a close friend of Harriet Beecher Stowe.

DANGER

With what a childish and short-sighted sense
Fear seeks for safety; reckons up the days
Of danger and escape, the hours and ways
Of death; it breathless flies the pestilence;
It walls itself in towers of defence;
By land, by sea, against the storm it lays
Down barriers; then, comforted, it says:
"This spot, this hour is safe." Oh, vain pretence!
Man born of man knows nothing when he goes;
The winds blow where they list, and will disclose
To no man which brings safety, which brings risk.
The mighty are brought low by many a thing
Too small to name. Beneath the daisy's disk
Lies hid the pebble for the fatal sling.

EMIGRAVIT

With sails full set, the ship her anchor weighs.
Strange names shine out beneath her figure head

What glad farewells with eager eyes are said!
What cheer for him who goes, and him who stays!
Fair skies, rich lands, new homes, and untried days
Some go to seek: the rest but wait instead,
Watching the way wherein their comrades led,
Until the next stanch ship her flag doth raise.
Who knows what myriad colonies there are
Of fairest fields, and rich, undreamed-of gains
Thick planted in the distant shining plains
Which we call sky because they lie so far?
Oh, write of me, not "Died in bitter pains,"
But "Emigrated to another star!"

FRANCES E. W. HARPER (1825–1911)

Frances Harper was born in Maryland of free Negro parents who died before she was three. She was raised by an uncle and educated at his school for free Negroes. In 1854, she began delivering anti-slavery lectures. After the Civil War, she toured the South, lecturing about temperance and the need for education for the freed slaves. Her poems and articles appeared in the *Liberator*, Frederick Douglass' paper, and other anti-slavery publications. Most of her income was donated to fugitive slaves and to the underground railroad.

A DOUBLE STANDARD

Do you blame me that I loved him?
   If when standing all alone
I cried for bread, a careless world
   Pressed to my lips a stone?

Do you blame me that I loved him,
    That my heart beat glad and free,
When he told me in the sweetest tones
    He loved but only me?

Can you blame me that I did not see,
    Beneath his burning kiss,
The serpent's wiles, nor even less hear
    The deadly adder hiss?

Can you blame me that my heart grew cold,
    That the tempted, tempter turned—
When he was feted and caressed
    And I was coldly spurned?

Would you blame him, when you drew from me
    Your dainty robes aside,
If he with gilded baits should claim
    Your fairest as his bride?

Would you blame the world if it should press
    On him a civic crown;
And see me struggling in the depth,
    Then harshly press me down?

Crime has no sex and yet today
    I wear the brand of shame;
Whilst he amid the gay and proud
    Still bears an honored name.

Can you blame me if I've learned to think
    Your hate of vice a sham,
When you so coldly crushed me down,
    And then excused the man?

Yes, blame me for my downward course,
    But oh! remember well,
Within your homes you press the hand
    That led me down to hell!

I'm glad God's ways are not your ways,
    He does not see as man;
Within his love I know there's room
    For those whom others ban.

I think before His great white throne,
    His theme of spotless light,
That whited sepulchres shall wear
    The hue of endless night.

That I who fell, and he who sinned,
    Shall reap as we have sown;
That each the burden of his loss
    Must bear and bear alone.

No golden weights can turn the scale
    Of justice in His sight;
And what is wrong in woman's life
    In man's cannot be right.

THE SLAVE MOTHER

Heard you that shriek? It rose
    So wildly in the air,
It seemed as if a burdened heart
    Was breaking in despair.

Saw you those hands so sadly clasped—
    The bowed and feeble head—
The shuddering of that fragile form—
    That look of grief and dread?

She is a mother, pale with fear,
    Her boy clings to her side,
And in her kirtle vainly tries
    His trembling form to hide.

He is not hers, although she bore
    For him a mother's pains;
He is not hers, although her blood
    Is coursing through his veins!

He is not hers, for cruel hands
   May rudely tear apart
The only wreath of household love
   That binds her breaking heart.

LET THE LIGHT ENTER

"Light! more light! the shadows deepen
   And my life is ebbing low,
Throw the windows widely open:
   Light! more light! before I go.

"Softly let the balmy sunshine
   Play around my dying bed,
E'er the dimly lighted valley
   I with lonely feet must tread.

"Light! more light! for Death is weaving
   Shadows 'round my waning sight,
And I fain would gaze upon him
   Through a stream of earthly light."

Not for greater gifts of genius;
   Not for thoughts more grandly bright,
All the dying poet whispers
   Is a prayer for light, more light.

Heeds he not the gathered laurels,
   Fading slowly from his sight;
All the poet's aspirations
   Center in that prayer for light.

Gracious Saviour, when life's day-dreams
   Melt and vanish from the sight,
May our dim and longing vision
   Then be blessed with light, more light.

JULIA WARD HOWE (1819–1910)

The *Atlantic Monthly* published Julia Ward Howe's "Battle Hymn of the Republic" in 1862, bringing her sudden fame. Over her husband's violent opposition to married women in political life, she became extremely active in the movements for world peace and women's suffrage. She helped found the New England Woman Suffrage Association, founded women's clubs throughout the country, and edited many magazines devoted to the cause. Her own literary work had been considered shocking and immoral to Boston critics when she was young; as she grew older, she continued to write and publish and came to be thought of as an institution in American life.

THE BATTLE HYMN OF THE REPUBLIC

Mine eyes have seen the glory of the coming of the
 Lord;
He is trampling out the vintage where the grapes of
 wrath are stored;
He hath loosed the fateful lightning of His terrible, swift
 sword;
   His truth is marching on.

I have seen Him in the watch-fires of a hundred circling
 camps;
They have builded Him an altar in the evening dews
 and damps;
I can read His righteous sentence by the dim and
 flaring lamps;
   His day is marching on.

I have read a fiery gospel, writ in burnished rows of
 steel:

"As ye deal with my contemners, so with you my grace
  shall deal;
Let the Hero, born of woman, crush the serpent with
  his heel,
        Since God is marching on."

He has sounded forth the trumpet that shall never call
  retreat;
He is sifting out the hearts of men before His
  judgement-seat:
Oh, be swift, my soul, to answer Him! be jubilant, my
  feet!
        Our God is marching on.

In the beauty of the lilies Christ was born across the
  sea,
With a glory in His bosom that transfigures you and
  me:
As He died to make men holy, let us die to make men
  free,
        While God is marching on.

FURTHERMORE

We, that are held of you in narrow chains,
Sought for our beauty, thro' our folly raised
One moment to a barren eminence,
To drop in dreary nothingness, amazed;

We, dwarfed to suit the measure of your pride,
Thwarted in all our pleasures and our powers,
Have yet a sad, majestic recompense,
The dignity of suffering, that is ours.

The proudest of you lives not but he wrung
A woman's unresisting form with pain,
While the long nurture of your helpless years
Brought back the bitter childbirth throes again.

We wait upon your fancies, watch your will,
Study your pleasure, oft with trembling heart,—
Of the success and glory of your lives
Ye think it grace to yield the meanest part.

Ev'n Nature, partial mother, reasons thus:
To these the duty, and to those the right";
Our faithful service earns us sufference,
But we shall love you in your own despite.

To you, the thrilling meed of praise belongs,
To us, the painfuller desert may fall;
We touch the brim, where ye exhaust the bowl,
But where ye pay your due, we yield our all.

Honour all women—weigh with reverend hand
The worth of those unproved, or overtried,
And, when ye praise the perfect work of One,
Say not, ye are shamed in her, but glorified.

EMMA LAZARUS (1849–1887)

The lines "Give me your tired, your poor . . .,"
which are inscribed on a plaque at the bottom of the
Statue of Liberty, were written by a woman who was
a poet, a Marxist, a scholar, a Jew and an active
Zionist. Emma Lazarus was familiar with ancient
Jewish history, having been brought up in a wealthy
and cultured Jewish family in New York, but it was
not until the Russian pogroms began in the 1880s
that she made an intense personal connection with
contemporary Judaism. She wrote poems and prose,
translated ancient Jewish poets and scholars, and did

some of the earliest work in American literature in the form of the prose-poem. She once wrote, "Until we are all free, we are none of us free."

VENUS OF THE LOUVRE

Down the long hall she glistens like a star,
The foam-born mother of Love, transfixed to stone,
Yet none the less immortal, breathing on.
Time's brutal hand hath maimed but could not mar.
When first the enthralled enchantress from afar
Dazzled mine eyes, I saw not her alone,
Serenely poised on her world-worshipped throne,
As when she guided once her dove-drawn car,—
But at her feet a pale, death-stricken Jew,
Her life adorer, sobbed farewell to love.
Here *Heine* wept! Here still he weeps anew,
Nor ever shall his shadow lift or move,
While mourns one ardent heart, one poet-brain,
For vanished Hellas and Hebraic pain.

THE NEW COLOSSUS

Not like the brazen giant of Greek fame,
With conquering limbs astride from land to land;
Here at our sea-washed, sunset gates shall stand
A mighty woman with a torch, whose flame
Is the imprisoned lightning, and her name
Mother of Exiles. From her beacon-hand
Glows world-wide welcome; her mild eyes command
The air-bridged harbor that twin cities frame.
"Keep, ancient lands, your storied pomp!" cries she
With silent lips. "Give me your tired, your poor,
Your huddled masses yearning to breathe free,
The wretched refuse of your teeming shore.
Send these, the homeless, tempest-tost to me,
I lift my lamp beside the golden door!"

ECHOES

Late-born and woman-souled I dare not hope,
The freshness of the elder lays, the might
Of manly, modern passion shall alight
Upon my Muse's lips, nor may I cope
(Who veiled and screened by womanhood must grope)
With the world's strong-armed warriors and recite
The dangers, wounds, and triumphs of the fight;
Twanging the full-stringed lyre through all its scope.
But if thou ever in some lake-floored cave
O'erbrowed by rocks, a wild voice wooed and heard,
Answering at once from heaven and earth and wave,
Lending elf-music to thy harshest word,
Misprize thou not these echoes that belong
To one in love with solitude and song.

ELLA WHEELER WILCOX (1850–1919)

As a child, Ella Wheeler was determined to escape the
poverty of her rural Wisconsin childhood by writing.
She began submitting poetry and prose to magazines
at the age of fourteen. A collection of her love poems
entitled *Poems of Passion* brought her notoriety, for
a Chicago publisher refused to publish it on moral
grounds and, in the ensuing publicity, the poet found
herself famous. She has been called a "phenomenon
of democracy." In the 1890s, she was devoted to
Hindu mysticism and, allegedly on instruction of her
dead husband's spirit, reached through mystical practice, she toured Allied Army camps in France during
the war, reading her poetry to soldiers. She suffered a

nervous breakdown in 1919 and died very soon after of cancer.

SOLITUDE

Laugh, and the world laughs with you;
  Weep, and you weep alone,
For the sad old earth must borrow its mirth,
  But has trouble enough of its own.
Sing, and the hills will answer;
  Sigh, it is lost on the air,
The echoes bound to a joyful sound,
  But shrink from voicing care.

Rejoice, and men will seek you;
  Grieve, and they turn and go.
They want full measure of all your pleasure,
  But they do not need your woe
Be glad, and your friends are many;
  Be sad, and you lose them all,—
There are none to decline your nectar'd wine,
  But alone you must drink life's gall.

Feast, and your halls are crowded;
  Fast, and the world goes by.
Succeed and give, and it helps you live,
  But no man can help you die.
There is room in the halls of pleasure
  For a large and lordly train,
But one by one we must all file on
  Through the narrow aisles of pain.

LIZETTE WOODWORTH REESE
(1856-1935)

Lizette Reese was born in a rural area in Maryland which, in her lifetime, grew to be the city of Baltimore. She recorded that growth in a memoir, *A Victorian Village*, published in 1929. For forty-eight years of her life, she was a teacher in public schools. Her first real notice as a poet came when E. C. Stedman included her work in a pioneering anthology of American poets. She published several volumes of poetry and prose during her lifetime and was quite well known, but fell into half-oblivion after her death.

A FLOWER OF MULLEIN

I am too near, too clear a thing for you,
A flower of mullein in a crack of wall,
The villagers half-see, or not at all,
Part of the weather, like the wind or dew.
You love to pluck the different, and find
Stuff for your joy in cloudy loveliness;
You love to fumble at a door, and guess
At some strange happening that may wait behind.
Yet life is full of tricks, and it is plain,
That men drift back to some worn field or roof,
To grip at comfort in a room, a stair;
To warm themselves at some flower down a lane:
You, too, may long, grown tired of the aloof,
For the sweet surety of the common air.

THE SECOND WIFE

She knows, being woman, that for him she holds
The space kept for the second blossoming,

Unmixed with dreams, held tightly in the folds
Of the accepted and long-proper thing—
She, duly loved; and he, proud of her looks
Shy of her wit. And of that other she knows
She had a slim throat, a nice taste in books,
And grew petuinas in squat garden rows.
Thus knowing all, she feels both safe and strange;
Safe in his life, of which she has a share;
Safe in her undisturbed, cool, equal place,
In the sweet commonness that will not change;
And strange, when, at the door, in the spring air,
She hears him sigh, old Aprils in his face.

I NEVER TALK OF HUNGER

I never talk of hunger. No.
I, once down to the last crust,
Would rather rip each bone from bone,
And cast me to the dust.

Never of battles. Have not I
Held the hot sword in hand?
Broken my body for a cause,
In a lost field, lost land?

There is no word in any tongue,
Can make clear to one or all,
My strange hunger, or that fight
My back against a wall.

CHARLOTTE PERKINS GILMAN (1860–1935)

Women and Economics: A Study of the Economic Relation Between Men and Women as a Factor in

Social Evolution has been called "the most influential book ever written by an American feminist." Its author, Charlotte Perkins Gilman, was a relative of Harriet Beecher Stowe who had left her husband and set out to earn her own living. *In This Our World* was her first published book and the following selections are taken from it. The volume was revised and enlarged several times. It is one of the first in American history to attempt to deal in poetry with what the author and an entire movement were then expressing in lectures and in prose. After a lifetime of productive work in the women's movement and a second marriage, suffering from cancer, she committed suicide.

SHE WALKETH VEILED AND SLEEPING

She walketh veiled and sleeping,
For she knoweth not her power;
She obeyeth but the pleading
Of her heart, and the high leading
Of her soul, unto this hour.
Slow advancing, halting, creeping,
Comes the Woman to the hour!—
She walketh veiled and sleeping,
For she knoweth not her power.

THE ANTI-SUFFRAGISTS

Fashionable women in luxurious homes,
With men to feed them, clothe them, pay their bills,
Bow, doff the hat, and fetch the handkerchief;
Hostess or guest, and always so supplied
With graceful deference and courtesy;
Surrounded by their servants, horses, dogs,—
These tell us they have all the rights they want.

Successful women who have won their way
Alone, with strength of their unaided arm,

Or helped by friends, or softly climbing up
By the sweet aid of "woman's influence";
Successful any way, and caring naught
For any other woman's unsuccess,—
These tell us they have all the rights they want.

Religious women of the feebler sort,—
Not the religion of a righteous world,
A free, enlightened, upward-reaching world,
But the religion that considers life
As something to back out of!—whose ideal
Is to renounce, submit, and sacrifice,
Counting on being patted on the head
And given a high chair when they get to heaven,—
These tell us they have all the rights they want.

Ignorant women—college-bred sometimes,
But ignorant of life's realities
And principles of righteous government,
And how the privileges they enjoy
Were won with blood and tears by those before—
Those they condemn, whose ways they now oppose;
Saying, "Why not let well enough alone?
Our world is very pleasant as it is,"—
These tell us they have all the rights they want.

And selfish women,—pigs in petticoats,—
Rich, poor, wise, unwise, top or bottom round,
But all sublimely innocent of thought,
And guiltless of ambition, save the one
Deep, voiceless aspiration—to be fed!
These have no use for rights or duties more.
Duties to-day are more than they can meet,
And law insures their right to clothes and food,—
These tell us they have all the rights they want.

And, more's the pity, some good women, too;
Good conscientious women, with ideas;
Who think—or think they think—that woman's cause
Is best advanced by letting it alone;

That she somehow is not a human thing,
And not to be helped on by human means,
Just added to humanity—an "L"—
A wing, a branch, an extra, not mankind,—
These tell us they have all the rights they want.

And out of these has come a monstrous thing,
A strange, down-sucking whirlpool of disgrace,
Women uniting against womanhood,
And using that great name to hide their sin!
Vain are their words as that old king's command
Who set his will against the rising tide.
But who shall measure the historic shame
Of these poor traitors—traitors are they all—
To great Democracy and Womanhood!

THE PROPHETS

Time was we stoned the Prophets. Age on age,
When men were strong to save, the world hath slain
   them.
People are wiser now; they waste no rage—
   The Prophets entertain them!

AMY LOWELL
(1874–1925)

Amy Lowell's heritage was an old American family
that included the poets Maria White Lowell and James
Russell Lowell; her grandfather's generation founded
the Lowell textile mills. She spent her time, until well
into her thirties, as a busy Boston debutante. In 1902,
the Italian actress Eleonora Duse played a Boston
season; Amy Lowell said afterwards that the sight of
Duse shocked her into writing poetry. Her first

volume was published ten years later, in the same year as the appearance of Harriet Monroe's *Poetry* magazine. Lowell met Monroe and, through her, the Imagist poets in London. She became a sort of administrator for Imagism, was largely responsible for the work of that school reaching a large audience. Amy Lowell edited three important anthologies of Imagist work from 1915 to 1917. Her life's work included literary essays, translations of Chinese poetry, a biography of Keats and many books of her own poems. Appreciation of women poets and a feminist attitude is present throughout her work. "A Fable for Critics," a parody of James Russell Lowell's poem, is mostly about, and in praise of, women poets.

VENUS TRANSIENS

Tell me,
Was Venus more beautiful
Than you are,
When she topped
The crinkled waves,
Drifting shoreward
On her plaited shell?
Was Botticelli's vision
Fairer than mine;
And were the painted rosebuds
He tossed his lady,
Of better worth
Than the words I blow about you
To cover your too great loveliness
As with a gauze
Of misted silver?
For me,
You stand poised
In the blue and buoyant air,
Cinctured by bright winds,

Treading the sunlight.
And the waves which precede you
Ripple and stir
The sands at my feet.

WITCH-WOMAN

"Witch!
Witch!
Cursed black heart,
Cursed gold heart striped with black;
Thighs and breasts I have loved;
Lips virgin to my thought,
Sweeter to me than red figs;
Lying tongue that I have cherished.
Is my heart wicked?
Are my eyes turned against too bright a sun?
Do I dazzle, and fear what I cannot see?
It is grievous to lose the heart from the body,
Death which tears flesh from flesh is a grievous thing;
But death is cool and kind compared to this,
This horror which bleeds and kindles,
These kisses shot with poison,
These thoughts cutting me like red knives.
Lord,
Thunderer,
Swift rider on the clashing clouds,
Ruler over brass heavens,
Mighty ruler of the souls of men,
Be merciless to me if I mistake this woman,
As I will be merciless if I learn a bitter truth.
I burn green oil to you,
Fresh oil from fair young olives,
I pour it upon the ground;
As it drips I invoke your clemency
To send a sign.
Witches are moon-birds,
Witches are the women of the false, beautiful moon.

To-night the sign,
Maker of men and gods.
To-night when the full-bellied moon swallows the stars.
Grant that I know.
Then will I offer you a beastly thing and a broken;
Or else the seed of both
To be your messengers and slaves forever,
My sons, and my sons' sons, and their sons after;
And my daughters and theirs throughout the ages
For your handmaidens and bedfellows as you command.
How the white sword flickers!
How my body twists in the circle of my anguish!
Behold, I have loved this woman,
Even now I cry for her,
My arms weaken,
My legs shake and crumble.
Strengthen my thews,
Cord my sinews to withstand a testing.
Let me be as iron before this thing,
As flashing brass to see,
As lightning to fall;
As rain melting before sunshine if I have wronged the
    woman.
The red flame takes the oil,
The blood of my trees is sucked into fire
As my blood is sucked into the fire of your wrath and
    mercy,
O just and vengeful God."

Body touches body. How sweet the spread of loosened
    bodies in the coil of sleep, but a gold-black thread is
    between them. An owl calls deep in the wood.
Can you see through the night, woman, that you stare
    so upon it? Man, what spark do your eyes follow in
    the smouldering darkness?
She stirs. Again the owl calling. She rises. Foot after
    foot as a panther treads, through the door—a minute
    more and the fringes of her goat-skin are brushing

the brushes. She pushes past brambles, the briars catch little claws in her goat-skin. And he who watches? As the tent-lap flaps back, he leaps. The bearer of the white sword leaps, and follows her. Blur of moonshine before—behind. He walks by the light of a green-oil oath, and the full moon floats above them both.

Seeded grass is a pool of grey. Ice-white, cloud-white, frosted with the spray of the sharp-edged moon. Croon—croon—the wind in the feathered tops of the grass. They pass—the witch-white woman with the gold-black heart, the flower-white woman—and his eyes startle, and answer the bow curve of her going up the hill.

The night is still, with the wind, and the moon, and an owl calling.

On the sea of a hill where the grass lies tilted to a sheer drop down, with the sea splash under as the waves are thrown upon a tooth of rock. Shock and shatter of a golden track, and the black sucking back. The draw of his breath is hard and cold, the draw of the sea is a rustle of gold.

Behind a curl of granite stone the man lies prone. The woman stands like an obelisk, and her blue-black hair has a serpent whisk as the wind lifts it up and scatters it apart. Witch-heart, are you gold or black? The woman stands like a marble tower, and her loosened hair is a thunder-shower twisted across with lightnings of burnt gold.

Naked and white, the matron moon urges the woman. The undulating sea fingers the rocks and winds stealthily over them. She opens the goat-skin wide— it falls.

The walls of the world are crashing down, she is naked before the naked moon, the Mother Moon, who sits in a courtyard of emerald with six black slaves before her feet. Six—and a white seventh who dances, turn-

ing in the moonlight, flinging her arms about the soft
air, despairingly lifting herself to her full height,
straining tiptoe away from the slope of the hill.

Witch-breasts turn and turn, witch-thighs burn, and the
feet strike always faster upon the grass. Her blue-
black hair in the moon-haze blazes like a fire of salt
and myrrh. Sweet as branches of cedar, her arms;
fairer than heaped grain, her legs; as grape clusters,
her knees and ankles; her back as white grapes with
smooth skins.

She runs through him with the whipping of young fire.
The desire of her is thongs and weeping. She is the
green oil to his red flame. He peers from the curl of
granite stone. He hears the moan of the crawling sea,
and sees—as the goat-skin falls so the flesh falls. . . .

And the triple Heaven-wall falls down, and the Mother
Moon on a ruby throne is near as a bow-shot above
the hill.

Goat-skin, here, flesh-skin there, a skeleton dancing in
the moon-green air, with a white, white skull and no
hair. Lovely as ribs on a smooth sand shore, bright as
quartz-stones speckling a moor, long and narrow as
Winter reeds, the bones of the skeleton. The wind in
the rusty grass hums a funeral-chant set to a jig.
Dance, silver bones, dance a whirligig in a crepitation
of lust. The waves are drums beating with slacked
guts. Inside the skeleton is a gold heart striped with
black, it glitters through the clacking bones, throwing
an inverted halo round the stamping feet.

Scarlet is the ladder dropping from the moon. Liquid is
the ladder—like water moving yet keeping its shape.

The skeleton mounts like a great grey ape, and its bones
rattle; the rattle of the bones is the crack of dead trees
bitten by frost. The wind is desolate, and the sea
moans.

But the ruby chair of Mother Moon shudders, and
quickens with a hard fire. The skeleton has reached

the last rung. It melts and is absorbed in the burning moon. The moon? No moon, but a crimson rose afloat in the sky. A rose? No rose, but a black-tongued lily. A lily? No lily, but a purple orchid with dark, writhing bars.

Trumpets mingle with the sea-drums, scalding trumpets of brass, the wind-hum changes to a wail of many voices, the owl has ceased calling.

"White sword are you thirsty?
I give you the green blood of my heart.
I give you her white flesh cast from her black soul.
Thunderer,
Vengeful and cruel Father,
God of Hate,
The skins of my eyes have dropped,
With fire you have consumed the oil of my heart.
Take my drunken sword,
Some other man may need it.
She was sweeter than red figs.
O cursed God!"

GERTRUDE STEIN (1874–1946)

"Patriarchal poetry might be what they wanted," Gertrude Stein wrote in the long poem from which this selection is exerpted, but patriarchal poetry is not what she gave them. Her operas, which along with her novels and other excursions in prose are far better known than her poetry, are about women. *Four Saints in Three Acts* (1927) has Saint Theresa as the protagonist and *The Mother of Us All* (1946) is about Susan B. Anthony. The reputation for obtuseness that discourages readers from reading Stein extends particularly to "Patriarchal Poetry," which one critic has complained is "not about ideas."

Stein was the daughter of a German émigré clothing-store merchant in Baltimore and spent her childhood shuttling back and forth between life with father and life with mother, life in America and life in Europe. She studied at Harvard Annex, later Radcliffe College, with Santayana and William James. Afterwards, she went to Johns Hopkins Medical School and left in her fourth year, without a degree. In 1909, living in Paris and presiding over her already-famous salon, she met Alice B. Toklas, who had volunteered to read proofs for the publisher of Stein's first novel, *Three Lives*. The two women lived together until Stein's death. *Tender Buttons*, her first book of poems (1914), brought her the title "The Mama of Dada." "Patriarchal Poetry" was written thirteen years later.

PATRIARCHAL POETRY

As long as it took fasten it back to a place where after all he would be carried away, he would be carried away as long as it took fasten it back to a place where he would be carried away as long as it took.

For before let it before to be before spell to be before to be before to have to be to be for before to be tell to be to having held to be to be for before to call to be for to be before to till until to be till before to be for before to be until to be for before to for to be for before will for before to be shall to be to be for to be for to be before still to be will before to be before for to be to be for before to be before such to be for to be much before to be for before will be for to be for before to be well to be well before to be before for before might while to be might before to be might while to be might before while to be might to be while before for might to be for before to for while to be while for before while before to for which as for before had for before had for before to for to before.

· · · · ·

Their origin and their history patriarchal poetry their origin and their history patriarchal poetry their origin and their history.

Patriarchal Poetry.

Their origin and their history.

Patriarchal Poetry their origin and their history their history patriarchal poetry their origin patriarchal poetry their history their origin patriarchal poetry their history patriarchal poetry their origin patriarchal poetry their history their origin.

That is one case.

Able sweet and in a seat.

Patriarchal poetry their origin their history their origin. Patriarchal poetry their history their origin.

Two make it do three make it five four make it more five make it arrive and sundries.

Letters and leaves tables and plainly restive and recover and bide away, away to say regularly.

Never to mention patriarchal poetry altogether.

Two two two occasionally two two as you say two two two not in their explanation two two must you be very well apprised that it had had such an effect that only one out of a great many and there were a great many believe in three relatively and moreover were you aware of the fact that interchangeable and interchangeable was it while they were if not avoided. She knew that is to say she had really informed herself. Patriarchal poetry makes no mistake.

· · · · ·

Elegant replaced by delicate and tender, delicate and tender replaced by one from there instead of five from there, there is not there this is what has happened evidently.

Why while while why while why why identity identity why while while why. Why while while while while identity.

Patriarchal Poetry is the same as Patriotic poetry is the same as patriarchal poetry is the same as Patriotic poetry is the same as patriarchal poetry is the same.

Patriarchal poetry is the same.

. . . . .

Let her be to be to be to be let her be to be to be let her to be let her to be let her be to be when is it that they are shy.

Very well to try.

Let her be that is to be let her be that is to be let her be let her try.

Let her be let her be let her be to be to be shy let her be to be let her be to be let her try.

Let her try.

Let her be let her be let her be let her be to be to be let her be let her try.

To be shy.

Let her be.

Let her try.

Let her be let her let her let her be let her be let her be let her be shy let her be let her be let her try.

Let her try.

Let her be.

Let her be shy.

Let her be.

Let her be let her be let her let her try.

Let her try to be let her try to be let her be shy let her try to be let her try to be let her be let her be let her try.

Let her be shy.

Let her try.

Let her try.

Let her be
Let her let her be shy.
Let her try.
Let her be.
Let her let her be shy.
Let her be let her let her be shy
Let her let her let her let her try.
Let her try.
Let her try.
Let her try.
Let her be.
Let her be let her.
Let her try.
Let her be let her.
Let her be let her let her try.
Let her try.
Let her
Let her try.
Let her be shy.
Let her
Let her
Let her be.
Let her be shy.
Let her be let her try.
Let her try.
Let her try.
Let her try.
Let her let her try
Let her be shy.
Let her try
Let her let her try to be let her try.
Let her try.
Just let her try.
Let her try.
Never to be what he said.
Never to be what he said.
Never to be what he said.
Let her to be what he said.

Let her to be what he said.

Not to let her to be what he said not to let her to be
what he said.

Never to be let her to be never let her to be what he
said. Never let her to be what he said.

Never to let her to be what he said. Never to let her
to be let her to be let her to be let her what he said.

· · · · ·

Patriarchal she said what is it I know what it is it is I
know I know so that I know what it is I know so I know
so I know so I know what it is. Very slowly. I know
what it is it is on the one side a to be her to be his to
be their to be in an and to be I know what it is it is he
who was an known not known was he was at first it
was the grandfather then it was not that in that the
father not of that grandfather and then she to be to be
sure to be sure to be I know to be sure to be I know to
be sure to be not as good as that. To be sure not to be
sure to be sure correctly saying to be sure to be that. It
was that. She was right. It was that.

Patriarchal Poetry.

A Sonnet

To the wife of my bosom
All happiness from everything
And her husband.
May he be good and considerate
Gay and cheerful and restful.
And make her the best wife
In the world
The happiest and the most content
With reason.
To the wife of my bosom
Whose transcendent virtues
Are those to be most admired
Loved and adored and indeed
Her virtues are all inclusive

Her virtues her beauty and her beauties
Her charms her qualities her joyous nature
All of it makes of her husband
A proud and happy man.

Patriarchal poetry makes no mistake makes no
mistake in estimating the value to be placed upon the
best and most arranged of considerations of this in as
apt to be not only to be partially and as cautiously considered as in allowance which is one at a time. At a
chance at a chance encounter it can be very well as appointed as appointed not only considerately but as it as
use.

Patriarchal poetry to be sure to be sure to be sure
candidly candidly and aroused patriarchal to be sure and
candidly and aroused once in a while and as a circumstance within that arranged within that arranged to be
not only not only not only not not secretive but as one
at a time not in not to include cautiously cautiously
cautiously at one in not to be finally prepared. Patriarchal poetry may be mistaken may be undivided may
be usefully to be sure settled and they would be after a
while as establish in relatively understanding a promise
of not in time but at a time wholly reconciled to feel
that as well by an instance of escaped and interrelated
choice. That makes it even.

. . . . .

Reform the past and not the future this is what the
past can teach her reform the past and not the future
which can be left to be here now here now as it is made
to be made to be here now here now.

Reform the future not the past as fast as last as first
as third as had as hand it as it happened to be why they
did. Did two too two were sent one at once and one
afterwards.

Afterwards.

How can patriarchal poetry be often praised often
  praised.
To get away from me.
She came in.
Wishes.
She went in
Fishes.
She sat in the room
Yes she did.
Patriarchal poetry.
She was where they had it be nearly as nicely in
  arrangement.
In arrangement.
To be sure.

                    .   .   .   .   .

  Patriarchal Poetry does not make it never made it
will not have been making it be that way in their behalf.
  Patriarchial Poetry insistance.
  Insist.
  Patriarchal Poetry insist insistance.
  Patriarchal Poetry which is which is it.
  Patriarchal Poetry and left it left it by left it by left it.
Patriarchal Poetry what is the difference Patriarchal
Poetry.
  Patriarchal Poetry.
  Not patriarchal poetry all at a time.
  To find patriarchal poetry about.
  Patriarchal Poetry is named patriarchal poetry.
  If patriarchal poetry is nearly by nearly means it to be
to be so.
  Patriarchal Poetry and for them then.
  Patriarchal Poetry did he leave his son.
  Patriarchal Poetry Gabrielle did her share.
  Patriarchal poetry it is curious.
  Patriarchal poetry please place better.
  Patriarchal poetry in come I mean I mean.

Patriarchal poetry they do their best at once more once more once more once more to do to do would it be left to advise advise realise realise dismay dismay delighted with her pleasure.

Patriarchal poetry left to inundate them.

Patriarchal Poetry in pieces. Pieces which have left it as names which have left it as names to to all said all said as delight.

Patriarchal poetry the difference.

Patriarchal poetry needed with weeded with seeded with payed it with left it without it with me. When this you see give it to me.

Patriarchal poetry makes it be have you it here.

Patriarchal Poetry twice.

Patriarchal Poetry in time.

It should be left.

Patriarchal Poetry with him.

Patriarchal Poetry.

Patriarchal Poetry at a time.

Patriarchal Poetry not patriarchal poetry.

Patriarchal Poetry as wishes.

Patriarchal poetry might be found here.

Patriarchal poetry interested as that.

Patriarchal Poetry left.

Patriarchal Poetry left left.

Patriarchal poetry left left left right left.

Patriarchal poetry in justice.

Patriarchal poetry in sight.

Patriarchal poetry in what is what is what is what.

Patriarchal poetry might to-morrow.

Patriarchal Poetry might be finished to-morrow.

Dinky pinky dinky pinky dinky pinky dinky pinky once and try. Dinky pinky dinky pinky dinky pinky lullaby. Once sleepy one once does not once need a lullaby. Not to try.

Patriarchal Poetry not to try. Patriarchal Poetry and lullaby. Patriarchal Poetry not to try Patriarchal poetry

at once and why patriarchal poetry at once and by by
and by Patriarchal poetry has to be which is best for
them at three which is best and will be be and why why
patriarchal poetry is not to try try twice.

Patriarchal Poetry having patriarchal poetry. Having
patriarchal poetry having patriarchal poetry. Having
patriarchal poetry. Having patriarchal poetry and twice,
patriarchal poetry.

He might have met.

Patriarchal poetry and twice patriarchal poetry.

ANNA HEMPSTEAD BRANCH (1875–1937)

The poet who became interested in mysticism, numer-
ology, the Caballa and orthodox Christianity came
from a solid New London, Connecticut, family. Her
father was a lawyer, her mother a poet. She had a
privileged life, graduated from Smith College in 1897
and devoted enormous time and energy to a Lower
East Side settlement, Christodora House, where she
tried to put into practice her conviction that poetry
was a semi-divine pursuit through which people could
achieve brotherhood and understanding.

THE MONK IN THE KITCHEN

I

Order is a lovely thing;
On disarray it lays its wing,
Teaching simplicity to sing.

It has a meek and lowly grace,
Quiet as a nun's face.
Lo—I will have thee in this place!
Tranquil well of deep delight,
Transparent as the water, bright—
All things that shine through thee appear
As stones through water, sweetly clear.
Thou clarity,
That with angelic charity
Revealest beauty where thou art,
Spread thyself like a clean pool.
Then all the things that in thee are
Shall seem more spiritual and fair,
Reflections from serener air—
Sunken shapes of many a star
In the high heavens set afar.

II

Ye stolid, homely, visible things,
Above you all brood glorious wings
Of your deep entities, set high,
Like slow moons in a hidden sky.
But you, their likenesses, are spent
Upon another element.
Truly ye are but seemings—
The shadowy cast-off gleamings
Of bright solidities. Ye seem
Soft as water, vague as dream;
Image, cast in a shifting stream.

III

What are ye?
I know not.
Brazen pan and iron pot,
Yellow brick and gray flag-stone
That my feet have trod upon—

Ye seem to me
Vessels of bright mystery.
For ye do bear a shape, and so
Though ye were made by man, I know
An inner Spirit also made
And ye his breathings have obeyed.

IV

Shape, the strong and awful Spirit,
Laid his ancient hand on you.
He waste chaos doth inherit;
He can alter and subdue.
Verily, he doth lift up
Matter, like a sacred cup.
Into deep substance he reached, and lo
Where ye were not, ye were; and so
Out of useless nothing, ye
Groaned and laughed and came to be.
And I use you, as I can,
Wonderful uses, made for man,
Iron pot and brazen pan.

V

What are ye?
I know not;
Nor what I really do
When I move and govern you.
There is no small work unto God.
He requires of us greatness;
Of his least creature
A high angelic nature,
Stature superb and bright completeness.
He sets to us no humble duty.
Each act that he would have us do
Is haloed round with strangest beauty.
Terrific deeds and cosmic tasks

Of his plainest child he asks.
When I polish the brazen pan
I hear a creature laugh afar
In the gardens of a star,
And from his burning presence run
Flaming wheels of many a sun.
Whoever makes a thing more bright,
He is an angel of all light.
When I cleanse this earthen floor
My spirit leaps to see
Bright garments trailing over it.
Wonderful lustres cover it,
A cleanness made by me.
Purger of all men's thoughts and ways,
With labor do I sound Thy praise,
My work is done for Thee.
Whoever makes a thing more bright,
He is an angel of all light.
Therefore let me spread abroad
The beautiful cleanness of my God.

VI

One time in the cool of dawn
Angels came and worked with me.
The air was soft with many a wing.
They laughed amid my solitude
And cast bright looks on everything.
Sweetly of me did they ask
That they might do my common task.
And all were beautiful—but one
With garments whiter than the sun
Had such a face
Of deep, remembered grace,
That when I saw I cried—"Thou art
The great Blood-Brother of my heart.
Where have I seen thee?"—And he said,
"When we are dancing 'round God's throne,

How often thou art there.
Beauties from thy hands have flown
Like white doves wheeling in mid air.
Nay—thy soul remembers not?
Work on, and cleanse thy iron pot."

VII

What are we? I know not.

SONNETS FROM A LOCK BOX

XIV

What witchlike spell weaves here its deep design,
And sells its pattern to the ignorant buyer.
Oh lacelike cruelty with stitches fine—
Which stings the flesh with its sharp mesh of fire.
God of the Thief and Patron of the Liar,
I think that it is best not to inquire
Upon whose wheel was spun this mortal thread;
What dyed this curious robe so rich a red;
With shivering hues it is embroiderèd.
With changing colors like unsteady eyes.
I think the filigree is Media's wreath.
Oh, treacherous splendor! In this lustrous prize
Of gold and silver weaving, madness lies.
Who purchases this garment—Sire—buys death.

XXV

Into the void behold my shuddering flight,
Plunging straight forward through unhuman space,
My wild hair backward blown and my white face
Set like a wedge of ice. My chattering teeth
Cut like sharp knives my swiftly freezing breath.
Perched upon straightness I seek a wilder zone.
My Flying Self—on this black steed alone—
Drives out to God or else to utter death.

Beware straight lines which do subdue man's pride!
'Tis on a broomstick that great witches ride.
Wild, dangerous and holy are the runes
Which shift the whirling atoms with their tunes.
Oh like a witch accursed shall she be burned
Who having flown on straightness has returned.

XXXI

I say that words are men and when we spell
In alphabets we deal with living things;
With feet and thighs and breasts, fierce heads, strong
    wings;
Material Powers, great Bridals, Heaven and Hell.
There is a menace in the tales we tell.
From out the throne from which all language springs
Voices proceed and fires and thunderings.
Oh when we speak, Great God, let us speak well.
Beware of shapes, beware of letterings,
For in them lies such magic as alters dream,
Shakes cities down and moves the inward scheme.
Beware the magic of the coin that sings.
These coins are graved with supernatural powers
And magic wills that are more strong than ours.

ADELAIDE CRAPSEY (1878-1914)

Totally unknown as a poet, her work not published
until after her death, Adelaide Crapsey spent her life,
after a childhood in Rochester, New York, and a
college education at Vassar, teaching, studying, and
writing poems. The fruits of her experimentation with
metrics can be seen in the poems and in *A Study in*

English Metrics, published in 1918. She spent the last years of her life teaching poetry at Vassar College and died, of tuberculosis, in a sanatorium at Saranac Lake.

CINQUAINS

Triad

> These be
> Three silent things:
> The falling snow . . . the hour
> Before the dawn . . . the mouth of one
> Just dead.

Trapped

> Well and
> If day on day
> Follows, and weary year
> On year . . . and ever days and years . . .
> Well?

Susanna and the Elders

> "Why do
> You thus devise
> Evil against her?" "For that
> She is beautiful, delicate;
> Therefore."

Niagara

> Seen on a Night in November

> How frail
> Above the bulk
> Of crashing water hangs,
> Autumnal, evanescent, wan,
> The moon.

EXPENSES

Little my lacking fortunes show
    For this to eat and that to wear;
Yet laughing, Soul, and gaily go!
    An obol pays the Stygian fare.

THE WITCH

When I was a girl by Nilus stream
    I watched the desert stars arise;
My lover, he who dreamed the Sphinx,
    Learned all his dreaming from my eyes.

I bore in Greece a burning name,
    And I have been in Italy
Madonna to a painter-lad,
    And mistress to a Medici.

And have you heard (and I have heard)
    Of puzzled men with decorous mien,
Who judged—The wench knows far too much—
    And hanged her on the Salem green?

THE LONELY DEATH

In the cold I will rise, I will bathe
In waters of ice; myself
Will shiver, and shrive myself,
Alone in the dawn, and anoint
Forehead and feet and hands;
I will shutter the windows from light,
I will place in their sockets the four
Tall candles and set them a-flame
In the grey of the dawn; and myself
Will lay myself straight in my bed,
And draw the sheet under my chin.

BLOSSOMING PLUM AND CHERRY

Blossoming plum and cherry
Flowering apple and quince
In spring time I was merry
I've learned weeping since
    Bitter weeping since.

(CINQUAIN) TO AN
UNFAITHFUL LOVER

What words
Are left thee then
Who hast squandered on thy
Forgetfulness eternities
I love?

LEONORA SPEYER
(1872–1956)

Before she was twenty, Leonora Speyer had established a brilliant career as a concert violinist, appearing with the New York Philharmonic and the Boston Symphony Orchestra. She married, lived in Paris and London, had four daughters and was divorced. In 1915, she returned to America and began to write poetry. Amy Lowell, a close friend, was the person responsible, according to the poet, for those first attempts. Leonora Speyer was quite well known in the twenties, a close associate of Harriet Monroe and the *Poetry* magazine circle, and a friend of Robert Bridges. In 1927, her second book of poems, *Fiddler's Farewell*, won the Pulitzer Prize.

THE LADDER

I had a sudden vision in the night,
I did not sleep, I dare not say I dreamed,
Beside my bed a curious ladder gleamed
And lifted upward toward the sky's dim height;
And every rung shone luminous and white,
And every rung a woman's body seemed
Out-stretched, and down the sides her long hair
        streamed:
And you, you climbed that ladder of delight.

You climbed sure-footed, naked rung by rung,
Clasped them and trod them, called them by their name,
And my name too, I heard you speak at last;
You stood upon my breast the while and flung
A hand up to the next—and then, oh shame,
I kissed the foot that bruised me as it passed.

SALOME

I danced for Herod, yes. My mother's eyes,
Watchful and wary, followed as I danced.
I never dropped my veils, but swayed, advanced,
And tripped the steps she taught me, maiden-wise.
I danced for Herod, yes! I never glanced
Toward the deep place where John with woeful cries
Lay chained; nor sought his loving. These are lies.
I sought to please my mother as I danced.

And then I ran to her—she knew my wish,
For I had often whispered it: the Charm,
The carven emblem older women wore
To capture love! (O head upon the dish
She bade me choose!) Along my nurse's arm,
All night I wept till I could weep no more.

WITCH!

Ashes of me,
Whirl in the fires I may not name.
Lick, lovely flame!

Will the fagot not burn?
Throw on the tired broom
Stabled still in my room.

I have ridden wide and well.
Shall I say with whom?
(Stop the town bell!)

Listen now,
Listen now if you dare:
I have lain with hope
Under the dreadful bough,
I have suckled Judas' rope
As it swung on the air—

Go find the silver pieces in the moon.
I hid them there.

LOLA RIDGE
(1873-1941)

One of the first poets to write of America's most un-
poetic metropolis, the "ghetto" of New York, Lola
Ridge was an Irish woman who lived in Australia
before coming to the United States. After her arrival
in 1907, she worked as an illustrator, model, factory
worker, advertising copywriter and producer of pulp
fiction. "The Ghetto," first published in the *New
Republic*, resulted in a lot of critical attention. Since
her death, her work has been largely ignored. The

poet was a committed anarchist, contributor to Emma Goldman's monthly magazine, *Mother Earth*, and editor of the radical literary magazine *Broom*. With Edna Millay and Dorothy Parker, she participated in agitation against the trial and imprisonment of Sacco and Vanzetti.

PALESTINE

Old plant of Asia—
Mutilated vine
Holding earth's leaping sap
In every stem and shoot
That lopped off, sprouts again—
Why should you seek a plateau walled about,
Whose garden is the world?

SPIRES

Spires of Grace Church,
For you the workers of the world
Travailed with the mountains . . .
Aborting their own dreams
Till the dream of you arose—
Beautiful, swaddled in stone—
Scorning their hands.

AMY LOWELL

Your words are frost on speargrass,
Your words are glancing light
On foils at play,
Your words are shapely . . . buoyant as balloons,
They make brave sallies at the stars.
When your words fall and grow cold
Little greedy hands
Will gather them for necklets.

RUSSIAN WOMEN

You swing of necessity into male rhythms
that at once become female rhythms;
you take high place
as hills take sun—
being inevitably there
in the path of the sun.
Yet in you there is no peace,
but infinite collisions,
impact of charged atoms
in ceaseless vibration.
In you unimagined circuits,
in you uncoiled
passion electric—
the stroke swift
and the recoil as swift . . .
in you the unidentified power—
hysteria directed,
the world force.

MINA LOY
(1882–1966)

Mina Loy was born in London into a middle-class
Victorian family, in spite of whom she traveled and
studied painting in England, Germany and France.
Most of her life she moved between Europe and
America. She made her first trip to New York in 1916,
and there she met up with the artistic, bohemian
group that included Alfred Kreymborg, Alfred Steig-
litz and Walter Conrad Arensberg. Afterward, in Paris
in the twenties, she was connected with American
expatriates and European *avant-gardistes*. She pub-

lished in small magazines and ran a shop, supported by Peggy Guggenheim, which sold original painted lampshade creations. *Lunar Baedeker*, from which the following poems are taken, was published in a small edition in 1923. She came back to America to stay in 1936. Her publications, for the rest of her life, were few and only recently has her work become available to a contemporary audience.

PARTURITION

I am the centre
Of a circle of pain
Exceeding its boundaries in every direction
The business of the bland sun
Has no affair with me
In my congested cosmos of agony
From which there is no escape
On infinitely prolonged nerve-vibrations
Or in contraction
To the pin-point nucleus of being
Locate an irritation   without
It is   within
Within
It is without.
The sensitized area
Is identical   with the extensity
Of intension

I am the false quantity
In the harmony of physiological potentiality
To which
Gaining self-control
I should be consonant
In time

Pain is no stronger than the resisting force
Pain calls up in me
The struggle is equal

The open window is full of a voice
A fashionable portrait-painter
Running up-stairs to a woman's apartment
Sings
   "All the girls are tid'ly did'ly
   All the girls are nice
   Whether they wear their hair in curls
   Or—"
At the back of the thoughts to which I permit crystal-
   lization
The conception   Brute
Why?
     The irresponsibility of the male
Leaves woman her superior Inferiority
He is running up-stairs

I am climbing a distorted mountain of agony
Incidentally with the exhaustion of control
I reach the summit
And gradually subside into anticipation of
Repose
Which never comes.
For another mountain is growing up
Which   goaded by the unavoidable
I must traverse
Traversing myself

Something in the delirium of night-hours
Confuses while intensifying sensibility
Blurring spatial contours
So aiding elusion of the circumscribed
That the gurgling of a crucified wild beast
Comes from so far away
And the foam on the stretched muscles of a mouth
Is no part of myself
There is a climax in sensibility
When pain surpassing itself
Becomes exotic
And the ego succeeds in unifying the positive and

negative poles of sensation.
Uniting the opposing and resisting forces
In lascivious revelation

Relaxation
Negation of myself as a unit
      Vacuum interlude
I should have been emptied of life
Giving life
For consciousness in crises   races
Through the subliminal deposits of evolutionary
   processes
Have I not
Somewhere
Scrutinized
A dead white feathered moth
Laying eggs?

A moment
Being realization
Can
Vitalized by cosmic initiation
Furnish an adequate apology
For the objective
Agglomeration of activities
Of a life
LIFE
A leap with nature
Into the essence
Of unpredicted Maternity
Against my thigh
Touch of infinitesimal motion
Scarcely perceptible
Undulation

Warmth   moisture
Stir of incipient life
Precipitating into me
The contents of the universe

Mother I am
Identical
With infinite Maternity
   Indivisible
   Acutely
   I am absorbed
   Into
The was—is—ever—shall—be
Of cosmic reproductivity

Rises from the subconscious
Impression of a cat
With blind kittens
Among her legs
Same undulating life-stir
I am that cat

Rises from the sub-conscious
Impression of small animal carcass
Covered with blue-bottles
—Epicurean—
And through the insects
Waves that same undulation of living
Death
Life
I am knowing
All about
   Unfolding

The next morning
Each woman-of-the-people
Tip-toeing the red pile of the carpet
Doing hushed service
Each woman-of-the-people
Wearing a halo
Of which she is sublimely unaware

LOVE SONGS:

IV

Evolution fall foul of
Sexual equality
Prettily miscalculate
Similitude

Unnatural selection
Breed such sons and daughters
As shall jibber at each other
Uninterpretable cryptonyms
Under the moon

Give them some way of braying brassily
For caressive calling
Or to homophonous hiccoughs
Transpose the laugh
Let them suppose that tears
Are snowdrops or molasses
Or anything
Than human insufficiencies
Begging dorsal vertebrae

Let meeting be the turning
To the antipodean
And Form   a blurr
Anything
Than seduce them
To the one
As simple satisfaction
For the other

V

Shuttle-cock and battle-door
A little pink-love
And feathers are strewn

VI

Let Joy go solace-winged
To flutter whom she may concern

CRAB-ANGEL

An atomic sprite
perched on a polished
monster-stallion
reigns over Ringling's   revolving
trinity of circus attractions

Something the contour
of a captured crab
waving its useless pearly claws

From a squat body
pigmy arms
and bow legs
with their baroque calves
curve in a bi-circular attitude
to a ballerina's ecstasy

An effigy of Christmas Eves
smile-cast among chrysanthemum curls
it seems a sugar angel
while from a rose flecked ruff of gauze
its manly legs
stamp on the vast rump of the horse

An irridescent speck
dripped from a rainbow
onto an ebony cloud

Crab-Angel   I christen you
minnikin of masquerade sex

Helen of Lilliput?
Hercules in a powder puff?

ALICE DUNBAR NELSON (1875–1935)

Alice Moore was born in New Orleans, Louisiana, and was very well educated, first at Straight College in New Orleans and later at several northern universities. She married Paul Laurence Dunbar in 1898. Dunbar was the first black poet to achieve large-scale literary acceptance in America. Together, the Dunbars made a collection of great literary works in the black heritage, to be performed on the stage. Alice Dunbar Nelson contributed this poem, one of the few she wrote. Most of her life, she taught school; her published writing consists mostly of short stories and newspaper columns.

I SIT AND SEW

I sit and sew—a useless task it seems,
My hands grown tired, my head weighed down with
    dreams—
The panoply of war, the material tread of men,
Grim-faced, stern-eyed, gazing beyond the ken
Of lesser souls, whose eyes have not seen Death,
Nor learned to hold their lives but as a breath—
But—I must sit and sew.

I sit and sew—my heart aches with desire—
That pageant terrible, that fiercely pouring fire
On wasted fields, and writhing grotesque things
Once men. My soul in pity flings
Appealing cries, yearning only to go
There in that holocaust of hell, those fields of woe—
But—I must sit and sew.

The little useless seam, the idle patch;
Why dream I here beneath my homely thatch,

When there they lie in sodden mud and rain,
Pitifully calling me, the quick ones and the slain!
You need me, Christ! It is no roseate dream
That beckons me—this pretty futile seam,
It stifles me—God, must I sit and sew?

ANGELINA WELD GRIMKÉ (1880-1958)

Her father was the son of Charleston, South Carolina's, aristocratic Henry Grimké and a black slave woman, Nancy Weston. In a sketch she wrote of her father, Angelina Grimké explained how Henry's sisters, Sarah and Angelina Grimké, "two utterly inexperienced women, carefully sheltered from birth, broke without a qualm with their traditions and their family, came North and joined themselves to the abolitionists." The younger sister, Angelina, acknowledged the familial connection of the poet's father. She was born in Boston, educated in Northern schools and taught English in a high school in Washington, D.C. A play, *Rachel*, was published in 1921, but her poems have never been collected.

TENEBRIS

There is a tree, by day,
That, at night,
Has a shadow,
A hand huge and black,
With fingers long and black.
   All through the dark,
Against the white man's house,
   In the little wind,

The black hand plucks and plucks
    At the bricks.
The bricks are the color of blood and very small.
    Is it a black hand,
    Or is it a shadow?

AT APRIL

Toss your gay heads,

    Brown girl trees;

Toss your gay lovely heads;

Shake your downy russet curls

All about your brown faces;

Stretch your brown slim bodies;

Stretch your brown slim arms;

Stretch your brown slim toes.

Who knows better than we,

With the dark, dark bodies,

What it means

When April comes a-laughing and a-weeping

Once again

At our hearts?

A WINTER TWILIGHT

A silence slipping around like death,
Yet chased by a whisper, a sigh, a breath;
One group of trees, lean, naked and cold,
Inking their crests 'gainst a sky green-gold;
One path that knows where the corn flowers were;

Lonely, apart, unyielding, one fir;
And over it softly leaning down,
One star that I loved ere the fields went brown.

GEORGIA DOUGLAS JOHNSON (1886–1967)

Born in Atlanta, Georgia, Georgia Douglas Johnson went to the University of Georgia and then to Oberlin Conservatory. She wanted to be a composer, but finding that road, as it has been said, "obstructed," she worked all her life, first as a schoolteacher and later in various government agencies in Washington. It was in the capital that she met and showed her work to several black intellectuals who helped her to publish. Novelist Jessie Fauset encouraged her to publish the first book of poems, *The Heart of a Woman,* in 1918 and W. E. B. Du Bois wrote an introduction for the second, *Bronze,* in 1922. She became a regular contributor to *The Crisis.*

THE HEART OF A WOMAN

The heart of a woman goes forth with the dawn,
As a lone bird, soft winging, so restlessly on,
Afar o'er life's turrets and vales does it roam
In the wake of those echoes the heart calls home.

The heart of a woman falls back with the night,
And enters some alien cage in its plight,
And tries to forget it has dreamed of the stars
While it breaks, breaks, breaks on the sheltering bars.

THE SUPPLIANT

Long have I beat with timid hands upon life's leaden
  door,
Praying the patient, futile prayer my fathers prayed
  before,
Yet I remain without the close, unheeded and unheard,
And never to my listening ear is borne the waited word.

Soft o'er the threshold of the years there comes this
  counsel cool:
The strong demand, contend, prevail; the beggar is a
  fool!

A PARADOX

I know you love me better cold
Strange as the pyramids of old
Responselessly.
But I am frail, and spent and weak
With surging torrents that bespeak
A living fire.
So, like a veil, my poor disguise
Is draped to save me from your eyes'
Deep challenges.
Fain would I fling this robe aside
And from you, in your bosom hide
Eternally.
Alas! you love me better cold
Like frozen pyramids of old
Unyieldingly?

CELIBACY

Where is the love that might have been
Flung to the four far ends of Earth?
In my body stamping around,
In my body like a hound
Leashed and restless—
Biding time!

COSMOPOLITE

Not wholly this or that,
But wrought
Of alien bloods am I,
A product of the interplay
Of traveled hearts.
Estranged, yet not estranged, I stand
All comprehending;
From my estate
I view earth's frail dilemma;
Scion of fused strength am I,
All understanding,
Nor this nor that
Contains me.

ANNE SPENCER
(1882-   )

Anne Spencer has lived all her life in Lynchburg,
Virginia, and has never published a book of poems.
She was educated at Virginia Seminary and worked
for many years as the librarian of the Dunbar High
School. Few biographical details are available; her
poetry has been recognized by editors of collections of
black literature, but is virtually unknown outside that
readership.

LETTER TO MY SISTER

It is dangerous for a woman to defy the gods;
To taunt them with the tongue's thin tip,
Or strut in the weakness of mere humanity,
Or draw a line daring them to cross;
The gods who own the searing lightnings,

The drowning waters, the tormenting fears,
The anger of red sins . . .
Oh, but worse still if you mince along timidly—
Dodge this way or that, or kneel, or pray,
Or be kind, or sweat agony drops,
Or lay your quick body over your feeble young,
If you have beauty or plainness, if celibate,
Or vowed—the gods are Juggernaut,
Passing over each of us . . .
      Or this you may do:
Lock your heart, then quietly,
And, lest they peer within
Light no lamp when dark comes down.
Raise no shade for sun,
Breathless must your breath come thru,
If you'd die and dare deny
The gods their godlike fun!

AT THE CARNIVAL

Gay little Girl-of-the-Diving-Tank,
I desire a name for you,
Nice, as a right glove fits;
For you—who amid the malodorous
Mechanics of this unlovely thing,
Are darling of spirit and form.
I know you—a glance, and what you are
Sits-by-the-fire in my heart.
My Limousine-Lady knows you, or
Why does the slant-envy of her eyes mark
Your straight air and radiant inclusive smile?
Guilt pins a fig-leaf; Innocence is its own adorning.
The bull-necked man knows you—this first time
His itching flesh sees from divine and vibrant health,
And thinks not of his avocation.
I came incuriously—
Set on no diversion save that my mind
Might safely nurse its brood of misdeeds

In the presence of a blind crowd.
The color of life was gray.
Everywhere the setting seemed right
For my mood!

Here the sausage and garlic booth
Sent unholy incense skyward;
There a quivering female-thing
Gestured assignations, and lied
To call it dancing;
There, too, were games of chance
With chances for none;
But oh! the Girl-of-the-Tank, at last!
Gleaming Girl, how intimately pure and free
The gaze you send the crowd,
As though you know the dearth of beauty
In its sordid life.
We need you—my Limousine-Lady,
The bull-necked man, and I.
Seeing you here brave and water-clean,
Leaven for the heavy ones of earth,
I am swift to feel that what makes
The plodder glad is good; and
Whatever is good is God.
The wonder is that you are here;
I have seen the queer in queer places,
But never before a heaven-fed
Naiad of the Carnival-Tank!
Little, Diver, Destiny for you,
Like as for me, is shod in silence;
Years may seep into your soul
The bacilli of the usual and the expedient;
I implore Neptune to claim his child to-day!

H.D.
(1886–1961)

Hilda Doolittle grew up in Pennsylvania, went to Bryn Mawr for a while and traveled to London, from which she never really returned. She became part of the "Imagist Movement," as it is still being called, constructing manifestoes with Ezra Pound and Amy Lowell. She married and divorced Richard Aldington, a member of the group. It has been said that she was the only true Imagist. She has been frozen in the Imagist category unfairly, however, for her later work has little of the remote Hellenism of her well-known poems. The volumes of poetry published in the 1940's deal directly and colloquially with the real world of war through which she was immediately living and take on the question of the artist's responsibility in such a time. H.D. wrote her own epitaph:

> Greek flower, Greek ecstasy
> reclaims for ever
> One who died
> following
> intricate songs' last measure

HELEN

> All Greece hates
> the still eyes in the white face,
> the luster as of olives
> where she stands,
> and the white hands.
>
> All Greece reviles
> the wan face when she smiles,

hating it deeper still
when it grows wan and white,
remembering past enchantments
and past ills.

Greece sees unmoved,
God's daughter, born of love,
the beauty of cool feet
and slenderest knees,
could love indeed the maid,
only if she were laid,
white ash amid funereal cypresses.

EURYDICE

I.

So you have swept me back,
I who could have walked with the live souls
above the earth,
I who could have slept among the live flowers
at last;

so for your arrogance
and your ruthlessness
I am swept back
where dead lichens drip
dead cinders upon moss of ash;

so for your arrogance
I am broken at last,
I who had lived unconscious,
who was almost forgot;

if you had let me wait
I had grown from listlessness
into peace,
if you had let me rest with the dead,
I had forgot you
and the past.

THE WALLS DO NOT FALL

I

An incident here and there,
and rails gone (for guns)
from your (and my) old town square:

mist and mist-grey, no colour,
still the Luxor bee, chick and hare
pursue unalterable purpose

in green, rose-red, lapis;
they continue to prophesy
from the stone papyrus:

there, as here, ruin opens
the tomb, the temple; enter,
there as here, there are no doors:

the shrine lies open to the sky,
the rain falls, here, there
sand drifts; eternity endures:

ruin everywhere, yet as the fallen roof
leaves the sealed room
open to the air,

so, through our desolation,
thoughts stir, inspiration stalks us
through gloom:

unaware, Spirit announces the Presence;
shivering overtakes us,
as of old, Samuel:

trembling at a known street-corner,
we know not nor are known;
the Pythian pronounces—we pass on

to another cellar, to another sliced wall
where poor utensils show
like rare objects in a museum;

Pompeii has nothing to teach us,
we know crack of volcanic fissure,
slow flow of terrible lava,

pressure on heart, lungs, the brain
about to burst its brittle case
(what the skull can endure!):

over us, Apocryphal fire,
under us, the earth sway, dip of a floor,
slope of a pavement

where men roll, drunk
with a new bewilderment,
sorcery, bedevilment:

the bone-frame was made for
no such shock knit within terror,
yet the skeleton stood up to it:

the flesh? it was melted away,
the heart burnt out, dead ember,
tendons, muscles shattered, outer husk dismembered,

yet the frame held:
we passed the flame: we wonder
what saved us? what for?

XLIII

Still the walls do not fall,
I do not know why;

there is zrr-hiss,
lightning in a not-known,

unregistered dimension;
we are powerless,

dust and powder fill our lungs,
our bodies blunder

through doors twisted on hinges,
and the lintels slant

cross-wise;
we walk continually

on thin air
that thickens to a blind fog,

then step swiftly aside,
for even the air

is independable,
thick where it should be fine

and tenuous
where wings separate and open,

and the ether
is heavier than the floor,

and the floor sags
like a ship floundering;

we know no rule
of procedure,

we are voyagers, discoverers
of the not-known,

the unrecorded;
we have no map;

possibly we will reach haven,
heaven.

THE BLUES

The blues is about separation and suffering. Women's blues is about slavery to no-good men, submission to physical violence, or its mirror, fantasies of becoming violent. The height of "popularity," meaning exposure in white culture, of this indigenous black musical literature, came after the First World War. These blues are the "classic blues" and the singers were almost all women. The poetry of the blues in this period is both traditional and original, particularly in terms of the songs that follow, where everyone from Ma Rainey to Billie Holiday draws imagery from an oral tradition that is not tied to gender, speaking in a language of common reference to black women and black men equally. The subject is the man-woman relationship. The setting is domestic; the emotional story about what is called infidelity. The theme is generally balanced or unbalanced power in sexual relationships. These songs are about domination. The women who made them present alternating moods of cynical submission or a rather tenuous bravura. For richness of poetic language, this genre has no counterpart in our cultural heritage.

GERTRUDE "MA" RAINEY (1886–1939)

The first to set the style for classic blues singers, the originator, was born Gertrude Pridgett in Columbus, Georgia. At fourteen, she made her first stage appearance in a local talent show. Legend says that Will "Pa" Rainey came through town with his traveling minstrel show and "discovered" her. By 1904, she had married Rainey and, as a song-and-dance team called "Rainey and Rainey, The Assassinators of the Blues," they were continually on the road, traveling the tent-show circuit. Separating from Rainey, she reached the height of her fame on her own in the twenties, when the Paramount Company recorded her and brought her inimitable voice, for the first time, to people outside the rural black South.

DON'T FISH IN MY SEA

My daddy come home this morning
Drunk as he could be
My daddy come home this morning
Drunk as he could be
I knowed by that, he's
Done gone bad on me
He used to stay out late, now
He don't come home at all
He used to stay out late, now
He don't come home at all
(No kidding, either.)
I know there's another mule
Been kicking in my stall

If you don't like my ocean
Don't fish in my sea
Don't like my ocean
Don't fish in my sea
Stay out of my valley
And let my mountain be

I ain't had no loving
Since god knows when
I ain't had no loving
Since god knows when
That's the reason I'm through with these
No good trifling men

You'll never miss the sunshine
Till the rain begin to fall
Never miss the sunshine
Till the rain begin to fall

You'll never miss your ham till a-
Nother mule be in your stall

SWEET ROUGH MAN

I woke up this morning
My head was sore as a board
I woke up this morning
My head was sore as a board
My man beat me last night
With five feet of chopped up cord

He keeps my lips split
God eyes as black as day
He keeps my lips split
God eyes as black as day
But the way he love me
Make me soon forget

Every night for five years
I've got a beaten from my man
Every night for five years
I've got a beaten from my man
People says I'm crazy
How to straighten you understand

My man, my man, Lawd
Everybody knows he's mean
My man, my man, Lawd
Everybody knows he's mean
Cause when he starts to loving
I wring, and twist and sing

Lawd, it ain't no big thing
About my man being rough
Lawd, it ain't no big thing
About my man being rough
But when it comes to loving
He sho can strut his stuff.

BESSIE SMITH
(1898–1937)

The girl who sang on the stage of the Ivory Theatre in Chattanooga, Tennessee, at the age of nine learned her first blues from "Ma" Rainey. Bessie Smith spent her youth on the road, traveling with the Rabbit Foot Minstrels and the Florida Cotton Blossoms. "Race recordings" brought her considerable fame and no small fortune. The Columbia Phonograph Company was, it is claimed, saved from bankruptcy by her success. "The Empress of the Blues" brought her music out of the country; she sang, at the height of her fame, in theatres and nightclubs more than in tent shows and as much in the urban black centers of the North as the cities of the South. In the twenties, she dominated the blues; in the thirties she was often broke and out of work. The Depression brought the decline of "race recordings" and Columbia dropped her. The car accident outside Clarksdale, Mississippi, that killed her happened during a tour she was making, trying for a comeback.

DIRTY NO GOODER BLUES*

Did you ever fall in love with a man that was no good
Did you ever fall in love with a man that was no good
No matter what you did for him he never understood
The meanest things he could say would thrill you
through and through

The meanest things he could say would thrill you
     through and through
And there was nothing too dirty for that man to do

He'd treat you nice and kind 'til he'd win your heart
     in hand
He'd treat you nice and kind 'til he'd win your heart
     in hand
Then he'd get so cruel that man you just could not stand

Lord, I really don't think no man love can last
Lord, I don't think no man love can last
They love you to death then treat you like a thing of
     the past

There's nineteen men living in my neighborhood
There's nineteen men living in my neighborhood
Eighteen of them are fools and the one ain't no doggone
     good

Lord, lord, lord, lord, lord, oh lord, lord lord
That dirty no-good man treats me just like I'm a dog

YOUNG WOMAN'S BLUES*

Woke up this mornin' when chickens was crowin' for
     days
And on the right side of my pilla my man had gone
     away
By the pilla he left a note reading I'm sorry Jane you
     got my goat
No time to marry, no time to settle down
I'm a young woman and ain't done runnin' 'round
I'm a young woman and ain't done runnin' 'round.

Some people call me a hobo, some call me a bum
Nobody knows my name, nobody knows what I've done
I'm as good as any woman in your town
I ain't high yeller, I'm a deep yella brown
I ain't gonna marry, ain't gonna settle down
I'm gonna drink good moonshine and run these browns
   down

See that long lonesome road
Lord, you know it's gotta end
I'm a good woman and I can get plenty men

IDA COX
(1889–1968)

Ida Cox was born in Knoxville, Tennessee, and from the age of fourteen, served the tough apprenticeship of the blues singer—tent shows, minstrel troupes, carnivals, small clubs, waterfront dives. She remained with the Rabbit Foot Minstrels most of her life and did not appear outside the Deep South. She formed her own touring company and was still on the road until late in the fifties. She retired and died in the town in which she had been born.

WILD WOMEN BLUES

I've got a different system
And a way of my own,
When my man starts kicking
I let him find another home.
I get full of good liquor
And walk the street all night,
Go home and put my man out

If he don't treat me right,
Wild women don't worry,
Wild women don't have the blues.

You never get nothing
By being an angel child,
You better change your ways
And get real wild.
I want to tell you something
I wouldn't tell you no lie,
Wild women are the only kind
That really get by,
'Cause wild women don't worry,
Wild women don't have the blues.

MEMPHIS MINNIE (1900–   )

One of the few blues singers to play her own accompaniment, usually on the guitar, Memphis Minnie was born across the river from New Orleans but, by fifteen, was singing in the streets of Memphis. She was discovered by one of the Columbia Phonograph Company's ubiquitous talent scouts—singing for dimes in the barber shops on Beale Street. In the early thirties, she left Memphis for Chicago. It was said that she sang and played guitar "like a man."

ME AND MY CHAUFFEUR BLUES

Won't you be my chauffeur
Won't you be my chauffeur
I want someone to drive me
I want someone to drive me
Down town

Baby drives so easy
I can't turn him down

But I don't want him
But I don't want him
To be riding these girls
To be riding these girls
A-round
You know I'm gonna steal me a pistol
Shoot my chauffeur down

Well I must buy him
Well I must buy him
A brand new V-8
A brand new V-8 Ford
And he won't need no passengers
I will be his load

(Yeah, take it away)

Going to let my chauffeur
Going to let my chauffeur
Drive me around the
Drive me around the
World
Then he can be my little boy
Yes I'll treat him good

SARA TEASDALE (1884–1933)

In Saint Louis, Missouri, at the turn of the century, Sara Teasdale, daughter of prosperous parents, lived in an elegant, still-Victorian culture. Her first books of poetry brought her considerable genteel attention, but her audience faded as she grew older and her work became less precious. Two women pervade her poems: Eleonora Duse (around whom there was a devoted cult of female admirers) and Christina Rossetti, whose work she studied throughout her life. She planned to write a biography of Rossetti. In the year that her last book of poetry was published (*Strange Victory*, 1933), she killed herself with an overdose of sleeping pills.

EFFIGY OF A NUN

Infinite gentleness, infinite irony
    Are in this face with fast-sealed eyes,
And around this mouth that learned in loneliness
    How useless their wisdom is to the wise.

In her nun's habit carved, patiently, lovingly,
    By one who knew the ways of womankind,
This woman's face still keeps, in its cold wistful calm,
    All of the subtle pride of her mind.

These long patrician hands, clasping the crucifix,
    Show she had weighed the world, her will was set;
These pale curved lips of hers, holding their hidden
        smile,
    Once having made their choice, knew no regret.

She was of those who hoard their own thoughts
        carefully,
    Feeling them far too dear to give away,
Content to look at life with the high, insolent
    Air of an audience watching a play.

If she was curious, if she was passionate
    She must have told herself that love was great,
But that the lacking it might be as great a thing
    If she held fast to it, challenging fate.

She who so loved herself and her own warring thoughts,
  Watching their humorous, tragic rebound,
In her thick habit's fold, sleeping, sleeping,
  Is she amused at dreams she has found?

Infinite tenderness, infinite irony
  Are hidden forever in her closed eyes,
Who must have learned too well in her long loneliness
  How empty wisdom is, even to the wise.

STRANGE VICTORY

To this, to this, after my hope was lost,
  To this strange victory;
To find you with the living, not the dead,
  To find you glad of me;
To find you wounded even less than I,
  Moving as I across the stricken plain;
After the battle to have found your voice
  Lifted above the slain.

CENTRAL PARK AT DUSK

Buildings above the leafless trees
  Loom high as castles in a dream,
While one by one the lamps come out
  To thread the twilight with a gleam.

There is no sign of leaf or bud,
  A hush is over everything—
Silent as women wait for love,
  The world is waiting for the spring.

ELINOR WYLIE
(1885–1928)

Until she was twenty-five, Elinor Wylie conformed
most decorously to her well-placed family's life style,
went to finishing schools and debutante parties,
married the son of a socially prominent family. In
1910, she abandoned her husband and son to elope
with Horace Wylie, a married man ten years older
than she. The scandal followed the Wylies to England,
where they lived for seven years and where Elinor
Wylie began to write poetry. She published a small
pamphlet of poems, but did not take herself seriously
as a writer. Returning to America, she began to write
in earnest and *Nets to Catch the Wind*, her first
"real" book of poems, was published in 1921. She
was then in her mid-thirties. That year, she moved to
New York City, received attention and acclaim for
her work, and began what turned out to be seven
extremely productive years in which she wrote three
more books of poetry and four novels. The only
book review Edna St. Vincent Millay wrote in her life
was of *Nets to Catch the Wind*. The two poets became extremely close friends and Millay wrote several
poems about her affection and admiration for Wylie.
Elinor Wylie's last book of poems was published post-
humously; she died of a stroke, having just made final
arrangements for the publication of *Angels and
Earthly Creatures*.

PROPHECY

I shall lie hidden in a hut
  In the middle of an alder wood,
With the back door blind and bolted shut,
  And the front door locked for good.

I shall lie folded like a saint,
  Lapped in a scented linen sheet,
On a bedstead striped with bright-blue paint,
  Narrow and cold and neat.

The midnight will be glassy black
  Behind the panes, with wind about
To set his mouth against a crack
  And blow the candle out.

SONNET

XII

In our content, before the autumn came
To shower sallow droppings on the mould,
Sometimes you have permitted me to fold
Your grief in swaddling-bands, and smile to name
Yourself my infant, with an infant's claim
To utmost adoration as of old,
Suckled with kindness, fondled from the cold,
And loved beyond philosophy or shame.

I dreamt I was the mother of a son
Who had deserved a manger for a crib;
Torn from your body, furbished from your rib,
I am the daughter of your skeleton,
Born of your bitter and excessive pain:
I shall not dream you are my child again.

LET NO CHARITABLE HOPE

Now let no charitable hope
Confuse my mind with images
Of eagle and of antelope:
I am in nature none of these.

I was, being human, born alone;
I am, being woman, hard beset;
I live by squeezing from a stone
The little nourishment I get.

In masks outrageous and austere
The years go by in single file;
But none has merited my fear,
And none has quite escaped my smile.

FALSE PROPHET

When I was forty, and two feathers sprung
Like crescents silver-curved from either temple,
Above a casque of bronze, I saw the simple
And casual shape of beauty; and my tongue
Spoke thus: "I am rejoiced I am not young
Lest this supreme and ultimate example
Of fine-spun flesh should very lightly trample
Upon my wounds; my withers are unwrung.

He might have been my son, save that my youth,
Bending the slender bow of its despair,
Loosed no such luminous arrow on the air;
His shaft was cut from some diviner bough:
And while my fainting heart perceived the truth,
My tongue spoke thus: "He cannot hurt me now."

EDNA ST. VINCENT MILLAY (1892-1950)

When Edna Millay was eight years old, her mother left her father, taking the three daughters, of whom Edna was the oldest, to Camden, Maine, to live. Cora Millay, her mother, has always been considered a major influence on the poet's work. At nineteen, prompted by her mother, Edna Millay entered a contest sponsored by a forthcoming anthology of modern verse, *The Lyric Year*. Her submission was "Renascence," which she had been working on since her high school years. Although it didn't win the contest, the poem nevertheless aroused such controversy that Millay found herself suddenly in the midst of literary New York and then at Vassar College, sponsored by a patron, Caroline Dow. After Vassar, she lived in Greenwich Village, acted with the Provincetown Players, and was very involved in left-wing politics. Her friends included John Reed, Edmund Wilson and Max Eastman. She began to publish her poetry and became, quite quickly, one of this country's first poets to win a wide mass audience for serious literary work. Her popularity, at its height in the twenties, declined as her work became more political. She often apologized for the "uncrafted" quality of some of her work around the time of the Second World War, explaining that the urgency of what she had to say superseded her desire to polish what she was writing. Although she is most famous for her sonnets, much of Millay's work was seriously political and often feminist.

SONNET XXXI

Oh, oh, you will be sorry for that word!
Give back my book and take my kiss instead.
Was it my enemy or my friend I heard,
"What a big book for a such little head!"
Come, I will show you now my newest hat,
And you may watch me purse my mouth and prink!
Oh, I shall love you still, and all of that.
I never again shall tell you what I think.
I shall be sweet and crafty, soft and sly;
You will not catch me reading any more:
I shall be called a wife to pattern by;
And some day when you knock and push the door,
Some sane day, not too bright and not too stormy,
I shall be gone, and you may whistle for me.

SONNET XLI

I, being born a woman and distressed
By all the needs and notions of my kind,
Am urged by your propinquity to find
Your person fair, and feel a certain zest
To bear your body's weight upon my breast:
So subtly is the fume of life designed,
To clarify the pulse and cloud the mind,
And leave me once again undone, possessed.
Think not for this, however, the poor treason
Of my stout blood against my staggering brain,
I shall remember you with love, or season
My scorn with pity,—let me make it plain:
I find this frenzy insufficient reason
For conversation when we meet again.

GENEVIEVE TAGGARD (1894–1948)

Genevieve Taggard's father was a fruit farmer, her mother a teacher. Many of her early years were spent in Hawaii, where the poet developed a strong and clear picture of white racism that would appear in her poetry. She attended the University of California at Berkeley, supported by contributions from her friends. At Berkeley, she became a socialist and when she came to New York afterwards, was associated with the radical left. She was a committed feminist. Her poetry frequently appeared in *The Liberator* and *The Masses*, and she was founder of an experimental magazine called *The Measure*. Her study, *The Life and Mind of Emily Dickinson*, was published in 1930. Genevieve Taggard died of hypertension.

EVERYDAY ALCHEMY

Men go to women mutely for their peace;
And they, who lack it most, create it when
They make, because they must, loving their men,
A solace for sad bosom-bended heads. There
Is all the meagre peace men get—no otherwhere;
No mountain space, no tree with placid leaves,
Or heavy gloom beneath a young girl's hair,
No sound of valley bell on autumn air
Or room made home with doves along the eaves,
Ever holds peace, like this, poured by poor women
Out of their heart's poverty, for worn men.

IMAGE

*Dedicated to the heroic memory of Christopher Caudwell,
author of* Illusion and Reality, *killed in action fighting
with the government forces at Madrid, 1937.*

Mask-face of old grief, death-mask, massive
Visage uttering Joy; Joy sputtering; glorious oracle!
Joy, red on tongue with wind on frozen forehead;
Mouth open, Joy just-spoken, grief just-broken;
Clarion throat eloquent, quenching cries; eyes
Wide, soul of Hallelujah, Ah,
Fury of song and drum and gong; fury
For the color of flags snapping on broomsticks,
Screw it in chromium on motor-cars,
Put the medallion on money,
Let it shake large and quiet in star-water.

WITH CHILD

Now I am slow and placid, fond of sun,
Like a sleek beast, or a worn one:
No slim and languid girl—not glad
With the windy trip I once had,
But velvet-footed, musing of my own,
Torpid, mellow, stupid as a stone.

You cleft me with your beauty's pulse, and now
Your pulse has taken body. Care not how
The old grace goes, how heavy I am grown,
Big with this loneliness, how you alone
Ponder our love. Touch my feet and feel
How earth tingles, teeming at my heel!
Earth's urge, not mine—my little death, not hers;
And the pure beauty yearns and stirs.
It does not heed our ecstasies, it turns
With secrets of its own, its own concerns,
Toward a windy world of its own, toward stark
And solitary places. In the dark,

Defiant even now, it tugs and moans
To be untangled from these mother's bones.

BABETTE DEUTSCH
(1895–   )

Babette Deutsch began to publish poetry while she
was a student at Barnard College. At the same time
and later she was involved in social causes, working
as secretary to Thorstein Veblen, publishing in *The
Masses* and *The Liberator*, and was participant in
John Dewey's Committee for Cultural Freedom. She
is truly a "woman of letters." In addition to her books
of poetry, Babette Deutsch has written novels, and
books for children, translated Russian and other foreign poems, and written literary criticism, also editing
several anthologies with her husband, the Slavonic
scholar and biographer Avrahm Yarmolinsky.

PETROGRAD

And there was stormy silence in that city,
A silence of the unborn where it moved
In darkness, piteous, but without pity,
Tearing the body that held it, the heart that loved.
Her sides were shaken with the weight she bore,
Dwarfing, with the huge shadow that it threw,
Hunger and empty death and puny war:
The red hour loomed. The lunging city knew.
Her cry smote on the dawn and she was mute;
Tossing in the bewildered agony
Of that impatient and impeded birth:
She was alone as any groaning brute.

Savage in solitary victory,
She challenges the leagued imperial earth.

(c. 1919)

LIONESS ASLEEP

Content that now the bleeding bone be swept
Out of her reach, she lay upon her side.
In a blonde void sunk deep, she slept, she slept
Bland as a child, slept, breathing like a bride.
Color of noons that shimmer as they sing
Above the dunes, her sandy flanks heaved slow.
Between her paws curled inward, billowing
Waves of desert silence seemed to flow.

The crowd was gone, the bars were gone, the cage
Thinned into air, the sawdust and the fleas
Winnowed by sleep to nothing. After food,
Absence possessed her: bliss keener than rage,
If slumber's prisoner at a bound could seize
This ghostly freedom, lapping it like blood.

NIKE AT THE METROPOLITAN

Great-winged, as thirstily as an athlete you
Lean your headless throat upon the wind.
Your blind breasts
Remember how they once frowned down the sea.
But the prow
That outfaced Ptolemy is now worn stone,
And here is worse—
A plaster image of that faceless thing.
It is this age's curse
To look at you, goddess of Samothrace, and think,
No cause is just.
Yet, with shorn arms you nurse
Whatever infant triumph men will bring
To rest in your opposing thrust.

A BULL

His sad brown bulk rears patient as the hills
Hunched like dark herders at the pasture's back.
Swaying, he will not topple like those clouds
Heavy with throttled thunders. Lust that thrills
The crowd, to see such power pricked and teased
Through hot blind plunges to a sandy death
While they breathe blood, rage flowering in their veins,
His poor tame suffering will not have appeased,
Who takes the sun's barbs in a sullen drowse.
The ritual of his fertility
Is simple; he was bred only to breed,
The homely husband to a score of cows.
Yet monstrous as a myth, his front denies
His humbled horns, as, hugely male, he stands
Hung with endurance as with iron weights.
Clustering flies mate round his red-rimmed eyes.

EPISTLE TO PROMETHEUS

VIII

*There are historical periods when it is most important for
the success of the revolution to pile up as many fragments
as possible—that is to blow up as many old institutions as
possible. But there are periods when enough has been
blown up, and it becomes necessary to turn to the
"prosaic" . . . work of clearing the ground of the fragments. And there are periods when it is most important to
tend carefully the germs of the new growth under the
fragments, on the soil that is yet full of rubbish.*

Lenin

Beauty is dead and rotten.
Goodness
lies in a ditch.
Truth is a painted whore.

Can a lost generation—
machine-guns spitting death across barbed fields
at men staled by their stinking trade,
four years
of spitting and being spat at by the guns—
can a lost generation remember
the world at morning?

Who now
dares open the grave to look at the corpse of morning?
This incorruptible
puts on corruption.
The tender flesh is vexed
past recognition,
the worm's in his heaven . . .

Let the dead future
bury its dead.
After the funeral
return to the empty house—
the door is open,
go into the unswept room,
go in and face
the iron day.

What's death
to the Promethean breed?
If Paris falls,
if Berlin crumbles, if
the stones cry aloud in the street,
and the fields feed
vultures long hungry for the immortal heart,
shall the rebel, shaken
from his old vigil,
hesitate, retreat,
or on the walls
of broken nations build his fires,
blowing
the embers of defeat.

Put by the dream.
Come to a huddle of houses
in a mean block.
Open the gate,
go up into a room
where a man is living on sour bread and hate.
He is short and shabby,
has nothing in his pockets but his fists.
He rises early,
goes late to bed, halts, twists
to a harsh music,
his nerves being tuned
to the voice of the machines,
the heavy hum,
the monotonous monstrous
cradle-song that crooned
his peace to sleep . . .
And in his ears the crying
of war's adorable bastard—
revolution.

The Czar
is shooting crows,
lean pickings for the emperor
of all the Russias.
The short shabby man
looks out of the window on a slum in Berlin,
London, Zurich, no matter,
looks out . . .
he knows
a trick worth two of that.
He looks out, sees
black hundreds fattening for his shooting-party,
turns from the window, clasps
his hand behind his back, goes
to the table, bends again to the task
of building up his arsenal of words,
the cobbled walls

morticed with sweat,
the powder-casks
safe,
the faithful stone opposing
all hammers but his own.

Gold is the sinews of war.
His credit? Good
with a handful of talkers,
smugglers of mad print,
clubmen who meet in cellars,
wageless workmen, soldiers
without guns.
The house of Morgan
does not know this banker,
does not know the mint
upon the barricades.
This cold-eyed merchant
buys
a throne with hunger,
iron troops with peace,
peasants with land, trades
war for civil war,
and barters, with a brief smile,
empire
for the wildfire that was the light of exile.

Where are the lares and penates
the hunted carry
from one hole to another?
They shall be set
above the seats of the mighty.
Despair, that gilded
the pediments of death,
has other work.
Hooligans harry
God from His high cloud,
and who now will forbear to sully
His torn disfigured shroud?

In the Red Square
under the time-eaten battlements
they will build
new shrines for old, but
first there shall be
wars, famine, plague, the scourging of the nations,
hard pangs of the unripe womb,
by these shall the faith live, the prophecy
be fulfilled,
while the dead prophet's mummy
seems faintly to smile
from the second exile of the tomb.

Sweet Plato, forgive them,
they know not what they do.

And is this too
your handiwork, Prometheus?
Was it you let fall
sparks among factory benches,
along the byways, under the broken roofs,
in muddy trenches on the eastern front, until
Peter's chill city caught,
the Winter Palace
smoked, and finally Smolny
spoke with red tongues?
Did you
channel the fire slow years underground
from Munich into Moscow?
Would you cast
from the Kremlin heights
a net of flame to snare
Asia, and at the second throw
catch fast
earth in the burning mesh?
Fisher of peoples, Titan of the charred hand,
do you dare?
You answer no questions.
Still I ask:

can one of your stature
stoop to the lousy bunk-house in the woods,
crouch in the blind foulness of the pit,
walk the mill's narrow aisles where animal thousands
are turned to the machines' magnificat?
I ask: will you,
schooled upon Caucasus,
teach in more modest prisons?
I ask how
will your thief's task be finished,
and by whom?
Prometheus, is it you
whom the dead prophet's mummy
hails, as with a smile,
from the final exile of the tomb?

(c. 1931)

JANET LEWIS
(1889-   )

Janet Lewis was born in Chicago and received a degree from the University of Chicago. She was there at the beginning of the Poetry Renaissance, and through the important Poetry Club at the University, met Elizabeth Madox Roberts and Harriet Monroe, founder of *Poetry* magazine. From her father, a teacher of English, Janet Lewis said she received her first education in English prose. She is better known as a novelist and short-story writer, but there is one slim volume of her poems in print. In the early twenties, she left Chicago for Santa Fe, New Mexico, where she met and married the poet/critic Yvor Winters.

HELEN GROWN OLD

We have forgotten Paris, and his fate.
We have not much inquired
If Menelaus from the Trojan gate
Returning found the long desired
Immortal beauty by his hearth. Then late,

Late, long past the morning hour,
Could even she recapture from the dawn
The young delightful love? When the dread power
That forced her will was gone,
When fell the last charred tower,

When the last flame had faded from the cloud,
And by the darkening sea
The plain lay empty of the armèd crowd,
Then was she free
Who had been ruled by passion blind and proud?

Then did she find with him whom first she chose
Before the desperate flight,
At last, repose
In love still radiant at the edge of night,
As fair as in the morning? No one knows.

No one has cared to say. The story clings
To the tempestuous years, by passion bound,
Like Helen. No one brings
A tale of quiet love. The fading sound
Is blent of falling embers, weeping kings.

HELEN, THE SAD QUEEN

(*From the French of Paul Valéry*)

Azure, 'tis I, come from Elysian shores
To hear the waves break on sonorous steps,
And see again the sunrise full of ships
Rising from darkness upon golden oars.

My solitary arms call on the kings
Whose salty beards amused my silver hands.
I wept; they sang of triumphs in far lands,
And gulfs fled backward upon watery wings.

I hear the trumpet and the martial horn
That wield the rhythm of the beating blade,
The song of rowers binding the tumult.

And the gods! exalting on the prow with scorn
Their ancient smile that the slow waves insult,
Hold out their sculptured arms to my sad shade.

GIRL HELP

Mild and slow and young,
She moves about the room,
And stirs the summer dust
With her wide broom.

In the warm, lofted air,
Soft lips together pressed,
Soft wispy hair,
She stops to rest.

And stops to breathe,
Amid the summer hum,
The great white lilac bloom
Scented with days to come.

THE MILLS AND THE MINES: WORKER-POETS

In the late nineteenth century, there were occasional
instances of direct expression of the lives of working

women by those who were living those lives. Usually
this expression took the form of songs. The songs
were about conditions in the textile mills of both
North and South. Several examples are printed here.
Their authors are unknown. A century later, in one
generation, three women organizers and songwriters
became quite visible, and unlike their earlier sisters,
they have not been forgotten. The tradition of class
struggle in life and in songwriting is what eventually
produced the worker-poets Gunning, Jackson and
Wiggins.

HARD TIMES COTTON MILL GIRLS

I've worked in a cotton mill all of my life
And I ain't got nothing but a Barlow knife,
It's hard times cotton mill girls,
It's hard times everywhere.

Chorus:

It's hard times cotton mill girls,
It's hard times cotton mill girls,
It's hard times cotton mill girls,
It's hard times everywhere.

In nineteen and fifteen we heard it said,
Go to the country and get ahead.
It's hard times cotton mill girls,
It's hard times everywhere.

Us girls work twelve hours a day
For fourteen cents of measly pay.
It's hard times cotton mill girls,
It's hard times everywhere.

When I die don't bury me at all,
Just pickle my bones in alcohol,

Hang me up on the spinning room wall,
It's hard times everywhere.

(Chorus)

HARD TIMES IN THE MILL

Every morning at half-past four
You hear the cook's hop on the floor.

Refrain:

It's hard times in the mill, my love,
Hard times in the mill.

Every morning just at five,
You gotta get up dead or alive.

Every morning right at six,
Don't that old bell just make you sick?

The pulley got hot, the belt jumped off,
Knocked Mr. Guyon's derby off.

Old Pat Goble thinks he's a hoñ
He puts me in mind of a doodle in the sun.

The section hand thinks he's a man,
And he ain't got sense to pay off his hands.

They steal his rings, they steal his knife,
They steal everything but his big fat wife.

My mobbin's all out, my ends all down
The doffer's in my alley and I can't get around.

The section hand's standing at the door
Ordering the sweepers to sweep up the floor.

Every night when I go home,
A piece of cornbread and an old jaw bone.

Ain't it enough to break your heart?
Hafta work all day and at night it's dark.

THE LOWELL FACTORY GIRL

When I set out for Lowell,
Some factory for to find,
I left my native country,
And all my friends behind.

Refrain:

Then sing hit-re-i-re-a-re-o
Then sing hit-re-i-re-a

But now I am in Lowell,
And summon'd by the bell,
I think less of the factory
Than of my native dell.

The factory bell begins to ring,
And we must all obey,
And to our old employment go,
Or else be turned away.

Come all ye weary factory girls,
I'll have you understand,
I'm going to leave the factory
And return to my native land.

No more I'll put my bonnet on
And hasten to the mill,
While all the girls are working hard,
Here I'll be lying still.

No more I'll lay my bobbins up,
No more I'll take them down;
No more I'll clean my dirty work,
For I'm going out of town.

No more I'll take my piece of soap,
No more I'll go to wash,
No more my overseer shall say,
"Your frames ars stopped to doff."

Come all you little doffers
That work in the Spinning room;
Go wash your face and comb your hair,
Prepare to leave the room.

No more I'll oil my picker rods,
No more I'll brush my loom,
No more I'll sour my dirty floor
All in the Weaving room.

No more I'll draw these threads
All through the harness eye;
No more I'll say to my overseer,
Oh! dear me, I shall die.

No more I'll get my overseer
To come and fix my loom,
No more I'll say to my overseer
Can't I stay out 'till noon?

Then since they've cut my wages down
To nine shillings per week,
If I cannot better wages make,
Some other place I'll seek.

No more he'll find me reading,
No more he'll see me sew,
No more he'll come to me and say
"Such works I can't allow."

I do not like my overseer,
I do not mean to stay,
I mean to hire a Depot-boy
To carry me away.

The Dress-room girls they needn't think
Because they higher go,
That they are better than the girls
That work in the rooms below.

The overseers they need not think
Because they higher stand,
That they are better than the girls
That work at their command.

'Tis wonder how the men
Can such machinery make,
A thousand wheels together roll
Without the least mistake.

Now soon you'll see me married
To a handsome little man,
'Tis then I'll say to you factory girls,
Come and see me when you can.

AUNT MOLLY JACKSON (1880–1961)

Aunt Molly Jackson spent her childhood going to union meetings with her father, who had sold the farm she was born on and gone to work in the mines. At fourteen, she married a coal miner. Complaining about the constant child-bearing of miners' wives and vowing "not to grow up to be a fool," she learned to read and write, and became a registered nurse and midwife. She was famous in Harlan County, Kentucky, as a woman who could take the place of several doctors. Mining accidents killed her father, her husband and her son. With other organizers, she was blacklisted, harassed and forced to leave Kentucky in 1931. She spent the years after that traveling the country, carrying the message of the miners' struggle. She eventually came to live in New York, where she was often seen at rallies for progressive causes, singing her songs.

I AM A UNION WOMAN

I am a union woman,
As brave as I can be;
I do not like the bosses,
And the bosses don't like me.

Refrain:

Join the NMU,
Come join the NMU

I was raised in old Kentucky,
In Kentucky borned and bred;
And when I joined the union
They called me a Rooshian Red.

When my husband asked the boss for a job
These is the words he said:
"Bill Jackson, I can't work you sir,
Your wife's a Rooshian Red."

This is the worst time on earth
That I have ever saw;
To get shot down by gun thugs
And framed up by the law.

If you want to join a union
As strong as one can be,
Join the dear old NMU
And come along with me.

We are many thousand strong
And I am glad to say,
We are getting stronger
And stronger every day.

The bosses ride fine horses
While we walk in the mud;
Their banner is a dollar sign
While ours is striped with blood.

SARAH OGAN GUNNING (1910–)

The half-sister of Aunt Molly Jackson is less well known. Her childhood, like the rest of the family's, was spent moving from one mining camp to another and she, too, became involved in union activity when she was young. She eloped at fifteen with a miner who developed tuberculosis. She, too, left Kentucky for New York and her husband died a few years after that. She was as militant as her sister and her organizer-songwriter brother, Jim Garland. Many of her songs were not recorded and did not reach a large audience until the early sixties. "I Hate the Company Bosses" was originally called "I Hate the Capitalist System." "Dreadful Memories" was written after she had left Kentucky and, in the East Side tenements of New York, looked back.

I HATE THE COMPANY BOSSES

I hate the company bosses,
I'll tell you the reason why.
They cause me so much suffering
And my dearest friends to die.

Oh yes, I guess you wonder
What they have done to me.
I'm going to tell you, mister,
My husband had T.B.

Brought on by hard work and low wages
And not enough to eat,
Going naked and hungry,
No shoes on his feet.

I guess you'll say he's lazy
And did not want to work.
But I must say you're crazy,
For work he did not shirk.

My husband was a coal miner,
He worked and risked his life
To try to support three children,
Himself, his mother, and wife.

I had a blue-eyed baby,
The darling of my heart.
But from my little darling
Her mother had to part.

Those mighty company bosses,
They dress in jewels and silk.
But my darling blue-eyed baby,
She starved to death for milk.

I had a darling mother,
For her I often cry.
But with them rotten conditions
My mother had to die.

Well, what killed your mother?
Oh tell us, if you please.
Excuse me, it was pellagra,
That starvation disease.

They call this the land of plenty,
To them I guess it's true
But that's to the company bosses
Not workers like me and you.

Well, what can I do about it,
To these men of power and might?
I tell you, company bosses,
I'm going to fight, fight, fight.

What can we do about it,
To right this dreadful wrong?
We're all going to join the union,
For the union makes us strong.

DREADFUL MEMORIES

Dreadful memories, how they linger,
How they ever flood my soul,
How the workers and their children
Die from hunger and from cold.

Hungry fathers, wearied mothers
Living in those dreadful shacks,
Little children cold and hungry
With no clothing on their backs.

Dreadful gun-thugs and stool-pigeons
Always flock around our door.
What's the crime that we've committed?
Nothing, only that we're poor.

When I think of all the heartaches
And all the things that we've been through
Then I wonder how much longer
And what a working man can do.

Really, friends, it doesn't matter
Whether you are black or white.
The only way you'll ever change things
Is to fight and fight and fight.

We will have to join the union,
They will help you find a way
How to get a better living
And for your work get better pay.

OLD SOUTHERN TOWN

I'm thinking tonight of an old southern town
And my loved ones that I left behind.
I know they are ragged and hungry, too,
And it sure does worry my mind.

Poor little children so hungry and cold,
The big mighty bosses so big and so bold,
They stole all our land and they stole all our coal.
We get starvation and they get the gold.

I know how it feels to be lonesome,
And I know how it feels to be blue.
I know how it is to be hungry,
And I've sure been ragged, too.

I'm thinking of brother and sister,
From the loved ones whom I had to part.
I'm thinking of their little children
Who is so near to my heart.

I'm thinking of heartaches and starvation
That the bosses has caused me and mine.
I'm thinking of friends and neighbors
And the loved ones that I left behind.

Now if I had these rotten bosses
Where the bosses has got me,
What I wouldn't do to them rascals
Would be a shame to see.

ELLA MAY WIGGINS (1889–1929)

Like most poor Appalachian women of her generation, Ella May's childhood saw the move from farm-

ing life to vagabonding from mine to mill to lumber
camp. At sixteen, she married a logger. A few years
later, he was crippled in an accident, leaving her the
sole provider for a family of nine children, four of
whom died of whooping cough. She moved the family
to cotton mill country and worked for ten years as a
spinner. She joined the National Textile Workers'
Union, engaged in ferocious struggle with the company bosses and used her own songs for organizing.
In 1929, at the bloodiest moment in the union
struggle, she was shot and killed on her way to a
union meeting at the mill in Gastonia, North Carolina.

ALL AROUND THE JAILHOUSE

All around the jailhouse
Waiting for a trial;
One mile from the union hall
Sleeping in the jail.
I walked up to the policeman
To show him I had no fear;
He said, "If you've got money
I'll see that you don't stay here."

"I haven't got a nickel,
Not a penny can I show."
"Lock her up in the cell," he said,
As he slammed the jailhouse door.
He let me out in July,
The month I dearly love;
The wide open spaces all around me,
The moon and stars above.

Everybody seems to want me,
Everybody but the scabs.
I'm on my way from the jailhouse,
I'm going back to the union hall.
Though my tent now is empty

My heart is full of joy;
I'm a mile away from the union hall,
Just a-waiting for a strike.

THE MILL MOTHER'S LAMENT

We leave our homes in the morning,
We kiss our children good bye
While we slave for the bosses
Our children scream and cry.

And when we draw our money
Our grocery bills to pay,
Not a cent to spend for clothing,
Not a cent to lay away.

And on that very evening,
Our little son will say:
"I need some shoes, Mother,
And so does sister May."

How it grieves the heart of a mother,
You everyone must know,
But we can't buy for our children
Our wages are too low.

It is for our little children,
That seem to us so dear,
But for us nor them, dear workers,
The bosses do not care.

But understand, all workers,
Our union they do fear;
Let's stand together, workers,
And have a union here.

MARIANNE MOORE
(1887-1972)

Marianne Moore grew up in the home of her grandfather, a Presbyterian minister. Her father had abandoned the family before her birth and she lived with
her mother until her mother's death. She was educated at Bryn Mawr College during the years when
M. Carey Thomas was its president; Thomas was one
of this country's most devoted and militant leaders
in the struggle for equal rights for education for
women. Entrance exams at Bryn Mawr were more
difficult than they were at Harvard or Yale. Hilda
Doolittle was a classmate of Marianne Moore's, but
the two poets were not friends. Around 1915, Moore's
poetry brought some recognition; five of her poems
were published in *Poetry* magazine and she was acclaimed as one of the "new" poets of her generation.
She worked at odd jobs, teaching first and then,
having moved to New York, as a part-time assistant
in the New York Public Library. "Marriage" was published separately in 1923. Two years later, her
reputation as poet and critic led to her being asked
to join the staff of *The Dial*. From 1926 until 1929,
she was editor of that publication, one of the most
influential and exciting magazines in American literary history. She devoted herself entirely to that job
and published no work of her own during those
years. Afterwards, she moved to Brooklyn and continued a life of enormous literary productivity. She
became known also, without compromising her in-
tegrity as a poet, as a beloved figure in mainstream
American culture. The Ford Motor Company asked

her to name a new model car and rejected her sug-
gestions for their own—the Edsel. Her knowledge of
baseball lore and her presence at baseball games
made Marianne Moore familiar to citizens who were
not avid readers of her rather intellectual and difficult
work.

MARRIAGE

This institution,
perhaps one should say enterprise
out of respect for which
one says one need not change one's mind
about a thing one has believed in,
requiring public promises
of one's intention
to fulfil a private obligation:
I wonder what Adam and Eve
think of it by this time,
this fire-gilt steel
alive with goldenness;
how bright it shows—
"of circular traditions and impostures,
committing many spoils,"
requiring all one's criminal ingenuity
to avoid!
Psychology which explains everything
explains nothing,
and we are still in doubt.
Eve: beautiful woman—
I have seen her
when she was so handsome
she gave me a start,
able to write simultaneously
in three languages—
English, German, and French—
and talk in the meantime;

equally positive in demanding a commotion
and in stipulating quiet:
"I should like to be alone";
to which the visitor replies,
"*I* should like to be alone;
why not be alone together?"
Below the incandescent stars
below the incandescent fruit,
the strange experience of beauty;
its existence is too much;
it tears one to pieces
and each fresh wave of consciousness
is poison.
"See her, see her in this common world,"
the central flaw
in that first crystal-fine experiment,
this amalgamation which can never be more
than an interesting impossibility,
describing it
as "that strange paradise
unlike flesh, stones,
gold or stately buildings,
the choicest piece of my life:
the heart rising
in its estate of peace
as a boat rises
with the rising of the water";
constrained in speaking of the serpent—
shed snakeskin in the history of politeness
not to be returned to again—
that invaluable accident
exonerating Adam.
And he has beauty also;
it's distressing—the O thou
to whom from whom,
without whom nothing—Adam;
"something feline,
something colubrine"—how true!

a crouching mythological monster
in that Persian miniature of emerald mines,
raw silk—ivory white, snow white,
oyster white and six others—
that paddock full of leopards and giraffes—
long lemon-yellow bodies
sown with trapezoids of blue.
Alive with words,
vibrating like a cymbal
touched before it has been struck,
he has prophesied correctly—
the industrious waterfall,
"the speedy stream
which violently bears all before it,
at one time silent as the air
and now as powerful as the wind."
"Treading chasms
on the uncertain footing of a spear,"
forgetting that there is in woman
a quality of mind
which as an instinctive manifestation
is unsafe,
he goes on speaking
in a formal customary strain,
of "past states, the present state,
seals, promises,
the evil one suffered,
the good one enjoys,
hell, heaven,
everything convenient
to promote one's joy."
In him a state of mind
perceives what it was not
intended that he should;
"he experiences a solemn joy
in seeing that he has become an idol."
Plagued by the nightingale
in the new leaves,

with its silence—
not its silence but its silences,
he says of it:
"It clothes me with a shirt of fire."
"He dares not clap his hands
to make it go on
lest it fly off;
if he does nothing, it will sleep;
if he cries out, it will not understand."
Unnerved by the nightingale
and dazzled by the apple,
impelled by "the illusion of a fire
effectual to extinguish fire,"
compared with which
the shining of the earth
is but deformity—a fire
"as high as deep
as bright as broad
as long as life itself,"
he stumbles over marriage,
"a very trivial object indeed"
to have destroyed the attitude
in which he stood—
the ease of the philosopher
unfathered by a woman.
Unhelpful Hymen!
a kind of overgrown cupid
reduced to insignificance
by the mechanical advertising
parading as involuntary comment,
by that experiment of Adam's
with ways out but no way in—
the ritual of marriage,
augmenting all its lavishness;
its fiddle-head ferns,
lotus flowers, opuntias, white dromedaries,
its hippopotamus—
nose and mouth combined

in one magnificent hopper—
its snake and the potent apple.
He tells us
that "for love that will
gaze an eagle blind,
that is with Hercules
climbing the trees
in the garden of the Hesperides,
from forty-five to seventy
is the best age,"
commending it
as a fine art, as an experiment,
a duty or as merely recreation.
One must not call him ruffian
nor friction a calamity—
the fight to be affectionate:
"no truth can be fully known
until it has been tried
by the tooth of disputation."
The blue panther with black eyes,
the basalt panther with blue eyes,
entirely graceful—
one must give them the path—
the black obsidian Diana
who "darkeneth her countenance
as a bear doth,"
the spiked hand
that has an affection for one
and proves it to the bone,
impatient to assure you
that impatience is the mark of independence,
not of bondage.
"Married people often look that way"—
"seldom and cold, up and down,
mixed and malarial
with a good day and a bad."
"When do we feed?"
We occidentals are so unemotional,

we quarrel as we feed;
self lost, the irony preserved
in "the Ahasuerus *tête-à-tête* banquet"
with its small orchids like snakes' tongues,
with its "good monster, lead the way,"
with little laughter
and munificence of humor
in that quixotic atmosphere of frankness
in which, "four o'clock does not exist,
but at five o'clock
the ladies in their imperious humility
are ready to receive you";
in which experience attests
that men have power
and sometimes one is made to feel it.
He says, " 'What monarch would not blush
to have a wife
with hair like a shaving-brush?'
The fact of woman
is 'not the sound of the flute
but very poison.' "
She says, "Men are monopolists
of 'stars, garters, buttons
and other shining baubles'—
unfit to be the guardians
of another person's happiness."
He says, "These mummies
must be handled carefully—
'the crumbs from a lion's meal,
a couple of shins and the bit of an ear';
turn to the letter M
and you will find
that a 'wife is a coffin,'
that severe object
with the pleasing geometry
stipulating space not people,
refusing to be buried
and uniquely disappointing,

revengefully wrought in the attitude
of an adoring child
to a distinguished parent."
She says, "This butterfly,
this waterfly, this nomad
that has 'proposed
to settle on my hand for life.'—
What can one do with it?
There must have been more time
in Shakespeare's day
to sit and watch a play.
You know so many artists who are fools."
He says, "You know so many fools
who are not artists."
The fact forgot
that 'some have merely rights
while some have obligations,'
he loves himself so much,
he can permit himself
no rival in that love.
She loves herself so much,
she cannot see herself enough—
a statuette of ivory on ivory,
the logical last touch
to an expansive splendor
earned as wages for work done:
one is not rich but poor
when one can always seem so right.
What can one do for them—
these savages
condemned to disaffect
all those who are not visionaries
alert to undertake the silly task
of making people noble?
This model of petrine fidelity
who "leaves her peaceful husband
only because she has seen enough of him"—
that orator reminding you,

"I am yours to command."
"Everything to do with love is mystery;
it is more than a day's work
to investigate this science."
One sees that it is rare—
that striking grasp of opposites
opposed each to the other, not to unity,
which in cycloid inclusiveness
has dwarfed the demonstration
of Columbus with the egg—
a triumph of simplicity—
that charitive Euroclydon
of frightening disinterestedness
which the world hates,
admitting:

> "I am such a cow,
> if I had a sorrow
> I should feel it a long time;
> I am not one of those
> who have a great sorrow
> in the morning
> and a great joy at noon;"

which says: "I have encountered it
among those unpretentious
protégés of wisdom,
where seeming to parade
as the debater and the Roman,
the statesmanship
of an archaic Daniel Webster
persists to their simplicity of temper
as the essence of the matter:

> 'Liberty and union
> now and forever';

the Book on the writing-table;
the hand in the breast-pocket."

JOSEPHINE MILES
(1911–   )

Born in Chicago, Josephine Miles went to California
for her education and has remained there, often being
called a "Bay Area" poet. Since 1940, she has taught
English literature at the University of California at
Berkeley. In addition to being an accomplished poet,
her critical writing is extensive and influential, and innovative in its application of scientific methodology
and statistics to the study of literature. She has continued to publish collections of poetry in recent years;
the selections here reflect the work she was doing
before mid-century.

DENIAL

Events like the weeping of the girl in the classroom
Bring to the demands of objects
Denial pure and simple.

Denies the sun, desk, hand, head of the girl,
Denies the book, letter, document,
Denies the ether of the natural will,

Any event like the crying of girl
In the chair in the sun
In the passion of denial.

PLAYERS

Into the spacious bay the sun of afternoon
Shone,
And there two people, a man with a beard and a
    woman without, were playing
At cards alone.

Lake traffic, line traffic, pine, plain traffic all around
  them
Presided,
Roared but soft, rushed but not
Into the window many-sided,

Looking for a game to play, a war to win, some sort of
  magnificent errand
To be done;
While the spadebeard took easily a trick
Already a century won.

GOVERNMENT INJUNCTION
RESTRAINING HARLEM COSMETIC CO.

They say La Jac Brite Pink Skin Bleach avails not,
They say its Orange Beauty Glow does not glow,
Nor the face grow five shades lighter nor the heart
Five shades lighter. They say no.

They deny good luck, love, power, romance, and
  inspiration
From La Jac Brite ointment and incense of all kinds,
And condemn in writing skin brightening and whitening
And whitening of minds.

There is upon the federal trade commission a burden of
  glory
So to defend the fact, so to impel
The plucking of hope from the hand, honor from the
  complexion,
Sprite from the spell.

DILYS BENNETT LAING
(1906–1960)

Dilys Bennett's father was a civil engineer whose work took the family to such remote places as the north of Scotland and the wilds of Ontario. As a child, she suffered two severe diseases that deepened her isolation from the outer world—polio, contracted when she was two years old, and a mastoid infection that left her partially deaf when she was twelve. She was a child prodigy, contributing poetry to periodicals before she was a teenager. In 1928, her family settled in Seattle and she began concentrating on her work. Through the editor of the magazine *Palms*, she met the poet Alexander Laing, whom she eventually married. The decade of the forties was her most productive period—four books of poetry and a novel were published. She was then living in the Vermont countryside, struggling with the restrictions of domesticity on her life as a creative artist. Although she was not famous, she was very much admired by poets. In the fifties, she published little. After her death of acute asthma in 1960, much unpublished work began to appear in literary magazines and her work is now known to a generation only just born at the height of her power.

EXCEPT YE BECOME . . . .

With how intense a fire the celibate
purifies suffering until she gleams:
a bare knife pointed at the breast of life.

But savager than this, the married prude
wraps her necessities in muslin fibs
and hangs wax fruit on Eden's groaning tree,

while children, beasts, and lovers, lax and whole,
walk muddyfooted into Kingdom Come.

TEN LEAGUES BEYOND THE WIDE WORLD'S END

I pursue him, the loved one all unsolved,
through mines of mercury, salt caves and folded stone,
down decimal steps of dream and sleep and death,
through flowering, breaking rocket-head of war
and long anxious ferment of peace.

I pursue him whom I might catch if ever
only by sitting still.
I know, I have taken with sliding rule and wavering scale
his height and shape not fixed but leaping and falling
like fire and shadow forever between child and man.
I know his voice, treble and bass, infantile and mature.
I know the chords of his changes from god to demon
within the scale of his humanity.

I think he is my lover or my child.
When I attempt to take him in my arms
he pulls away from me with a boy's pride
and walks to the edge of the burning world with a gun
   in his hand.

OCEAN FABLE

There is a fish
whose anus is his mouth.
In his beginning is his end.
He is his own foe and friend

and the reply to his own wish.
This creature of primeval mud
is born forever in the blood.
But higher up, in swifter tides,

the murderous swordfish stabs and slides.
They say the complex octopus

is subtly brained and amorous.
I, tidal in my acts and wishes,

perceive how hierarchies of fishes
kill and make love in me. My God,

grant me the rage of shark or cod
but mark my exits, one for dung,

another for the mind and tongue,
and let the fish whose shape is O
cease breeding self in night below.

MARGARET WALKER (1915–   )

A minister's daughter born in Birmingham, Alabama, Margaret Walker was educated in church schools, at the Gilbert Academy in New Orleans and at Northwestern University. In the late thirties, she worked for the WPA Writers' Project in Chicago, compiling information about the near North Side of that city and its rapidly growing black slums. Dropped from the WPA payroll in 1939, she decided to go back to graduate school to earn a degree in English so she could teach. She studied at the Writers' Workshop at the University of Iowa. Her thesis was a book of poems. That book, *For My People*, won the Yale University Younger Poets award in 1942. The selections that follow are from *For My People*. Margaret Walker has since published another book of poems and a novel, *Jubilee*, on which she had worked for nearly thirty years. *Jubilee* is one of the few works in our literature that deals with the Civil War from the point of view of black reality.

LINEAGE

My grandmothers were strong.
They followed plows and bent to toil.
They moved through fields sowing seed.
They touched earth and grain grew.
They were full of sturdiness and singing.
My grandmothers were strong.

My grandmothers are full of memories
Smelling of soap and onions and wet clay
With veins rolling roughly over quick hands
They have many clean words to say.
My grandmothers were strong.
Why am I not as they?

DARK BLOOD

There were bizarre beginnings in old lands for the making of me. There were sugar sands and islands of fern and pearl, palm jungles and stretches of a never-ending sea.

There were the wooing nights of tropical lands and the cool discretion of flowering plains beneath two stalwart hills. They nurtured my coming with wanderlust. I sucked fevers of adventure through my veins with my mother's milk.

Someday I shall go to the tropical lands of my birth, to the coasts of continents and the tiny wharves of island shores. I shall roam the Balkans and the hot lands Africa and Asia. I shall stand on mountain tops and gaze on fertile homes below.

And when I return to Mobile I shall go by the way of
Panama and Bocas del Toro to the littered streets and
the one-room shacks of my old poverty, and blazing
suns of other lands may struggle then to reconcile the
pride and pain in me.

GWENDOLYN BROOKS (1917–)

When she was a child growing up on the South Side
of Chicago, Gwendolyn Brooks was known as a "girl
who wrote," which was a peculiar thing. In her home,
however, the writing was encouraged. Her father
bought her a small desk to write on and her mother
gave her the works of Paul Laurence Dunbar, saying
that Gwendolyn would be the female Dunbar when
she grew up. She has poetry journals dating from
her eleventh year. Brooks attended a poetry class run
by Inez Cunningham Stark for young blacks in Chicago and through Stark her work came to the attention of a white poetry audience. *A Street in Bronze-
ville* was published by a white publisher and read
mostly by white readers in 1945; *Annie Allen* won
the Pulitzer Prize in 1950. Brooks was the first black
writer to win that prize. Beginning in the late sixties,
the poet underwent what she describes as a deep
change of consciousness and became identified with
the new Black Arts movement. Her work in support
of young, militant black poets has been prodigious.
She has said about her attitude toward the black world
during the forties and fifties: "I thought that integra-
tion was the solution. All we had to do was keep on

appealing to the whites to help us, and they would."
The selections that follow are taken from her "early"
work.

the mother

Abortions will not let you forget.
You remember the children you got that you did not get,
The damp small pulps with a little or with no hair,
The singers and workers that never handled the air.
You will never neglect or beat
Them, or silence or buy with a sweet.
You will never wind up the sucking-thumb
Or scuttle off ghosts that come.
You will never leave them, controlling your luscious
    sigh,
Return for a snack of them, with gobbling mother-eye.

I have heard in the voices of the wind the voices of my
    dim killed children.
I have contracted. I have eased
My dim dears at the breasts they could never suck.
I have said, Sweets, if I sinned, if I seized
Your luck
And your lives from your unfinished reach,
If I stole your births and your names,
Your straight baby tears and your games,
Your stilted or lovely loves, your tumults, your
    marriages, aches, and your deaths,
If I poisoned the beginnings of your breaths,
Believe that even in my deliberateness I was not
    deliberate.
Though why should I whine,
Whine that the crime was other than mine?—
Since anyhow you are dead.
Or rather, or instead,
You were never made.
But that too, I am afraid,

Is faulty: oh, what shall I say, how is the truth to be
   said?
You were born, you had body, you died.
It is just that you never giggled or planned or cried.

Believe me, I loved you all.
Believe me, I knew you, though faintly, and I loved, I
   loved you
All.

the birth in a narrow room

Weeps out of Kansas country something new.
Blurred and stupendous. Wanted and unplanned.
      Winks. Twines, and weakly winks
Upon the milk-glass fruit bowl, iron pot,
The bashful china child tipping forever
Yellow apron and spilling pretty cherries.

Now, weeks and years will go before she thinks
"How pinchy is my room! how can I breathe!
I am not anything and I have got
Not anything, or anything to do!"—
But prances nevertheless with gods and fairies
Blithely about the pump and then beneath
The elms and grapevines, then in darling endeavor
By privy foyer, where the screenings stand
And where the bugs buzz by in private cars
Across old peach cans and old jelly jars.

kitchenette building

We are things of dry hours and the involuntary plan,
Grayed in, and gray. "Dream" makes a giddy sound,
   not strong
Like "rent," "feeding a wife," "satisfying a man."

But could a dream send up through onion fumes
Its white and violet, fight with fried potatoes
And yesterday's garbage ripening in the hall,
Flutter, or sing an aria down these rooms.

Even if we were willing to let it in,
Had time to warm it, keep it very clean,
Anticipate a message, let it begin?

We wonder. But not well! not for a minute!
Since Number Five is out of the bathroom now,
We think of lukewarm water, hope to get in it.

MURIEL RUKEYSER
(1913–   )

Muriel Rukeyser was once asked what she did besides
writing and she responded, "mainly reading poems
with people: undergraduates; 2-year-olds; drop-outs;
the old; the blind, etc." Her engagement with poetry is
a full-time, life-time one. She began publishing her
work while at Vassar College; her most recent book
of poems came out last year. She is that rare poet, a
person with particular understanding of science, author of biographies of Willard Gibbs and Thomas
Hariot. Rukeyser has lived most of her life in New
York City, leaving from time to time on journeys of
passionate dedication to radical social change: to Spain
during the Civil War, to marches on Washington, to
jail, to Hanoi. Historically, she is one of this country's
most important poets and one of the first and most
persistent women to possess the consciousness that
shapes this collection.

ANN BURLAK

Let her be seen, a voice on a platform, heard
as a city is heard in its prophetic sleep when
one shadow hangs over one side of a total wall

of houses, factories, stacks, and on the faces
around her tallies, shadow from one form.

An open square shields the voice, reflecting it
to faces who receive its reflections of light as
change on their features. She stands alone, sending
her voice out to the edges, seeing approach people
to make the ring ragged, to fill in blacker
answers.

       This is an open square of the lit world
whose dark sky over hills rimmed white with evening
squares lofts where sunset lies in dirty patterns
and rivers of mill-towns beating their broken bridges
as under another country full of air.
Dark offices evening reaches where letters take the light
even from palest faces over script.
Many abandon machines, shut off the looms,
hurry on glooming cobbles to the square. And many
are absent, as in the sky about her face, the birds
retreat from charcoal rivers and fly far.

The words cluster about the superstition mountains.
The sky breaks back over the torn and timid
her early city whose stacks along the river
flourished darkness over all, whose mottled sky
shielded the faces of those asleep in doorways
spread dark on narrow fields through which the father
comes home without meat, the forest in the ground
whose trees are coal, the lurching roads of autumn
where the flesh of the eager hangs, heavier by
its thirty bullets, barbed on wire. Truckdrivers
swing ungrazed trailers past, the woman in the fog
can never speak her poems of unemployment,
the brakeman slows the last freight round the curve.
And riveters in their hardshell fling short fiery
steel, and the servant groans in his narrow room,
and the girl limps away from the door of the shady
    doctor.
Or the child new-born into a company town

whose life can be seen at birth as child, woman, widow.
The neighbor called in to nurse the baby of a spy,
the schoolboy washing off the painted word
"scab" on the front stoop, his mother watering flowers
pouring the milk-bottle of water from the ledge,
who stops in horror, seeing. The grandmother going
down to her cellar with a full clothes-basket,
turns at the shot, sees men running past brick,
smoke-spurt and fallen face.
                        She speaks of these:
the chase down through the canal, the filling-station,
stones through the windshield. The woman in the bank
who topples, the premature birth brought on by tear-gas,
the charge leaving its gun slow-motion, finding those
who sit at windows knowing what they see;
who look up at the door, the brutalized face appraising
strangers with holsters;   little blackened boys
with their animal grins, quick hands salvaging coal
among the slag of patriotic hills.

She knows the field of faces at her feet,
remembrances of childhood, likenesses of parents,
a system of looms in constellation whirled,
disasters dancing.
                 And behind her head
the world of the unpossessed, steel mills in snow flaming,
nine o'clock towns whose deputies' overnight power
hurls waste into killed eyes, whose guns predict
mirages of order, an empty coat before the blind.
Doorways within which nobody is at home.
The spies who wait for the spy at the deserted crossing,
a little dead since they are going to kill.
Those women who stitch their lives to their machines
and daughters at the symmetry of looms.

She speaks to the ten greatest American women:
The anonymous farmer's wife, the anonymous clubbed
    picket,
the anonymous Negro woman who held off the guns,

the anonymous prisoner, anonymous cotton-picker
trailing her robe of sack in a proud train,
anonymous writer of these and mill-hand, anonymous
    city-walker,
anonymous organizer, anonymous binder of the illegally
    wounded,
anonymous feeder and speaker to anonymous squares.
She knows their faces, their impatient songs
of passionate grief risen, the desperate music
poverty makes, she knows women cut down
by poverty, by stupid obscure days,
their moments over the dishes, speaks them now,
wrecks with the whole necessity of the past
behind the debris, behind the ordinary
smell of coffee, the ravelling clean wash,
the turning to bed, undone among savage night
planning and unplanning seasons of happiness
broken in dreams or in the jaundiced morning
over a tub or over a loom or over
the tired face of death.
                        She knows
the songs: *Hope to die, Mo I try, I comes out,*
Owin boss mo, I comes out, Lawd, Owin boss mo
food, money and life.
                    Praise breakers,
praise the unpraised who cannot speak their name.
Their asking what they need as unbelieved
as a statue talking to a skeleton.
They are the animals who devour their mother
from need, and they know in their bodies other places,
their minds are cities whose avenues are named
each after a foreign city. They fall when cities fall.
They have the cruelty and sympathy of those
whose texture is the stress of existence woven
into revenge, the crime we all must claim.
They hold the old world in their new world's arms.
And they are the victims, all the splinters of war
run through their eyes, their black escaping face

and runaway eyes are the Negro in the subway
whose shadowy detective brings his stick
down on the naked head as the express pulls in,
swinging in locomotive roars on skull.
They are the question to the ambassador
long-jawed and grim, they stand on marble, waiting
to ask how the terms of the strike have affected him.
Answer: "I've never seen snow before. It's marvellous."
They stand with Ann Burlak in the rotunda, knowing
her insistent promise of life, remembering
the letter of the tear-gas salesman: "I hope
this strike develops and a damn bad one too.
We need the money."
                  This is the boundary
behind a speaker: Main Street and railroad tracks,
post office, furniture store. The soft moment before storm.
Since there are many years.
And the first years were the years of need,
the bleeding, the dragged foot, the wilderness,
and the second years were the years of bread
fat cow, square house, favorite work,
and the third years are the years of death.
The glittering eye all golden. Full of tears.
Years when the enemy is in our street,
and liberty, safe in the people's hands,
is never safe and peace is never safe.

Insults of attack arrive, insults
of mutilation. She knows the prophetic past,
many have marched behind her, and she knows
Rosa whose face drifts in the black canal,
the superstitions of a tragic winter
when children, their heads together, put on tears.
The tears fall at their throats, their chains are made
of tears, and as bullets melted and as bombs let down
upon the ominous cities where she stands
fluid and conscious. Suddenly perceives
the world will never daily prove her words,

but her words live, they issue from this life.
She scatters clews. She speaks from all these faces
and from the center of a system of lives
who speak the desire of worlds moving unmade
saying. "Who owns the world?" and waiting for the cry.

INDEX OF AUTHORS

INDEX OF FIRST LINES

ABOUT THE EDITOR

Louise Bernikow, a poet in her own right, is author of *Abel* and is widely known as an outspoken feminist journalist and scholar. A graduate of Barnard College, she is a Columbia University Ph.D. candidate who has taught at Juilliard, CCNY, and Queens College. She is a frequent guest speaker on campuses and her articles have appeared in *Ms.* and *University Review*.

VINTAGE BELLES—LETTRES